SAM HANNA BELL

NOVEMBER 1946
Sam Hanna Bell was a features producer and writer for BBC Northern Ireland
from 1945 until his retirement in 1969.

SAM HANNA BELL
A BIOGRAPHY

SEAN McMAHON

THE
BLACKSTAFF
PRESS

BELFAST

First published in 1999 by
The Blackstaff Press Limited
Blackstaff House, Wildflower Way, Apollo Road
Belfast BT12 6TA, Northern Ireland
with the assistance of
The Arts Council of Northern Ireland

ARTS
COUNCIL
of Northern Ireland

Typeset by Techniset Typesetters, Newton-le-Willows, Merseyside

Printed in England by Biddles Limited

A CIP catalogue record for this book
is available from the British Library

ISBN 0-85640-665-1

For Angélique, Fergus, young Sam, Philip and Edmund

CONTENTS

PROLOGUE 1

1 Ulster–Scot 4

2 5 India Street 13

3 Reading and Writing – and the ARP 20

4 *Summer Loanen* 33

5 Features Producer 43

6 Miss Reside 57

7 The Festival of Britain 64

8 *December Bride* 71

9 Plays and Features 83

10 *An Old Ulster Custom* 94

11 Rodgers, Campbell and Thompson 102

12 *The Hollow Ball* 113

13 The Diarist 121

14 Sam Hanna Bell MA (*honoris causa*), MBE 136

15 The Theatre in Ulster 143

16 *A Man Flourishing* 148

17 'Retired' Broadcaster 159

18 *Within Our Province* and *Tatler Tales* 169

19 Literary Miscellany 175

20 *Across the Narrow Sea* 183

21 The Artificer 190

22 Young Sam 194

Bibliography 200

Index 217

ACKNOWLEDGEMENTS

My thanks are due particularly to Fergus Hanna Bell, who provided all his father's papers for my use, and with unwearying kindness answered all my often personal questions about his family; to his wife Angélique, who imposed what order she could on the papers; and to Dr Sophia Hillan King, Assistant Director of the Institute of Irish Studies at Queen's University Belfast, who was most helpful to me in my work over the last two years.

I am also indebted to John Boyd, Douglas Carson, Mary Delargy, Robert Greacen, David Hammond, Denys Hawthorne, Deborah Keys, John Killen, Maurice Leitch, Grainne Loughran, Pat Loughrey, Tony McAuley, G.P. McCrudden, Roy McFadden, Linda McGarrity, Clare McVeigh, David Millar, Michael O'Donnell, Richard Sherry, Noreen Sherry-Dorman and Anne Tannahill.

I am indebted to Deborah Keys for permission to include the bibliography she compiled as part of her 1982 MA dissertation on Sam Hanna Bell.

Note: Quotations from diaries, letters, drafts and memos have been slightly edited to give consistency of capitalisation and punctuation, and misspellings have been silently corrected, but the original wording and abbreviations have been retained.

PROLOGUE

WE MET REGULARLY, about once a month, and usually on a Saturday. He would be waiting on the Victorian sofa on the first floor of the Linen Hall Library (of which he had been made a honorary member), just at the top of the first flight of steps. The figure was neat, tweedy, impeccably dressed, clinically clean and tidy. There would be a tweed hat and a cane beside him on the seat and he'd have a typescript in his hand and a book or two for me to review lying beside the hat. As I ran up the stairs, disdaining in those athletic years the lift, I would see and admire the magnificent profile; he'd rise and greet me with that remarkable second-tenor voice, still after sixty years retaining echoes of his Clyde Valley origins, a little bit louder now to keep pace with his deafness. The moustache would be stroked and the eyebrows, used for comic or minatory effect, would bristle.

We would talk about some piece I had written for his Literary Miscellany in the *Ulster Tatler*: a commissioned reappraisal of some of his admired literary friends, Peadar O'Donnell, Joe Tomelty, Michael J. Murphy, Alexander Irvine; a light essay to counterbalance the overstocks of poetry; a book review. Talk about further commissions, the state of the Literary Miscellany, his own work (in those years mainly, though not entirely, programmes for schools) would follow. These were the years of *Golden Boat for a Sea God* – the story of the finding of the Broighter Hoard and the protracted legal problems that followed –

1

and the fascinating 'John Steinbeck and Derry', a feature which had to be aborted when Steinbeck's publisher refused to allow quotations from the novelist's works. It was, however, the work done for such series as *Today and Yesterday in Northern Ireland* that represented at least a silver age that could stand comparison with his own golden age as a staff features writer and producer.

Business over, we would walk round to the special table in the Chalet d'Or restaurant in Fountain Street reserved for the unofficial club of which he was the rather more genial Dr Johnson – the gerontic residue of the table in Campbell's Coffee House of forty years earlier. Regulars like Shep and Norman McCaw, Norman Harrison and Sam Christie would already be ensconced. John Hewitt might be there, the essence of bleak integrity, and Joe Tomelty, from whom one received a bear hug and the whispered admonition 'Remember you're British!', or Robert Greacen, the Notting Hill exile from Erin on one of his many trips home. Ronnie Adams and John Killen, the bright sparks of the Linen Hall, would look in and the crack (in those years the non-Gaelic perversion *craic* had not been invented) was all that word should mean.

We shivered during the winter of 1980–81, enjoyed the warm summer of 1984. Politics was a rare topic and happily shelved for stories, light-hearted discussions about Ulster history and literature, and occasional self-revelation. Around one o'clock he and I would leave and go to Boots, braving the heavy security of the time, so that he could buy diabetic chocolate and sweets for Mildred. We would stand on the steps of the library waiting for Fergus to pick him up, chatting about family matters. Towards the middle of the 1980s he joked about the possibility of him becoming a father-in-law, and the thought of the filming of *December Bride*, including one memorable trip to the location at Killinchy, entertained him greatly. Other times I would leave him to his bus or if I (rarely) had my car with me I would follow the instructed serpentine route to the spot just off the Upper Newtownards Road where he had left his dark blue Fiesta.

I have mentioned Dr Johnson and can say that I would have been only too happy to have been a Boswell, treasuring the shards of biographical fact that crumbled from ordinary conversations. He was, however, mordantly suspicious and dismissive of autobiography (a diary entry for 22 November 1973 reads 'Good title for autobiography – Hit the road, Jack, and don't come back no more, no more, no more, no more'), opting rather for perfection of the work, in Yeats's dichotomy. The work remains and so does the reputation of greatness, but some account of the life is overdue.

1
ULSTER-SCOT

S AM HANNA BELL WAS BORN IN GLASGOW on 16 October 1909 and
baptised in the United Free Church of Scotland on Christmas Eve
of that year by the Reverend C.R. Ferguson. His father, James
Hanna Bell, was Scots but of County Antrim extraction and his
mother, Jane Ferris McCarey McIlveen, came from Raffrey, a small iso-
lated village about seven miles to the north of Crossgar, County Down,
on the road between Saintfield and Killyleagh. The copy of his birth
certificate shows that Samuel Bell was born at '11h. 30m. a.m. at 550
Tollcross Road, Tollcross'. The occupation of his father, who recorded
the birth on 2 November 1909, was given as 'mercantile clerk', and the
certificate states that he and the mother, 'Jane Bell née McIlveen were
married on 6 July 1908 at Crossgar, Co. Down, Ireland'.

Sam's paternal grandfather had left his home at Killyglen, near Kil-
waughter, County Antrim, a village three miles from Larne on the road
to Ballymena, and gone to Scotland to seek work. His son James, born
on 8 August 1879, was a rather austere autodidact (a characteristic inherited by Sam); having mastered French, Latin and enough Greek to read
Saint Paul in the original, he worked as a journalist with the *Glasgow
Herald*. (Among Sam's books are two prizes won by his father for written exercises in religious knowledge: leatherbound copies of Milton's
poems in 1891 and those of Wordsworth in 1892 – quite a handling
for a boy of twelve or thirteen but treasured by both father and son.)

Later James became manager and editor of the Greenock edition.

James's yearly holidays were spent in County Antrim at Killyglen; in that golden age of the steamship the hop across the narrow sea between Scotland and Ireland was short if not always tranquil – stabilisers were a luxury still to come. (A postcard sent by him in August 1907 remarks on the stormy journey to Ardrossan.) It was on one of these trips 'home' that he got to know his cousin Jane McIlveen (born on 13 August 1883 and therefore almost exactly four years James's junior). They were married in Raffrey Presbyterian Church.

Postcards preserved from the period and franked with halfpenny stamps show that the father was as precise and elegant a penman as the son was to prove, and that wooing in those days was as decorous as we have always assumed it to have been. The addressee was 'Miss Jane McIlveen' (though this was modified at times to 'Jenny' or 'Jennie') and most of the cards were sent to 102 Templemore Avenue, Belfast. The earliest in the collection is dated 3 October 1903 and the latest was sent on 27 May 1908, six weeks before the wedding, when Jenny's address was 37 Upper Frank Street, Belfast. It was obviously sent after a quick visit to Ireland:

> Dear Jenny
> Got home very early and had a welcome snooze before beginning my daily 'toil'. Among those who came across was the blind Italian from Bangor, who likely reaped a poor harvest there. And now he returns to the generous Scot!
> Kindest regards
> J.

In none of the cards was the farewell greeting more passionate than this 'Kindest regards', but the use of the single initial was an advance on the usual 'J.H.B.'

One postcard sent on 20 June 1904 to Templemore Avenue read thus:

> Dear Jenny,
> I hope this will be a welcome change from the usual scenes. The original, of course, belongs to the Corporation so that I had to make this do.
> Regards to one and all
> J.H.B.

'This' was a monochrome reproduction of a highly appropriate painting called *The Farmer's Daughter* – an indication that they shared the same dry sense of humour. The ready legibility of postcards probably prevented any greater intimacy.

Their first born, Sam, was the eldest of three sons; his younger brothers were christened Robert MacIlveen and Charles Hunter. Holidays in Ireland continued, mostly spent at the mother's family home, as was the usual custom. In a diary entry for 23 September 1957, Sam records:

> Mother told me how when she ran out to tell Uncle Sam McIlveen, who was ploughing the knowe field at Raffrey, that the *Titanic* had foundered he exclaimed, 'Nonsense, she couldn't sink!' He had worked on the ship in the Queen's Island and was to have sailed in her (now in Vancouver).

(Sam would have been two and a half in 1912, and the likeliest cause of Jenny's presence in Raffrey in April was that she was pregnant with Rab, as the second brother was to be known.)

The Bells would have been a douce middle-class family, Presbyterian but not illiberal, with respect both for kirk and schoolhouse. Undated cards indicate that Mr J.H. and Mrs J.H. Bell of 550 Tollcross Road, Glasgow, were registered communicants of Victoria United Free Church. Little other information exists about the family's life. Master Samuel Bell got an Easter card from 'Unca Sam' on 11 April 1914 and a birthday postcard on his fifth birthday headed 'Dear Little Nephew' from Aunt Mary in Glasgow. The family left Glasgow for Greenock, the most westerly of the shipbuilding towns of the Clyde, in 1915, and another card from Uncle Sam sent on 4 May 1916 came from a wartime field post office and was addressed to 18 Denholm Street, Greenock. In it the dear nephew was thanked for his 'Easter wishes in verse'. Two years later, the eight-year-old Sam's settled world was turned upside down when his father died suddenly, aged only thirty-eight. According to family lore, the cause of his death was an undiagnosed brain tumour.

It is vain to speculate what might have been the nature of Sam's life if it had not been for his father's premature death. It is likely he would have had the university career that he later envied his graduate colleagues. He might even have gone for the Church. The most likely career would have been journalism and/or radio leading to television, with

6

perhaps the same output of novels, though subvented by a different arts council. Sam, who was taken with mother and brothers to his grandfather's farm, had had a native Scots father and he spoke with a strong accent which never entirely left his speech throughout his life.

The family tradition that it was Grandmother McIlveen who crossed to the Clyde to bring them back is confirmed by a note from T.P. Inglis, who must have been a colleague of James Bell. He wrote on 30 May 1918 from the *Herald* office in Greenock giving the 35-year-old widow detailed instructions about obtaining travel permits for the journey to Ireland:

> Both your mother & yourself will have to go to the police office personally with your photographs ... The photographs should be fairly recent without hat or cap ... No permits are required for children under 16 years of age.

Among the family papers is the travel permit issued to Mrs Bell, widow, to enable her to make the wartime journey back to her childhood home.

The change in the family's circumstances was severe. In addition to bereavement Jane had to face the severe economic facts of widowhood thirty years before the setting up of the welfare state. From being the wife of a securely placed editor/manager of one of Scotland's leading newspapers, with offices in Paisley and Edinburgh as well as Glasgow and Greenock, she found herself in a position of dependence, once again a daughter in her father's house instead of mistress in her own. She never quite relinquished the bitterness associated with her position, and the understandable resentment was engrained when after three years she moved to Belfast, to a house off Botanic Avenue owned by a relative, and supported her young family by taking in sewing and lodgers.

In a pencilled draft of an autobiographical note Bell wrote for the publisher of his first novel, Denis Dobson, we find these paragraphs:

> I was born in Tollcross, Glasgow, in 1909. My father, James Hanna Bell, was a Scottish journalist of Co. Antrim stock. He and his forebears had crossed and re-crossed the Irish Sea for generations. He married his cousin, Jane McCarey McIlveen of Co. Down. On the death of my father in 1918 I was 'brought back' to the farm of my maternal grandfather, Robert McIlveen, a staunch Presbyterian, whose seers were Emerson, Carlyle and William Law, his poet Robert Burns.

During the few years of childhood that I spent there I saw a pattern of rural life that had existed for three hundred years vanish under the impact of the motor bus and the tractor. Districts whose inhabitants considered it an adventure to jog into the monthly cattle fair in the nearest small town were suddenly aerated by modern transport, and men and women to whom Belfast had been no more than a distant furnace glow in the evening sky were soon referring to its thoroughfares as familiarly as their own roads and loanens and loughside tracks. It was from that remote and idyllic past that I drew my novel *December Bride*.

For the bright eight-year-old the change from the bustle of a heavily populated industrial region to the remoteness and Sabbatarian restrictions of the County Down farm was striking. Clydeside, from Gourock to Glasgow, was even then a conurbation, and the society to which the young Sam was accustomed was considerably more variegated than the mainly Presbyterian, solidly Protestant region in which he was to spend his early adolescence. The Clyde Valley had many Irish Catholic immigrants, come mainly from Donegal and Derry to work in the yards. Moreover, the eager pupil could not help compare unfavourably the standards of education available in the 'low whitewashed schoolhouse' in County Down with what he had been used to at home, and he missed companions of his own age to play with in the long summer evenings. As he recalled in a script entitled 'A Country Childhood', 'You can't go tramping across four or five fields just to ask a neighbour to come out to play. And more important, when a fellow came home from school he had to take his share of the work around the farm.' At times he found the strictness of the Sabbath intolerable. He once had his ears boxed by Grandfather McIlveen for whistling on a Sunday and he did not reckon much to the six-mile journey, often undergone twice on the Lord's Day, to the Presbyterian meeting house for service.

He admitted that there were far more rigid worshippers than the McIlveens. Some, like the Covenanters of old, severely curtailed their Sabbath journeys and took their sparse midday meal picnic-style in the churchyard. They held it more seemly to wait for evening service than to make the double journey. Something of the flavour of the life is caught in the chapter 'To Crack by the Hearth' in *Erin's Orange Lily* (1956), Bell's companionable gallimaufry on Ulster's already changing folk life. The grandfather had five acres, one of them 'marred by a whin knowe', and he carried on a harness-making business in a lean-to at the gable of the house. One of his daughters was an agent for several linen firms in Belfast; she distributed, collected and paid for embroidery work done by the women of the district. Bell does not say so but this is the kind of work that his mother later did in Belfast; it is likely that she was glad of any work her sister could give her.

Robert McIlveen was a man of proper *gravitas* and his house, because of his own and his daughter's clients, was a place where neighbours met and where inevitably politics, weather and crops were discussed. The times were troubled in the years running up to the 1920 Government of Ireland Act and the establishment of Northern Ireland. They were characterised by civic unrest and armed Protestant vigilantes, originally members of the Ulster Volunteer Force (UVF) and eventually became the Ulster Special Constabulary. There was sectarian violence across Northern Ireland, but it was worst in Derry and Belfast. Raffrey, however, was well-cushioned from trouble, since its position in an almost solid Bible belt meant that there were few Catholics around. There was, nevertheless, an inevitable awareness of the existence of 'papishes'; in 'Summer Loanen', the title story of Bell's first book, a collection of short stories published in 1943, an irate farmer shouts at a trespassing boy, 'I'll tell your Grandma you're skiltin' the fields with a papish, my bold Jimmie Orr.' It should be noted, however, that none of the three children in the story considers the farmer's words either a significant threat or a reason not to meet again.

The McIlveen house was a little bit like the *céilí* houses of Catholic areas, with inevitable straitlaced modifications. Those rendezvous, called *tithe airneáil* (literally houses for night visiting) in the coastal gael-tachts, supplied most of the winter social life of rural communities countrywide. The staple entertainments were storytelling, music and singing and, of course, gossip. From them too, as in Sam's grandfather's house, 'several of the young men and women found that their home-ward road lay over the same paths'. The clients who came and stopped for a chat were happy to listen to the man of the house read from the newspaper, but it was not a fireside where people would linger too late. They knew, since it was the practice in their own homes, that with the departure of the last visitors the table would be laid for supper and that the saying of grace after eating would merge into evening prayer. After reading a few verses from the family bible the paterfamilias would kneel; so too, with a judicious air of piety, would the rest of the family, the younger ones cute enough to go down without reluctance and to rise without visible signs of relief.

Sam, who worshipped literature, notes that the only books apart from the Good one that his grandfather read were Emerson's *Essays*, Law's *A Serious Call to a Devout and Holy Life*, and Burns's *Poems*. (The affection general among Presbyterians in Ulster for the tempestuous Ayrshire lo'er o' the lassies was partly a form of nostalgia for their spiritual home.) The younger generation were permitted to read the books they won as Sunday School prizes. (Such prizes and the expectations of elders that they should be won form the theme of 'This We Shall Maintain', a story written in July 1941 and like 'Summer Loanen' first published in *The Bell*. 'This We Shall Maintain' drew from Seán O'Faoláin, the editor, the unusual praise, written to Bell on a postcard, 'Beautiful. Beautiful.' It noted the compensating fact that most third prizes were 'interesting books'.)

In addition to the mention of the Raffrey house in *Erin's Orange Lily* there are other reminiscences, some preserved as a result of general conversations, others to be found in the texts of teachers' notes for various educational programmes that Bell wrote in the years after his retirement from the BBC. He recalls that because of his family's annual Irish holidays in the years before his father's death, the translation from city streets to country loanens was not as traumatic as it might have been. In 'A Country Childhood' he wrote:

> The countryside was not unknown to me before that. My father came from the hills above Kilwaughter and my mother from a townland not far from Strangford Lough in Co. Down. From as far back as I can remember we made an annual trip from Scotland to holiday in Ulster. We were doing no more than treading a path beaten over the sea by generations of my father's ancestors. Therefore, when, on his death in 1918, we came to live with my mother's parents in Co. Down, I felt that I was 'returning home'.
>
> I was in time to glimpse the hem of a vanishing way of life. It would have been possible for an 18th-century countryman to recognise almost all the domestic furniture we used, and some of the clothes that we wore. As a schoolboy I was dressed in those knee-breeches to be seen in the illustrations to William Carleton's tales. A farmwife was considered superior if she had a kitchen range and I remember an old

woman who lived alone in a two-roomed cabin that had an earthen floor, black and hard, polished under generations of bare feet. The postman walked, the thatcher thatched, men still swung a flail and shook a winnowing sheet.

As suggested above, the schoolhouse would have struck the young Scots immigrant as providing the greatest contrast with what he had been accustomed to in Greenock.

The National School to which we trudged up and down the drumlin road was one long room with a black stove in the middle. We ciphered on slates; the maps on the wall, yellow and shiny as apple-skin, delineated long-vanished states and petty kingdoms. Big or little, we trembled under the eye of 'The Mester', William Rankin, who lived under the same roof as his school.

Yet for all its isolation the life had its excitements and its holidays, accounts of which would form the material for future essays, articles and radio and television programmes, and which were also to be assimilated with dramatic effect into the stories of *Summer Loanen, December Bride* and the play *That Woman at Rathard* (Lyric Theatre, 1967) which was quarried from it. Raffrey, with its drumlins and access to Strangford Lough, was as suitable a tutor for the poetic child as 'Caledonia, stern and wild' was for Scott. Lying in bed listening to the 'bumbling drone of voices from the kitchen, the muted explosions of laughter, the chink of the teacups' that followed, say, a cockle-raking expedition, was part of an aesthetic education. Then, as Bell recalled in *Erin's Orange Lily*, 'The talk would fall away into silence until someone would take up the story again, someone else would answer, and we would fall asleep to the antiphon of neighbours' voices round the hearth.'

By Sam's twelfth birthday in 1921 the family had suffered another reluctant flitting, and for the next score of years his address was officially (and for most of them actually) 5 India Street, Belfast. As he put it in the opening sentence of 'A Country Childhood', 'I was born in a city, Glasgow, and eventually came to live in another city, Belfast.' Yet the few country years were at least as significant for his work as the remainder when his base was urban. Belfast was important to him; it provided the locale for *The Hollow Ball* (1961) and was as much a character as the people in *A Man Flourishing* (1973) which told the story of its evolution from radical sea port to stolid Victorian city. Yet he never forgot the experience of rural life, and it was his realisation of the rate at which it was changing and his fear that much folklore and knowledge might be lost that caused him to make the changing countryside and its ways the subject of many of his finest radio programmes.

2
5 INDIA STREET

FOR THE NEXT TWENTY YEARS the chronological sequence of Sam Hanna Bell's life is unclear. Few papers from the period are extant and any information is derived from anecdote and conversational aside. A picture emerges of, if not actual hardship, then necessary frugality. The Bell boys were intelligent but fatherless, and welfare provision in the pre-Beveridge years was barely enough for subsistence. The widow's pension was necessarily supplemented by sewing and the taking in of lodgers. And her resident brother helped meet the rent. (Little mention is made by Sam of this uncle and he may have moved on.) From what wispy information we have, we can build up a picture of a clever adolescent, conscious of his lack of education and resentful of his mother's roomers. This resentment was shared by his mother, who only three years before had been enjoying a comfortable bourgeois life in the Clyde Valley and now spent her evenings engaged in eye-straining needlework.

During adolescence and early manhood the boy was to become an omnivorous reader, consciously providing for himself the education he could not attain conventionally. He set himself a rigorous course of reading, with all the autodidact's ruthlessness and lack of guidance. Many years later, he commented upon this to Deborah Keys in conversations during her research for her MA dissertation 'Sam Hanna Bell: A Study of His Contribution towards the Cultural Development of the

13

Region' (1982). She reported: '. . . looking back on these formative years, he says he feels he lacked the discipline and guidance which would have enabled him to benefit fully from his reading.' In this self-assessment, as ever, he was much too hard upon himself: he had devoured the usual classics of English literature: the great dramatists and novelists, especially Shakespeare and Dickens; Hardy was an especial favourite, and it is not fanciful to think that he considered himself another Jude Frawley, though happier and more fortunate.

He later brought an equal respect, even awe, to the great European masters, read necessarily in translation. That was fine for Dostoevsky, Cervantes or Dante (whose works had been written in languages not usually offered by the secondary schools of the time), but it rankled a little with Bell that some of the friends of his maturity, like John Boyd (b. 1912), could read French novels in the original and did not conceal the fact, while J[ames] J[oseph] Campbell (1910–79), a classical scholar, was not only conversant with Aeschylus and Virgil but actually edited Cicero. It should be noted, however, that in 1923 the bright school-leaver of fourteen carried a leaving certificate that showed a proficiency in arithmetic, English, geography, geometry, algebra and science that was much greater than today's GCSE requirements. It was by any standards a working education and had whetted his appetite for more. What is not clear is why both Rab and Charles were able to attend Belfast Royal Academy while Sam had to make do with All Saints' Public Elementary at the corner of University and Wolseley streets. (Rab became an electrical engineer on apprenticeship and after periods in Coventry and Rugby with British Thompson Houston was transferred to the Larne branch. Charles became a quantity surveyor and lived all his life in the Isle of Man.)

Here it may do no harm to insert another paragraph from the pencilled draft of 'autobiographical detail' required by publisher Denis Dobson:

> I was brought into the city, attended a series of National Schools and parted from them without any inextinguishable heart-pangs on the part of the teachers or myself. For the next twenty years I was in and out of almost as many jobs: potato salesman, advertisement writer, night watchman, art student, freelance reporter, toy salesman, welfare worker; every one of them, I was soon to realise, a window through which I could watch the comings and goings of my fellow men.

An awareness of the contrast between his own knowledge and talent and the performance of many who had had the privilege of the education denied him was some consolation to the proud, self-consciously gifted youth, but until he was established in the BBC he dearly wished for some academic standing. His demeanour was reserved, his conversation serious and much concerned with literature and left-wing politics. He became active in the socialist cause, and by the middle of the thirties, Auden's 'low dishonest decade', he had a much greater experience of working-class city life than most of his radical friends. The list of his occupations from the time he left school till the outbreak of war in 1939 reads like a parody of the Jack London school of muscular literacy.

He worked variously as a labourer (at the construction of the Belfast graving dock), as a night watchman at the harbour, as a potato grader, and as a laboratory technician holding post-mortems on cows for the Ministry of Agriculture. He worked in a wholesale woollen business as a clerk, as a 'counter-jumper' in a gentleman's outfitter's, as a salesman, and as a booking clerk in the Belfast office of the Canadian Pacific Railroad.

During this period, Bell attended the College of Technology to study drawing. He admitted that he wasn't particularly good but he 'liked the crack'. The course intensified an interest in art that made him afterwards seek out the company of such artists as William Conor (1881–1968), John Luke (1906–75) and later Rowel Friers (1920–98), Mercy Hunter (1910–89) and George MacCann (1909–67). His own beautiful calligraphy was one relic of the classes. His artistic ambitions were genuine. Among his papers is a handwritten account of his career prepared at the instigation of his friend J.J. Campbell. A piece of paper attached to the manuscript reads, 'These are the rough notes of information supplied to QUB at J.J. Campbell's request. October 1962.' The account begins, 'My original intention was to be a painter but from the mid-thirties until 1940 I wrote a number of short stories most of which were broadcast by the BBC or published in various literary journals.'

The job of night watchman gave greater opportunities for reading than some of the others, and it provided the background for part of 'The Broken Tree', one of the finest stories in *Summer Loanen*:

The weekends were hardest on him. From noon on Saturday until Sunday evening he stayed in the huts gazing into the fire or wandering aimlessly round the yard. From the hut door he had a vista across the city to the checkered hills that rose above the valley. Hungrily he watched the seasons through the frame of the gaunt walls. He knew how it was with the fields, whether they lay asleep and rustling drenched in the white sunlight, or trampled by the pillars of rain which strode along the hills . . .

The voice kept shouting, *Hans! Hi, Hans* . . . He sat on the bench, shaking his head and blinking his eyes. A policeman stood in the door, rain streaming from his cap and coat. 'Your lamps are blown over,' he said, 'you'd better come out and have a look at them.' He pulled on a coat and followed the policeman. The lamps were out except one which lay on its side, the flame spurting wildly in the wind. It shone on the slim long heads of the picks, and drew a line of crimson down the shafts, polished by the hands of the labouring men. He set the lamp upright again, and went round the yard, lighting the others, one by one.

Other stories in the collection reflect the variety of his work experience. 'Bound Limp Cloth', for example, describes the rise 'by the normal geologic process' of Eugene from apprentice to second assistant in the dress department of Messrs Hamilton. The discovery of the Little Library of the World's Greatest Books in the stockroom unsettles Eugene to the extent that he is in danger of losing his job. Significantly, the story deals with the knocking out of his head of 'this reading non-sense' by Miss Turley, who marries him. ('And now instead of drifting along, questioning, uneasy, independent, Eugene is a sensible married man, and grows daffodils on a plot on the Lagan Embankment.') The story is slight but surely deeply significant to the apprentice writer, since it could so easily have been autobiographical. Yet its opening sentence shows with what interest Bell regarded the vocational skills of any job; that interest was to be a characteristic of many programmes he was to make: 'There's a trick to spinning off a frocklength of georgette or mar-ocain at one turn of the wrists. Most drapers' assistants can judge it pret-ty accurately.'

The most telling details of Bell's life in the Belfast years before the outbreak of war may be gathered from his only 'modern' novel, *The Hollow Ball* (1961). A novel, of course, is no more reliable as autobio-graphy than any other fiction derived from a writer's own life. Yet certain aspects of this one are so immediate and so evidently based upon raw-nerve reaction that the reader can with confidence accept them as originating in fact. Set in the 1930s, *The Hollow Ball* describes the careers of two Protestant friends who in different ways are shackled by the conditions of their working-class backgrounds and their ways of escaping from the misery and injustice of their lot. David Minnis is the acquiescent elder son of a widow, 'a woman giving her life for them unstintingly, ungraciously'; he is given 'his start' in Messrs Hamilton's wholesale woollen warehouse on the recommendation of her lodger, Mr Rankin. Life has driven humour out of Mrs Minnis's life, and in the bleakness of her situation she has forgotten what it is like to be young. She is anxious that her son will keep the position ('You've got to make a better effort here than you did in the potato place'), and ever fearful of the future she tries to impose her own misery on him.

> He was fond of his mother. Yes, she worked away at her sewing to keep them, and he was fond of her, but my God she drove him nearly daft with the things she said! Casting up to him about his last job like that!

David Minnis is rather less sophisticated than Bell, and his mother lacks a *gravitas* that one may assign with reasonable justice to Jane McIlveen Bell (to whom *Summer Loanen* was dedicated), but edgy conversations were surely not unknown in the India Street house. The description of Hamilton's too – with its storerooms and their bewildering variety of goods, the unexpected stench of blankets in storage, the sharp practice, the raggedy camaraderie among the junior employees, and the rigid hierarchy of staff structure – has an insider authenticity.

David's friend and co-worker Bonar Law McFall is used to illustrate another aspect of Bell's own current preoccupations. To the innocently solipsistic David the way out of the misery of poor streets and his badly paid, dead-end job seems to be to develop his talent as a footballer and seek fortune through the 'hollow ball'. His preacher father died when he was six and his only ideals apart from those inculcated by the denunciatory sermons in the gospel hall where his father used to minister are the stark financial ones of his mother's genteel poverty. Boney, despite his extreme unionist name – derived from Andrew Bonar Law, the Canadian-Scottish head of the Unionist Party, prime minister from October 1922 to May 1923 and the greatest British opponent of Home Rule – is a working-class radical. He is very much his father's son in this, and the source of his loyalist name is the conservative Mrs McFall. ('My mother's that way inclined.') The father is a nightwatchman, like Hans in 'The Broken Tree', and an autodidact: 'His trouble is that he's devoured three libraries, covers and all.' He has a daunting library of left-wing books bearing 'such unappetizing titles as *The Mind in Chains*, *Anti-Duhring*, *Labour in Irish History*, *Fundamental Problems in Marxism* and a pile of dusty journals called *New Masses*'.

The father's hobby is the compilation of 'Thoughts', 'trumpet calls from Marx, Paine, Gorki, Voltaire, Shelley and other great liberators of the human spirit', the whole to be published as *The Radicals' Almanac*. Incidentally the novel's epigraph, written by Bell and the subject of confused correspondence with his editor, Doreen Henderson, at Cassell, is taken from that eventually unpublished work:

> Looking back from some vantage point we delude ourselves that we can see a pattern in our lives; but we have been impelled to this stage by events with which we were powerless or afraid to interfere.

Boney's slight public disparagement of his father's preoccupation conceals a strong belief in radical politics as a means of amelioration of working-class conditions; inevitably he is sacked from his position for being associated with an attempt to organise the workers in Hamilton's.

Northern Ireland shared in the worldwide economic depression of the period. By 1932 there were at least 100,000 unemployed, and the miserable means-tested system of Outdoor Relief so incensed its recipients (and non-recipients) that Protestant and Catholic workers united in opposition to it. In Belfast they celebrated their victory together too and together mourned their companions shot during clashes with the police in the Lower Falls. Unfortunately by 1935 the old atavism had resurfaced and it was in sectarian clashes that Belfast workers died. The McFall father and son characters belong in this world, and their fraternal concern that crosses the confessional divide was shared by Bell, as was the father's reading list; Boney's subsequent membership of the then radical IRA and his death *ar son na hÉireann* also has historical precedent. As in *Summer Loanen*, the descriptions in *The Hollow Ball* of left-wing meetings, which combine seriousness, formality and farce, have an unmistakable air of authenticity.

New Masses may be a fictitious title but it is typical of the periodicals that Bell himself read and indeed contributed to. His name was associated with a socialist news-sheet called *Labour Progress*. It originated from an office in Belfast's Church Lane, which runs from High Street to Arthur Square. This office was a focus of left-wing activity in the 1930s, and was the Northern Ireland distribution centre for Victor Gollancz's Left Book Club, the brochure for which first appeared in February 1936 promising to select important left-wing writings to offer its subscribers in a cheap format. By May the Left Book Club had 9,000 subscribers, and in spite of its founder's intentions it gained a reputation for extremism from the start. The editorial board's first two choices helped establish this view since they were strongly communist in attitude. *France Today and the People's Front* was written by Maurice Thorez, the general secretary of the French Communist Party. *Out of the Night: A Biologist's View of the Future* by H.J. Müller, suggested genetic selection in a future socialist society. Later choices mitigated this extremism somewhat and many were more appropriate to Gollancz's own political stance, anti-fascist and politically in favour of a welfare state. The club itself, its work done, was wound up in 1948.

There is no suggestion that Bell and his friends were put off by the communist flavour of the Left Book Club's more extreme choices. Like many young intellectuals of the period throughout Britain and Ireland, they were Marxists. Some indeed were card-carrying members of the Communist Party. In insular Belfast their primary concern was not so much the stemming of the rise of fascism in Italy and Germany (and its potential threat in Britain, Ireland and Romania, with their Black-Blue- and Green-shirts) as the amelioration of the appalling conditions of life in working-class Ireland, especially in the towns and cities of which they had first-hand experience. But the monolithic governmental structure of the state of Northern Ireland made any kind of constitutional agitation at a local level seem pointless, and in the years before the war there was little for their comfort in Westminster: the original spur for the creation of the Left Book Club had been the landslide Tory general election victory of 1935.

3
READING AND WRITING – AND THE ARP

D URING THE 1930S SAM HANNA BELL gradually became confident of his avocation of writing. The first paragraph of the
1962 autobiographical sketch ends with the sentence: 'Encouraged by Seán O'Faoláin, then editor of *The Bell*, and later by the novelist
F.L. Green, I turned my attention seriously to writing.' *The Bell*'s
clangour was first heard across the Irish meadows in October 1940
and, encouraged by his friend Denis Ireland (1894–1974), Bell sent
material to the Dublin master; his first story, 'Summer Loanen',
appeared in December 1941, when he was thirty-two.

In fact, the book-devouring Bell, had turned his hand to writing
some time before 1937. There were not many outlets for aspiring writers in the Ulster of the 1930s but one institution that needed material
was BBC Northern Ireland. Its charter committed it to provide a certain
amount of local matter, and one daily programme that needed a steady
supply of stories, plays and features was *Children's Hour*. Among Bell's
contract papers is one dated 'Monday 25 September' for a story called
'The Slaying of the Black Beast' for which 'Samuel Bell' received 'a
copyright fee of one guinea and a half'. The year was almost certainly
1936 because two stories – 'The Princess of the Isles' and 'How Ilveen
Hanna Kept His Promise' which earned two guineas each – were accepted on 25 February 1937 by Ursula Eason, the *Children's Hour* organiser. She was to prove a friend at court eight years later when a career as

a broadcaster began to seem possible. A script called 'Who Buried Cock Robin?' was returned on 19 March 1937 but 'The Champion of Ulster', a story about Cuchulainn, was accepted and broadcast on 7 June. In February 1938, Bell wrote giving permission to a James J. Casey, a physical education teacher, to dramatise the story for a pageant for a school in Termonfeckin, County Louth. (The rough draft of his letter was written on a torn form designed for Canadian Pacific referees, placing the much-employed Bell in their offices at 14 Donegall Place at that period.) The event was successful and appropriately presented in the county most closely associated with the Ulster hero. Bell always wrote well for children.

As the 1930s advanced, Belfast, had it been aware of them, could boast of a coterie of young men who met to discuss all aspects of art and literature. Their poets' pub was a decorous coffee shop situated at a convenient distance from the Linen Hall Library, which since its foundation as the Belfast Society for Promoting Knowledge in 1792 had been a centre of radical thought and an intellectual powerhouse in the city. This excellent institution had grown out of the Belfast Reading Society founded in 1788, and it had admitted 'Roman Catholics to a full and immediate participation in the rights enjoyed by their fellow citizens and countrymen' almost from the beginning. Membership of this institution was almost *de rigueur* for lay scholars and the apprentice artists of the city, and Campbell's Coffee House in Donegall Square North was practically next door. Bell, in conversation many years later with Deborah Keys, described its regulars with some amusement as 'young men consumed with a terrible thirst for culture'.

The company might include 'Richard Rowley', the pen name of Richard Valentine Williams (1877–1947), who had run his family's cotton handkerchief business until its collapse in 1931 and then became (not inappropriately) chairman of the Unemployment Assistance Board. He was a dialect poet who had written a mock-heroic verse play, *Apollo in Mourne*, in 1926 and was to become Bell's first publisher when in 1943 his Mourne Press issued *Summer Loanen*. Other members of the informal club were John Boyd when he could spare the time from teaching, Joseph Tomelty (1911–95) who had left his trade of decorating to become an actor and playwright, and the co-founder of the Ulster Group Theatre, Denis Ireland, who like Rowley had retired from a family business; for many years Ireland was a freelance journalist. Another member was Jack Loudan, the Armagh playwright who was to be Amanda McKittrick Ros's biographer. There were also the artists Willie Conor, Padraic Woodis (1898–1991), Gerard Dillon (1916–71) and George Campbell (1917–79), with occasional visits from the poet John Hewitt (1907–87), who was Keeper of Art at the Ulster Museum. Part-timers Bob Davidson, the local representative for Cadbury's chocolate, who shared a flat with Bell at 8 Wellington Park, and the engineer John D. Stewart who wrote stories and plays, worked for some time in the South Pacific, and on his return to Belfast in the late 1960s made a good living as an expert witness in legal cases involving traffic accidents. Separated brethren who looked in when they made visits north from Dublin were 'Lynn Doyle' – Leslie A. Montgomery (1873–1961), the humorist and novelist; 'Rutherford Mayne' – Samuel Waddell (1878–1967), the chief playwright of the Ulster Literary Theatre; and Cathal O'Shannon (1889–1969), the socialist.

An appreciation written by Robert Greacen (b. 1920) in *Brief Encounters* (1991) records his first impressions of Bell, aged thirty. Greacen was then a mature nineteen and already a determined poet:

> I first met Sam Hanna Bell around the start of the war in 1939. The meeting came about most probably through my friend John Boyd – then a teacher and later a playwright – who put me in touch with several older writers and intellectuals of a generation slightly older than mine. . . .
>
> On Saturday nights Sam and Bob [Davidson] kept open house. The literati and some politicos of the Left assembled there, armed with bottles of stout, for discussion that could begin with Karl Marx and end with D.H. Lawrence. We would drink and argue the night away behind black-out curtains. Football might come in for comment. Had not Bob Davidson . . . once played soccer at professional level and for Linfield at that? . . . But mainly our chat – or chatter – centred on the arts and politics. Sam, like most of us there, had a commitment to democratic socialism.
>
> I remember Sam as an intense young man with gingery, bristly hair. He had a seriousness of purpose and a directness of approach that was very appealing. Unlike some who talked of what they would some day write, including the 'Great Ulster Novel', Sam was already getting on with the job and learning through trial and error – and extensive reading – the craft of fiction.

Davidson's company car was a marvellous possession and one good use it was put to was to drive groups of friends to a cold-water cottage near Murlough Bay in northeast Antrim. (The place had been a favourite of the controversial patriot Roger Casement who was executed for his part in the Easter Rising.) Not all members of the group were as radical or anti-establishment as Bell, and Casement's career was a topic of frequent and heated argument. Though the Sea of Moyle is not exactly the Mediterranean, the guests of both sexes were fond of skinny-dipping, as John Boyd recalls in the second volume of his autobiography, *The Middle of My Journey* (1990).

> Among the friends I made was Sam Hanna Bell, who was a couple of years older than myself, and a friend of Bob Davidson. . . . The three of us had spent holidays at Murlough Bay, where we had the company of Eva Gorstein, who later emigrated to South America, Peggy Lowenthal, who married an Austrian skiing instructor and settled later in Vienna, and Linde Ewalt, who was then a medical student at Queen's and later married Bob Davidson. The Murlough holidays began before the war started, and some of our number, including Bob's younger sister Georgie and her husband, an Englishman, kept returning to Murlough year after year long after the war was over. . . .
>
> Murlough Bay is one of the most isolated parts of Northern Ireland. The roomy, sheltered cottage we rented was beside the bay, protected by Torr Head to the south and Fair Head to the north. It was a romantic place, having associations with Roger Casement who, according to the old people, had slept in the cottage and loved to scramble over the scree and along the shore. . . . We were, of course, escapists from the war raging outside Ireland; and we seldom discussed it. Sometimes we saw convoys of ships in the North Channel on their way to America, but that was all. War was tacitly a *verboten* subject. Eva and Linde, émigrés from Germany, never talked of their experiences there, and certainly none of us ever questioned them about their past. That amazes me now, considering how inquisitive I was. My explanation is that personal relations obsessed us and we gave our attention to little else.
>
> We escaped to Murlough as often as we could, during the summer, at Easter and even at Christmas, and we bathed at all seasons in the cold sea. Adjacent to the cottage lay the tiny beach, sometimes stony but always sandy in summer, when we used the beach most of all. The first summer the German girls surprised us by swimming naked and

the rest of us immediately followed their lead. The beauty of the sight of young women running naked in and out of the sea still remains with me as a symbol of our freedom.

It was from here that Bell sent his mother a postcard dated 17 August 1943 and postmarked 'Ballycastle'. It showed Fair Head and read:

This is the sort of scenery I've been living in this past few days. I'm having a splendid time. This scene is taken just above the cottage in Murlough. I got the proofs from Mourne Press last week. It should be out shortly.

'It' was his first collection of stories.

Another regular at both Murlough and the Chalet d'Or was E[myr] Estyn Evans (1905–89) who had become a lecturer in geography at Queen's University in 1928 (he was to become honorary director of the Institute of Irish Studies there when it was founded in 1966). Bell and he became very friendly; they had in common a deep interest in Irish myth, legend and folkways. Evans's books and Bell's radio programmes did much to preserve records of a passing way of life. Evans's wife recalls that each envied the other: Bell's freedom from the burden of fixed hours, Evans's steady job and academic prestige.

Bell's frequent changes of job continued; it is not clear whether it was restlessness or dismissals that caused them. As we have seen, in 1937–38 he was bookings clerk for the Canadian Steamship and Railway Company, the romantic associations of the title somewhat diluted by the fact that his place of work was no log cabin Hudson's Bay outpost but an office in Donegall Place. That job ended with the outbreak of war and Bell, though by now almost thirty, was placed on the reserve list. His friend Bob Davidson was appointed Chief Welfare Officer for the city and he offered Bell a job in his department; in time he would become Davidson's deputy.

Bell wrote a brief chapter of autobiography for a special edition of the *Honest Ulsterman*, No. 64 (January 1980). The issue's general title was 'The War Years in Ulster (1939–45)' and Bell's contribution described his involvement with *Labour Progress*.

The work was carried out on Sunday mornings. . . . Ostensibly it was a Labour Party organ, but the Party leaders viewed it with suspicion, then hostility, when we became too acid about prominent Unionists. It was an education in politics. The Nazi invasion of the USSR may have thrown other editorial bodies into momentary confusion. We stencilled ARMS FOR THE PEOPLE!! on our orange-coloured top sheet and similar operatic slogans on succeeding issues. Stuffed up jumpers and down boiler suits the paper was carried into factories and the ship-yard. Not one copy was confiscated or one distributor apprehended. From this we concluded that our paper wasn't as seditious and inflammatory as we had thought.

Bell had become an air raid warden and his account of the air raids of April 1941 is similarly brief. His sector was 'bounded approximately by Botanic Avenue and the Lagan' but there were few incidents to report, a stick of incendiaries in McClure Street and a landmine in the Ormeau Park.

> We wrestled with street doors blown halfway down hallways. From under the stairs in a house we extricated an old woman still clutching a miniature Union Jack. Some thought the tree-lined avenues and streets misled the Luftwaffe into thinking that here the countryside began. Others held that we were saved by our proximity to the Malone Road.

(Serving in one of those ARP relief stations at the time was a young man in his twenties who in his time had helped to sell the *Socialist Appeal* and who would make a splash in the literary world in 1955 with *Judith Hearne*.)

An identity card showing Bell's proof of membership of the Belfast Civil Defence Authority and dated 24 November 1942 describes him as 'Assistant to Emergency Meals Superintendent'. The special edition of the *Honest Ulsterman* on the war years cited above contains a brilliant impressionistic piece by the poet Roy McFadden (b. 1921) which has two brief 'under-fire' snapshots of Bell: 'Sam Hanna Bell, embattled in his tin hat, offered good advice on the use of the stirrup pump,' he recorded, and – during an apparently characteristic literary conversation in Lisburn – 'Joe [Tomelty] has been reading Chekhov, Sam Hanna Bell said, rubbing the war-wound of his helmet-weal.' An example of Bell's terseness is contained in McFadden's poem 'Sound Sense':

> Lucas used to gloss his party piece,
> MacDiarmid's 'Watergaw',
> By stressing how its *chitterin licht*
> Conveyed the stuttering flight
> Of water fowl skimming a river's breeze:

Till finally a plastic Scot complained:
Translated *Rainbow*. But
He hardly faltered in defence:
Just veered, and took his stance
On sound suggesting more than language meant.

Sam Bell it was who raised a somnolent head,
Insulted back to life,
Bitter from heavy reading and
The need to comprehend.
Tit, fart and *willy* were the words he said.

Bell's essay contains a brief mention of the founding of the Mourne Press, Richard Rowley's contribution to Ulster culture. According to Bell, Rowley announced its formation to the company in Campbell's. Bell does not give the date of the announcement but the press's most significant titles – *The White Mare and Other Stories* by Michael McLaverty (1904–92), who was already well known as a novelist, and *Summer Loanen and Other Stories* by Bell – appeared in 1943, the latter decorated with a pencil-drawn profile of the author by Doris V. Blair. Also mentioned in the laconic essay is the birth of *Lagan*, a literary journal that as a complement to *The Bell* would concentrate on 'Ulster writings'.

In 1943 John Boyd, Bob Davidson and I put together and published a literary magazine. . . . The first number was put into the hands of the Belfast *News-Letter*, part of whose operations had been moved to 36 Windsor Park. The printers worried if paper would be available and we worried with them. Word came at last that part of the issue could be collected. I borrowed a carrier-bike from Charlie Mooney's pub, filled the iron basket with the first few dozen copies, and re-turned elated to 8 Wellington Park, where . . . most of the editing had been done. While stoutly disclaiming that a literary renaissance was coming up over Ben Madigan, we thought that writers would be glad to see their work in print. The pervading isolation must have engendered some feeling of comradeship among us. I can think of no other plausible reason, for at that age we should have been concerned with our own work and not [with] editing the work of others. *Lagan* was the success it deserved to be and appeared annually till 1946.

That dismissive peroration with its ironic ambivalence was uttered by a 70-year-old man with much of his 'own work' safely behind him. The 34-year-old ARP official who summoned *Lagan* out of the air in 1943 was anything but dismissive at the time. Though he had not the title of editor, nor was he a significant contributor, the idea was his. It was he, too, who pressurised John Boyd into accepting the position of editor. Boyd was initially resistant, no doubt feeling like Bell that editing was a long day's journey from being a creative writer. He was, however, the most critically equipped of the founding trio, with degrees in literature and a consuming interest in European literature, especially French. As he records in *The Middle of My Journey*: 'In Paris in 1935 I had seen and listened to speeches by the foremost European writers, I had brought home volumes by Proust and Gide and Mauriac . . .'

Bell had already had two stories published by Seán O'Faoláin in *The Bell* and had them fervently praised. He had great admiration for the older man who was already Ireland's premier man of letters with an exemplary record in the fight for artistic freedom in what he had called the 'Grocers' Republic'. And the tinkling of his two-year-old *Bell* was reaching the remotest parts of de Valera's protectionist state. This did not inhibit Bell in the least from launching his own – or Ulster's own – equivalent.

His attitude was rather that of another sanguine Ulsterman, Bulmer Hobson, who founded *Ulad*, a noted predecessor of *Lagan*, in 1904. As Bell records in *The Theatre in Ulster* (1972), Hobson and David Parkhill had gone to see the 'theatre people' in Dublin in 1902 aware of the excitement that Yeats, Gregory, Martyn, Gonne, Æ, the Fays and the rest had generated since the founding of the Irish Literary Theatre in 1899. Hobson and Parkhill were founder members of the Protestant National Association which was trying to spread the ideas and principles of the United Irishmen in Ulster in the aftermath of the fall of Parnell. They thought of drama as a means of propaganda and they especially wanted permission to do Yeats's *Cathleen ni Houlihan*, which was about the rising of 1798. Though most of the Dublin group were cordial and helpful, Yeats was 'haughty and aloof' and permission was refused. But Hobson was nineteen and was not to be put down by an old man of thirty-seven. On the train home he turned to Parkhill and cried, 'Damn Yeats, we'll write our own plays.' And the Ulster Literary Theatre dates from that cry.

Bell's instinct told him that there would be an audience for a northern equivalent of *The Bell*. (O'Faoláin, conscious of the otherness of the

Northern Ireland state, published several Ulster numbers, beginning with the issue of July 1941.) Many of those who were asked to contribute to the four issues of *Lagan* had also written material for *The Bell*, including Michael McLaverty, Joe Tomelty, W.R. Rodgers (1909–69), Roy McFadden, Robert Greacen, Maurice James Craig (b. 1919), Denis Ireland and John Hewitt. This is hardly surprising: *The Bell* was the pre-eminent Irish literary journal of the period and the natural outlet for Irish writers, especially poets and short-story writers. Yet Bell knew the ferment of creativity among his friends and was confident that they would make *Lagan* as dynamic and worthy as *The Bell* but with an Ulster accent. (The young poets McFadden and Greacen had already published a poetry pamphlet called *Ulster Voices* which had been praised by both the *Irish Times* and the *Belfast Telegraph*. They were encouraged by the success of the first issue 'to present a second Folio' in summer 1943 which had three poems by John Hewitt, verse by the editors and a piece by John Boyd, 'Murlough Bay', noting 'the rounded rocks of Tor' and the 'cowl-like mist' on Fair Head. In all there were four of these Folios. Later McFadden and Barbara Hunter were to edit twenty issues of *Rann* (1948–53), an influential journal of poetry and criticism – the title was the Irish word for stanza – which also published one of the first bibliographies of Ulster writers.)

Though Boyd was the editor and did much editorial work he was *primus inter pares*: Bell and Davidson did their share, and because they worked together and shared a flat they probably had more time to spare than the married teacher. The magazine's manifesto is contained in its first editorial, which though ostensibly the work of the reluctant editor, must have been hammered out by the trio and contained the credo of its onlie begetter:

> An Ulster literary tradition that is capable of developing and enriching itself must spring out of the life and speech of the province; and an Ulster writer cannot evade his problems by adopting either a superimposed English or a sentimental Gaelic outlook. He must, therefore, train his ears to catch the unique swing of our speech; train his eyes to note the natural beauty of our hills and the unnatural ugliness of our towns: above all he must study the subtle psychology of our people.

These attitudes were deeply imbedded in Bell's psyche and became the composite lodestar of his broadcasting career. *Within Our Province,* the series title of a number of programmes made between 1949 and 1953, marks the spiritual and literary territory of all Bell's work. It was not provincial; the universality of *December Bride* and *The Hollow Ball* prove that; but it was regional and deeply cherished. Just as Thoreau assured his detractors that he had 'travelled a good deal in Concord' (relishing the pun) so Bell's parish and his world was the Ulster he knew, the distinctiveness of which he wished to preserve.

John Boyd admits his own reluctance to the editor and blames 'the persuasive tongue of Sam Hanna Bell' for his elevation. He regarded Belfast as 'an incredibly provincial city' and could not take any local writer seriously. Bell, however, was adamant, and he was correct in his view as to the most appropriate editor. Boyd was the trained literary man and the seasoned critic: rejection or editorial suggestions would be more acceptable coming from him than coming from a former chocolate salesman or an ARP welfare officer.

The title *Lagan* was Bell's, intended to celebrate the river in whose basin a majority of Ulster people lived. The title also had the advantage of being non-denominational. It was not arrived at without considerable discussion. An entry in an unpublished diary kept by David Millar, a teacher friend of Boyd, records that the question was discussed on the morning after a party in the Wellington Park flat.

> Sunday 27 December 1942
> I slept in the flat overnight and suffered from the effects of a short sleep and a hangover. This morning the new literary magazine, *The Harp*, was discussed. Urged on by Bob and Sam, Jack Boyd took on the job of editor.

In retrospect Bell was not entirely happy about the final title. As he admitted to Deborah Keys, the word *Lagan* meant nothing outside Northern Ireland. There was no reason why *Lagan* should have any significance for potential readers in Cork or Galway, let alone in Britain. Still, *Lagan* it became, and as Boyd puts it; 'The three of us put up the cash — £10 each. We supplemented this sum with a few cheap advertisements, found a printer in Lisburn, and the first issue appeared in 1942.' This account, besides mistaking the year, seems at variance with Bell's 1980 recollection that it was printed by the *Belfast News-Letter*. Perhaps numbers after the first were printed in Lisburn.

The 2,000 copies of the first number sold out even though they were printed on porridgy paper with bits of tree still adhering rather in the manner of the recently popular wood-chip wallpaper. *Lagan* was perhaps more of an anthology than a magazine for original material. Bell called it such in the piece in the *Honest Ulsterman*, noting that it was subtitled 'A Collection of Ulster Writings'. The editorial already quoted from gave the founders a chance to consider the nature of the Ulster writer and to have relatively harsh words to say about Ulster writing.

> The fact is that Ulster has been drained of her most talented writers; no vital tradition has been fostered (a Gaelic tradition, more or less subterranean, has been overlooked or made exclusive); and instead of a vital tradition a debased tradition has been perpetuated and encouraged by such means as powerful newspapers, puerile films, trashy magazines, feeble dramatic societies, and the trivial local productions of the BBC.

Elsewhere the artificial nature of the Northern Ireland state is glanced at: '[The Ulster writer] must be conscious of the inherent contradictions in our society, and of the intricate relationship between a maladjusted society and a maladjusted individual.' And a self-congratulatory cosiness is excoriated: 'It is nonsense to talk at present of a literary renaissance for the standard of writing is not high; it is however rising, the result perhaps of the war and the disintegration of firmly held political beliefs . . .'

The first number had stories by Joe Tomelty, Michael McLaverty, Bob Davidson, and Boyd himself, as well as the longest and strongest story from *Summer Loanen*, 'The Broken Tree'. W.R. Rodgers, Maurice James Craig, Robert Greacen, John Hewitt and Roy McFadden contributed poems, and Hewitt in his persona as art historian had a piece entitled 'Some Observations on the History of Irish Paintings'. It was a very creditable performance and the serious young men who produced it took some modest pride in their baby. The editorial had a postscript not without a touch of mock diffidence: 'It is hoped that further numbers of "Lagan" will appear, and prospective contributors are invited to send their manuscripts to John Boyd, Ballymacash, Lisburn.' The fact that the journal was as much anthology as 'little magazine' is indicated by the acknowledegments made to other publishers for the material by McFadden, McLaverty and Rodgers.

Later numbers, having as co-editors Jack Loudan, David Kennedy, Roy McFadden and John Hewitt, presented a more elegant appearance;

the paper was better and the covers bore a minimalist etching by James Watson of a barge being poled under a Lagan bridge. All four numbers had decorations by William Conor, who was indulgent to the young men and prodigal with his sketches. The third number printed a piece called 'The Green Springcart' by Bell which was part of his work in progress for *December Bride*.

The editorial of the fourth and final number began with the slightly depressed and prophetic sentence '*Lagan* has survived the war: and the problem now is to survive the peace.' The editor felt that the aim stated in the first number – 'to begin a literary tradition springing out of the life and speech of this province' – had 'not yet been achieved'. Bell in his later autobiographical sketch described *Lagan* as an 'outlet of expression for Irish writers at home and in the Forces'. The war over, there was never going to be a great public for a small literary magazine, though the later experiences of *Rann* and *Threshold* showed that there was a real if limited market. *Lagan*, like all the 'little magazines who died to make verse free', had a short life, though it survived longer than some others. The last number sold fewer than 500 copies and the outstanding bills were paid rather ingeniously by the expedient of having its four trustees do a programme for the new Talks Producer at BBC Northern Ireland, John Boyd, and using their fees to pay the debts. John Hewitt, who was poetry editor, either forgot about the arrangement or decided that the fee was properly his, and had to be reminded strongly about the agreed arrangement. By the time *Lagan* came to its honourable conclusion, Bell himself was already established as Features Producer for the BBC's Northern Ireland region (see Chapter 5).

The period of *Lagan*, the Folios of Greacen and McFadden, and later *Rann*, seems in retrospect a kind of golden age of Ulster writing. So much of the work done then has lasted, and the names of the period still glitter. The young(ish) participants were talented, opinionated and vocal; and the regular discussions about life, literature and the price of beer were often heated. A little of that fire remained to blaze forth in a short public spat in the columns of the *Irish Times* in January 1978. Bell had been interviewed by Elgy Gillespie, and the published article gave the impression that he had said that only he, Hewitt, Tomelty and McLaverty had kept writing alive at the time. Roy McFadden wrote a characteristically trenchant rebuttal to the paper on 4 January beginning with the sentence, 'Sam Bell must be in his dotage.' McFadden went on

31

to give a comprehensive literary history of the 1940s and early 1950s. In fact, as Gillespie made clear in a letter published two days later, Bell had mentioned other names including those of Greacen, McFadden and her father Leslie Gillespie, but she had 'excised them from a sense of modesty and from a desire to avoid the sort of back-scratching orgy so familiar to those who know, read and love literary magazines'. McFadden's reply (published on 12 January) gave yet more detail of the literary lights of the time and added:

> ... now that Elgy Gillespie has elected to damp down a sputter of twigs before we have had time to warm our hands, let me wish Mr Bell a long and happy supping of the gruel of trimmed memories, and venture an ambition that Miss Gillespie will strain towards a proper immodesty on any future improperly inhibiting occasion.

Bell snarled a bit in private – no man aged sixty-eight and a half likes to be thought of as doting – but there the matter ended. Robert Greacen, in a kind of supplementary (17 January 1978), referred to 'the literary battle raging between Ms Elgy Gillespie in Dublin and Mr Roy McFadden in Belfast', but by then the field was empty.

4
SUMMER LOANEN

THOUGH SAM HANNA BELL was essentially a novelist, his literary apprenticeship was in short fiction. Bell was no easy writer, and he was already thirty-four years old by the time his collection *Summer Loanen and Other Stories* was published, in 1943. He had already had some encouragement with the stories that O'Faoláin had praised and published. 'This We Shall Maintain' was written in response to a letter received from O'Faoláin on 28 April 1942 asking for more stories of the standard of 'Summer Loanen'. 'The one we printed was beautiful – one of the best we have ever had – and I've been hoping you would send another,' O'Faoláin wrote. Gerry Morrow, his friend and temporary literary agent, and one of a family that had played a significant part in the story of the Ulster Literary Theatre, wrote him a letter on 15 June:

> Seán O'F. says that your second story is 'LOVELY. Perfect. Divine.'
> Thought I'd let you know – you Gorgeous Beast!

By the summer of the following year Bell was correcting proofs of his first book. They were sent on 11 August by Rowley, with instructions to mark on the galleys exactly what order the stories were to appear in. Bell intended to take the book's title from the story 'Always Raise Your Hat to a Hearse', but Rowley (and A.W. Emerson, the printer) were against it. Rowley wrote:

I implore you to reconsider your first choice – It's too long – it suggests mournful thoughts – it isn't attractive. I'm convinced that 'Summer Loanen' or 'The Broken Tree' would be much better. 'Summer Loanen' for my choice.

His concluding paragraph was encouraging: 'In looking over the proofs I'm more than pleased with the book. It's really good stuff, & if the public has any taste it ought to do well.'

Bell considered calling the book 'The Broken Tree', the title of a story that, as we have seen, had deep symbolic significance for him. It was also much the longest story in the book, more than twice the length of the others. It is an account of how the accidental death of a cow and a series of related misfortunes drive a small farmer from the land he loves to the city. Hans Gault had up till then stubbornly resisted his wife's plea to accept a job from his brother-in-law ('I'm tired av livin' in all this clabber and mud') because that would mean 'livin' in a brick box in some street'. Now, disappointed even by the brother-in-law, in his job as a night watchman he alone is discontented. ('Maisie was happy in their new home. In the mornings Hans would lie, listening drowsily to her and the woman next door conversing in the back, their mouths full of clothes pegs.')

As ever the technical details of vocational skills are described with textbook precision. The farm year with its ploughing, sowing and the rest, and the sights and sounds that make the back-breaking work worthwhile are marvellously evoked. The description of the attempt to lift the stricken cow from the deep ditch in which she has fallen is meticulous. The sapling that is used as a pulley mount is too young to bear the weight:

> Slowly the cow came up out of the ditch, and as hands stretched out to swing her on to the grass the tree screamed, slivered down and broke. For a moment the gross body hung arched in the air, then fell, the neck striking a ridge in the sheugh face.

Here too is the masterly use of east Ulster dialect that characterises Bell's great novel *December Bride* and has made his work one of the authorities regularly referred to in the recent dictionary of colloquial Irish, Bernard Share's *Slanguage* (1997). Such sentences as 'Hans, Hans, yer wee coo's cowped in the sheugh!' have a kind of rough poetry.

Summer Loanen contains ten stories in all, which vary in quality and kind from slight sketches to seasoned stories that deserve their place in any representative anthology. The *Bell* stories dealt with childhood, but elsewhere there is a clear attempt to get away from this source of inspiration. 'Bound Limp Cloth', 'Thursday Nights', 'A Fish without Chips', 'Two Blades of Grass' and 'Dark Tenement' are attempts, not always successful, to deal with the urban life of young adults. Bell was conscious of the siren call of childhood as a theme for stories, especially for Irish writers. David Millar's diary entry for Monday 14 June 1943 records a conversation with Bell in Mooney's bar in Cornmarket:

> Sam discoursed on the art of the short story. He differentiated between theme and plot. Emphasised the need for hard work. He was hostile to what he called 'spit on the floor realism'. Stick to Ireland. There's plenty of material there for the writer . . .
>
> I told Sam I was planning to write short stories and an autobiography. He poo-pooed the idea of writing an autobiography and said that the short stories should be about adults rather than children.
>
> He advised me to go out with some ordinary decent girl to gain experience and disapproved of going away to live in a foreign country. He believes in self-assertion. You must assert, dogmatise, break down opposition in order to maintain one's individuality.

In fact the stories about childhood in *Summer Loanen* are the most successful. The title story and 'This We Shall Maintain' have a clarity based on the unblinking observation of the child that others lack. The adult stories are less fully understood. Even so, they are significant as the first faltering moves towards the extended prose fictions that were to be Bell's true *métier* as a writer.

'A Fish without Chips' is a tale of two young apprentices, Charlie and Davie, who are learning the trade of toolmaking under the unlovely eye of a brutal foreman, Big Archie Glass. Davie moves from fraternal indifference to possible matchmaker when he fixes a date with his sister for Charlie. A clumsy accident which results in a broken set of calipers consumes all the money that Charlie had intended to use for the trip to the pictures. He stands in the rain opposite the cinema watching in fear and frustration as the girl waits in vain; the next day at work he has to defend himself from being beaten by Davie for standing his sister up. The last scene shows Big Archie, whose bullying insistence on being paid had caused the crisis, urging them on. ('They closed, reeled and

went down. Big Archie sent a sliver of tobacco juice on to the struggling boys. "Bate hell out av him, boy," he said with fine impartiality.')
The story is about immaturity, the demands of a barely understood and self-conscious chivalry, the malevolence of the old in envy of the young, and shopfloor *machismo*. In a letter to Bell Gerald Morrow (a contributor to *Lagan* as well as Bell's agent) compared the story to 'Two Gallants', from Joyce's *Dubliners* (1914). It is hard to see similarities except in the general principle that women are kinder and stronger than men.

One of the stories, 'Thursday Nights,' paints an interesting picture of life in wartime Belfast. The chief character, Maureen Croskery, is one of the salesladies of Messrs Hamilton's, the department store that also forms the background of 'Bound Limp Cloth' (see Chapter 2) and is described in memorable detail in *The Hollow Ball* as David Minnis's place of apprenticeship. The store is a fictional representation of Sinclair's in Royal Avenue where Bell learned not only the secrets of the trade but also the complicated hierarchy of the staff. The first paragraph of 'Thursday Nights' has a piece of wry observation: 'As she approached the fancies the three other girls leant forward on the glass-topped counter, supporting themselves on their fingers (they all wore engagement rings, and one was really engaged . . .).' The description of quitting time in the store continues the wry humour and suggests that Bell if he had wished could have written an 'institutional' novel about Hamilton's, conveying the life of the place through the interlinked stories of owners, staff and regular customers, much as Arnold Bennett did with *Imperial Palace*, J.B. Priestley did with *Angel Pavement* and Vicki Baum did with *Grand Hotel* (all published in 1930). Such a novel would have lacked the high seriousness of *December Bride* and *The Hollow Ball* but might have been more popular.

> At five minutes to six a bell trills among all the departments on all three floors of Messrs. Hamiltons. Young ladies with black bags under their arms, and young men with surreptitious cigarettes in their palm, dash from behind counters, up stairs into cloakrooms. A narrow side entrance beside the time clock is open to allow the staff to depart. Here, slim young ladies in elegant costumes punch time-cards, and go out to meet their steadies.

The Belfast of the middle 1940s had as many unsteadies as steadies. In

'Thursday Nights', Maureen and her steady Jimmie have always met on Thursday evenings and had tea before going to the pictures. On this particular Thursday she dismisses him, not unkindly, because she has a date with an army officer. She spends the evening at the Khaki Klub, one of several such institutions organised to meet the needs of Allied forces which are bringing a whiff of the exotic to the staid industrial city. At the club she dances with a whole command structure ('she once was carried round the floor on a major-general's stomach'), virtually ignoring her escort, Lieutenant Peter Newman. When they reach her home decorously early by taxi he is sent off, with the words, 'Oh, no, not Thursday. I'm booked every Thursday. Give me a phone soon.' The piece is much more than just a sketch; it sums up the heady confusion that the war brought but it also reassures about the essential Ulster level-headedness of the successful saleslady and her sisters throughout Northern Ireland. It is a vein that Bell rarely used again.

'Two Blades of Grass' first appeared in an anthology, *Now in Ulster*, which was edited by Arthur and George Campbell. It deals with the funeral of a girl of nineteen, the daughter of the narrator's wife's cousin:

> Apart from godwillsits like starvation and war, I thought, it's frightening to think that people can die at nineteen. When old people die we don't panic. It seems natural . . . But not at nineteen, and not if it's a woman. No woman is ugly both inside and outside at nineteen, and God knows we could do with all the beautiful insides we've got.

The narrator first visits the wrong wake house, going through the reverential motions and vainly trying to find Bob, the girl's father, and to recognise the dead girl's boyfriend ('it was safe to assume that this girl would have a boy. I felt sure I could spot him just by the look on his face.'). The correct funeral is at the Crumlin Road end of Ankara Street, and there the narrator has no difficulty in finding either Bob or the boy ('He stood with a brown hat drooping from his oil-stained fingers. A cornerboy, he had taken on overnight the dignity of a man.') The piece is slight but extremely accurate in its observation.

The penultimate story, 'Dark Tenement', is about a kind of nighttown, Belfast. Robert, a young man on the town, allows himself to be picked up by a prostitute on Christmas Eve, buys liquor after hours, and spends the night in a filthy tenement. The story ends on Christmas morning with the singing of 'Gloria in Excelsis Deo!' coming from a church ablaze with festive lighting, and with Robert's dramatic apostrophe to an unheeding statue. This is sentimental. Yet Bell is able to capture the risk and appeal of low life, as one himself acquainted with the night.

'Summer Loanen', 'Always Raise Your Hat to a Hearse', 'Old Clay New Earth' and 'This We Shall Maintain' are characterised by remarkable confidence. Though city-born, Bell had spent his formative years in the heart of a countryside that cared little for towns. In the title story three small children – brother and sister, Jimmie and Nannie Orr, and another boy, Francie McCoy – enjoy the endless glory of a summer day in the fields only to have the shadow of sectarianism blight it. As with all Bell's country tales, the writing is marked by precise observation which extended to animals: 'Every few seconds she [a goat] would shake her bearded head free of the clegs and flies that sipped at the rims of her old eyes.'

'Always Raise Your Hat to a Hearse' is a comic character sketch, a kind of prose 'Finnegan's Wake' (the American-Irish ballad, not the Joycean work-in-progress). The victim of an accident in the city is taken for Banjo Reilly, an itinerant thatcher well known from Ardglass to Belfast. The real Reilly turns up hale as ever five days after the funeral while the obsequies are still continuing. He wreaks a just vengeance on Shuey Ogle the publican, who alone of the neighbours did not attend the wake. Though the piece is light-hearted, again the sense of rural community is strong. (Banjo is a comic precursor of the thatcher Charlie Gomartin, the father of Sarah Gomartin who is the eponymous December bride of Bell's first novel.)

'Old Clay New Earth' is a threnody on death and interment, in which none of the grisly details of fresh openings of family graves is spared:

As the preacher drew back there was a sudden dislodgement of the soil, and a round clay-filled thing hampered by muddy streamers trundled to my feet. I heard the man behind me catch his breath and glimpsed his aged distorted face over my shoulder. 'It's Tammy's first yin,' he breathed, 'I wud ha' kenned her by the long black hair!' I looked up to where Tom stood; he was gazing over the lough, following the flight of three swans as they toiled across the sky. With a twist of the blade the digger spun the skull back into the earth.

'This We Shall Maintain', the story that so impressed O'Faoláin, is about the shock and hurt of Aunt Lottie when her nephew Joe secures only third prize 'for answering in scripture at Sabbath School': 'Her sibilant whisper followed him down the aisle, "a Third Prize fur a McGimpsey".' The grief is all the deeper in that the first-prize winner is Aggie Gaw and 'the failure was moral rather than scholarly'. There is a cruel Calvinism in the aunt's bedtime sentence: 'I thank the Good Man yer father's no' livin' tae see this day.' (The story was broadcast from Belfast on 11 November 1952.)

Bell had sent some of his stories to Michael McLaverty for his opinion. McLaverty, five years older than Bell, was already established as a writer with two of his most popular novels, *Call My Brother Back* (1939) and *Lost Fields* (1941) already in print. McLaverty's answer, written on 23 June 1943, was friendly and expert. His comments on Bell's stories were unflinching, and his prescriptions are interesting in that though the results would have improved the stories they would have been McLaverty rather than Bell stories. In the 'The Broken Tree' McLaverty felt that 'when I had come to the lovely line *The soft evening wind came to him over the aching stubble of the field* I was surprised to find that the story had not ended.' This would have meant cutting five eighths of the text.

> The death of the cow is a fine bit of work and I'd advise you to use it as the core of a short story and confine it to two characters: Hans (you should change his name) and his young wife you could make both of them in love with the farm, and so heighten the tragedy and poignancy of the cow's death. As the basis of another story you could use with great delicacy the description of the countryman's uprooted life in the city . . .

This was all very well, but it was not what Bell intended. McLaverty also suggests that 'Two Blades of Grass' should be called 'The Funeral': 'there's nothing to be gained by wrapping your title in obscurity: think of Chekov's titles – The Wife, Easter Eve, Ward No. 6, etc.' The final paragraph of McLaverty's letter suggests a number of magazines that might accept the stories and encourages: 'Keep sending them out; keep on writing; and don't let rejection slips discourage you – I have had as many in my days as would make a fire-screen.'

Bell's response was appreciative and respectful but he made very few changes, if any. He did make an interesting admission:

> I note your remarks about a disciplined acquaintance with form. I've read few of the masters and to tell the truth I sit down to a book of stories, or for that matter to any work of fiction, with a sense of discomfort (maybe it's the Covenanter in me!) but I realise that the study of form is essential. The astringent artistic conscience – ah!

Summer Loanen was published for four shillings and sixpence by the Mourne Press in the autumn of 1943 at the same time as McLaverty's *The White Mare and Other Stories*, and it is interesting to compare the two books. Five of the six McLaverty stories had already been published, and 'The Game Cock', 'The White Mare' and 'Moonshine' (later 'The Poteen Maker') are among the best that McLaverty ever wrote. None of Bell's stories is of the same quality. McLaverty's best short stories are much superior to his novels. For Bell short stories were tentative essays towards his true literary genre, the novel.

Summer Loanen was reviewed in the second number of *Lagan* by 'R.D.' who wrote that the 'stories are of mixed and uneven quality but each convinces that the writer has a natural grace of style, an observant eye, a range of mood and some capacity to convey emotion'. R.D. found that:

> The best stories in the collection are the childhood studies, 'Old Clay New Earth', and 'The Broken Tree'. They share a unity of outlook which is interesting and there are moments of deep insight. The evocation of the rural scene is rich in well-turned phrases and creative imagery. 'Old Clay New Earth' contains a profound impression of a rural burial but it is marred by a horrific incident which tears the close-knit prose and draws the imagination away from the predominating solemnity of the occasion.

Fifty years on, it is possible to observe that not only is the 'horrific incident' entirely typical of the writer that Bell intended to be but it is what changes an ordinary 'colour' piece into a memorable experience. It is also hard to agree that the sketches of Belfast working life in 'Dark Tenement', 'Two Blades of Grass', 'Thursday Nights' and 'Bound Limp Cloth' are 'slight but amusing'. The book was reviewed at the same time as *The White Mare* and the reviewer's opinion that the McLaverty stories were superior was obvious. Nevertheless, his concluding paragraph is far from dismissive of Bell:

This group of stories indicates Mr Bell's talent for story telling but there is too much striving after effect. He has yet to learn that melo-dramatic incident impoverishes whatever sensitive impression is con-veyed. It is a fault attending many promising writers, it is not serious and when his approach is less unsure better things can be expected in the future.

Bell would naturally have read the review – he may well have com-missioned it. His way with his subsequent fiction was to take a long time over each of his four novels. The dates of publication are signifi-cant: *December Bride* (1951), *The Hollow Ball* (1961), *A Man Flourishing* (1973), *Across the Narrow Sea* (1987). Admittedly he was a working man; the day job did take up a lot of his time, especially in the years from 1945 to 1969 spent at the BBC. Yet he revised and pondered and restructured until the final versions suited his exacting mature standards.

Gerry McCrudden, who was a colleague and collaborator (they wrote a comic play together called *The Sliddry Dove*), remembers a nice example of this relentless precision. They worked together on many radio features, Bell as producer, Gerry as studio manager. Once they required a particular sound effect, that of the long drawer of a bread van being pulled out so that the bread server could show his wares. (In a region famous for the variety of its small breads this was an essential selling ploy.) None of the studio effects satisfied Bell, so he and Gerry borrowed an Ormo Bakery van, drove it to the Lagan embankment, and after sixteen tries got the sound that satisfied. Another of Gerry's reminiscences sheds light on Bell's attitude to writing. Once a young woman sought his advice on the matter of creative writing. 'Get your-self a copy of Roget's *Thesaurus*, for a start,' he suggested. 'There you'll find many subtle alternatives to your first choice of words.' Some time later the neophyte showed him an example of her work. It went some-thing like this: 'The farmer trudged wearily behind his plough. When he reached the top of the hill he turned andante and went down again.'

Years later in a letter written on 6 January 1978 to David Marcus (b. 1924), then editor of the New Irish Writing section in the *Irish Press*, Bell referred to *Summer Loanen*. Marcus had shown fraternal interest in Literary Miscellany, the 'little magazine' enfolded within the glossy pages of the *Ulster Tatler* that Bell had begun to edit, and mentioned the fact that in a list of Bell's works in an *Irish Times* profile by Elgy Gillespie, *Summer Loanen* was not mentioned. Bell responded:

The kernel was a couple of stories S. O'F had taken for *The Bell*. I have a copy somewhere but I haven't seen it in the secondhand lists for years. Apart from two or three of the tales I should think the rest reveal the prentice thumb.

5

FEATURES PRODUCER

THE FINAL NUMBER OF *LAGAN* included a poem by Louis MacNeice, the star of the famous Features Section of the BBC in London, which was run by Laurence Gilliam (1907–64). MacNeice had been born in Belfast 'between the mountains and the gantries' and was the son of the eventual Church of Ireland Bishop of Down, Connor and Dromore, a liberal from Connacht and a strong supporter of Home Rule. MacNeice had maintained strong ties with Northern Ireland, and in spite of education at an English preparatory school, Marlborough and Oxford, never quite lost his Ulster accent. He inherited his father's radicalism. In 1945 radio was still king, and when MacNeice made an extended visit to Ireland that year, Gilliam gave him a brief to look for new people and commission scripts for broadcasting from local writers.

Coincidentally, this was at a time when BBC management was attempting, following the extreme concentration of broadcasting in London of the war years, both to encourage regional development and to adjust to life under the new Labour government by recruiting staff from a broader range of social backgrounds than hitherto. Thus it was that the working-class Sam Hanna Bell came to be appointed to the BBC – to the surprise of some in the local management.

Thanks to Ursula Eason, Bell had already had stories, talks and children's plays broadcast and it was she who urged him one night at a party to apply for a new post that would be created as part of the BBC's plan to extend the Northern Ireland service. Each of the applicants was asked by MacNeice (who was put in charge of recruitment) to write a sample script. MacNeice met Bell on 28 May 1945 and they discussed possible topics which MacNeice passed on to Ursula Eason who chose the 'script about the Drift from the Land'. In a letter written on 29 May MacNeice suggested to Bell that the topic would make a half-hour feature 'consisting of say three or four dramatised episodes set in a sort of discussion framework'. The next day he sent Bell one of his own scripts. It was offered not as a model but to give 'some ideas about linking of scenes'.

Bell settled down to write the script with (for him) some speed though it was a topic that he had been considering for some time. There were interruptions – for a voice test, and several interviews – but nevertheless the script was finished and MacNeice took it with him on holiday to Keel on Achill Island and returned it to Bell on 6 August with congratulations on his temporary appointment on 3 August and three foolscap pages of detailed comments, which were deprecated with characteristic charm: 'Here follow,' he wrote, 'some page by page notes (disregard them if they irritate).' In fact Bell had not been appointed to the post mentioned by Ursula Eason: MacNeice had so liked the material that Bell was appointed as a temporary Features Producer answerable to him in London (though based in Belfast) and not at the censorial mercy of the management in Ormeau Avenue.

A contract followed on 7 August. The accompanying letter required him to send two photographs so that 'an official BBC pass may be issued'. As he used to recall with some pain, his position was made deliberately menial; he was paid weekly and he had to collect his wage in a little brown envelope 'like one of the cleaners'. The word 'temporary' was removed from his title in an offer from Marshall addressed to 5 India Street which arrived on 26 February 1946.

The broadcasting region in which Bell was to work for nearly a quarter of a century was 'the most contrary region' (as Rex Cathcart called his excellent 1984 history of BBC Northern Ireland). The word 'contrary' is used here in a double sense: 'opposite to the norm' and (its usual connotation in Ulster, with the stress on the second syllable) 'perverse, argumentative, troublesome'. The service had started on 15 September 1924 from a studio in 31 Linenhall Street as '2BE, the Belfast Station of the British Broadcasting Company' as its first announcer, the young Tyrone Guthrie (1900–71), described it. The British national anthem was played next, and then the station went off the air – the most contrary region had begun with a technical fault. Its sister system in Dublin, often its rival, ever its enemy in the eyes of the Stormont government and (it seemed) of the BBC Northern Ireland establishment, did not begin broadcasting until the following January.

The first significant manager of the new service in Belfast was Gerald Beadle who was appointed Station Director by John Reith, the BBC's Managing Director, in 1926. As Cathcart discreetly put it, Beadle 'was absorbed into the Unionist regime quite quickly, a process which other heads of the BBC in Northern Ireland were to experience in the future. It was a situation in which any sense of autonomy which the broadcaster might have could be lost.' Beadle's successor was George L. Marshall, who took over on 19 September 1932. He had been a school friend of Reith but he showed none of Reith's resolution in the matter of broadcasting independence. He was to remain Station Director for fourteen years and in his hands, it may be said, the region was made safe for the Unionist establishment. In 1937 he objected to a programme, *The Irish*, which the BBC Northern Region intended to produce:

> My first reactions would have been that the very title itself was highly undesirable, linking under one name two strongly antipathetic states with completely different political outlooks. There is no such thing today as an Irishman. One is either a citizen of the Irish Free State or a citizen of the United Kingdom of Great Britain and Northern Ireland. Irishmen as such ceased to exist after the partition. If it is intended to devote a programme exclusively to the Irish Free State, the programme should be labelled as such. . . . I would suggest that consultation might be desirable, so as to avoid giving offence.

The nice sending of the half a million nationalists living in Northern Ireland who did not consider themselves citizens of the UK into limbo precisely reflected the politics of the region. The nature of the programmes that Marshall's station had produced before and during the war had been a mockery of the BBC charter. Frequently it had seemed that its greatest priority had been to placate the Unionist government. But even Marshall could not ignore the postwar mood. As Cathcart puts it:

> He had after all systematically endeavoured for more than thirteen years to impose a policy of non-controversial broadcasting. Yet even

he was not totally immune to the opening up of broadcasting which was going on in the BBC across the water. If a measure of controversial discussion was to be allowed, then he would define the basic political parameters. Marshall declared in public that 'BBC programme policy in Northern Ireland is not to admit any attack on the constitutional position of Northern Ireland'.

That final sentence remained the essence of BBC Northern Ireland's policy. John Boyd was appointed Talks Producer in 1946 and, as he recorded in *The Middle of My Journey*, he soon found that

> The staff in Broadcasting House contained only a few Catholics, of whom none held senior posts, and none were producers. This was no accident but a deliberate policy of exclusion. Catholics were considered to be untrustworthy for posts of responsibility, and many years had to pass before the question of religious discrimination was confronted.

At first the war, which had broken down so many of the old ways, seemed to have little effect in Northern Ireland. But change did happen slowly, and in it both Bell and Boyd were to play significant parts. Edna Longley, in her book *The Living Stream* (1994), puts it thus: 'MacNeice constantly used his own clout in the London Features Department to fortify Bell and Boyd in their constructive subversion of the unionist grip on BBC Northern Ireland.' Douglas Carson, in an appreciation written after Bell's death, agreed:

> He fought his corner with determination. . . . The struggle, however, distracted and angered him. He had joined the tabernacle which preached public service, and was treated like a heretic because he believed.

I suspect that the 'subversion' was not always intentional, but the freedom that Bell and Boyd insisted upon to reflect the life of Ulster as it actually was lived was inevitably subversive of the monolith. Bell played a small, but significant role, too, in combating discrimination. There were no Catholic producers when he joined; twenty years later there was just one, Gerry McCrudden, who had been greatly helped by Bell's literary cooperation with him, and by Bell's efforts to secure him promotion.

Bell's reference to his appointment in his 'rough notes' is sparse:

In 1945 Louis MacNeice visited Northern Ireland and commissioned a number of broadcast scripts from local writers. After the production of my script 'Their Country's Pride' (which dealt with the problem of the drift from the land), I joined the BBC as Features Producer in Northern Ireland Region.

There seems to be some confusion about the programme's title, which came from Goldsmith's 'The Deserted Village'. The relevant lines are:

Ill fares the land to hastening ills a prey,
Where wealth accumulates and men decay:
Princes and lords may flourish, or may fade;
A breath can make them as a breath has made;
But a bold peasantry, their country's pride,
When once destroy'd, can never be supplied.

(The choice of Goldsmith was a good one since the village that was the original inspiration for the poem was Lissoy in County Westmeath where the poet spent most of his childhood; both MacNeice and Bell knew that, even if the management in Portland Place or Ormeau Avenue did not.) There is no record of any programme called *Ill Fares the Land* having been produced. Yet that is the name of the script that MacNeice approved, according to Jon Stallworthy's life of the poet. A feature called *Their Country's Pride*, however, was broadcast on 17 August 1949 (presumably as a repeat). This was the title used by MacNeice in a letter he wrote from Achill four years earlier giving detailed notes about the feature.

page 1. I think you need a signature tune. (Something folk – N. Ireland equivalent of the English 'Farmer's Boy' – to be done simply and straight, say on a fiddle).
    This should appear at the beginning, e.g. –

Announcer: Their Country's Pride.
    (up sig. tune and hold behind Commentator. After 'can never be supplied' bring it back up again & f/o [fade out]; the children's voices emerging from it.)

By the summer of 1948, Bell was a member of the 'Established Staff'. Marshall wrote to him at 2 Crescent Gardens on 26 May 1948. The letter was headed *'Establishment of Unestablished Staff'*, and gave details of salary ('£770, rising subject to satisfactory service by increments of

£40 per annum to a maximum of £890') and pension (5 per cent on the first £400 a year and 7.5 per cent on salary in excess). The starting dates offered were 'with effect from 1st June 1948 or from 1st October 1947 or from the first day of any quarter falling from between these two dates as you may prefer'. Bell chose 1 June.

MacNeice found a recruit he wanted to take back to London in W.R. ('Bertie') Rodgers who had been minister in Loughgall, County Armagh, at one of the oldest Presbyterian churches in Ireland, from 1935 to 1946. Bertie had been born in Belfast, and *The Return Room*, a lyrical sound picture inspired by his childhood, was to become one of Bell's most famous programmes. (It was finally broadcast, after a long genesis, on 23 December 1955, repeated twice on the Northern Ireland Home Service and three further times on the Third Programme.) Rodgers had published *Awake and Other Poems* in 1941 and was already known to Radio Éireann listeners for his broadcasts. Later poems such as 'The Net' and 'Lent' combine strong faith and sensuality. The two qualities warred within his nature and the stress found its outlet in drinking, sometimes to excess. Stallworthy records, quoting Dan Davin's *Closing Times* (1975):

> ... the pulpit in Loughgall was so high that, on those Sundays when Saturday had been the night before, Bertie – as even the staid parish knew its pastor – could stoop in a pause of his preaching, some cautiously contrived caesura, and retch gently, invisible to his devout and Sunday-sombre flock.

Freed by MacNeice from the constricting life of the manse, for six years from 1946 till 1952 Rodgers wrote much material of Irish interest for the Third Programme; he continued to write for it after his resignation from the Features Department. His interviews with notable Irish writers were published as *Irish Literary Portraits* by the BBC in 1972. (This book was Mildred's gift to Bell on his sixty-third birthday.)

Bell was to stay in Belfast and originate programmes which would be the regional equivalent of those that made the Features Department in London justly famous. Like Rodgers, he experienced almost unbearable stresses, mainly the product of being a socialist and freethinker in a Unionist institution. And he took the same remedy. He had plenty of ideas of what his product should be. As he puts it in his 'rough notes':

> Having had the good fortune to spend most of my childhood on an

Ulster farm I had a pretty thorough knowledge of how country people live their lives. From this knowledge I have been able to introduce the pattern and occupations of the province into broadcasting. My broadcast series *It's a Brave Step* and *Country Bard* first heard in 1950 are still drawing on the voices and verse of country people. *Within Our Province*, a series of documentaries on industry, transport and social problems, started in 1948 [and] ran to over twenty programmes ... written by experts.

By the time that *Their Country's Pride*, the script that won Bell his position, was rebroadcast in August 1949, the various series produced by Bell that were to make the postwar BBC Northern Ireland vastly different from the prewar service had been established. *Country Magazine* ran from 15 May 1949 until 29 June 1954. The programmes brought ordinary people to the microphone for the first time. The magazine format allowed for news, gossip, serious agricultural discussion, music, song, and that mysterious element, surely an Ulster invention, 'crack'. Its popularity grew as it became clear that all the people of the region were eligible to take part. Other series followed: *Country Bard* (21 January 1951–1 June 1962), *Music on the Hearth* (30 October 1953–14 September 1956) and *Talking Round the Hearth* (5 October–9 November 1961) are examples.

It's a Brave Step had two runs: 8 June–14 September 1949 and 18 June 1957–21 July 1958. The programme was location-centred; it did for rural areas what *Country Town* (12 June–1 December 1955) had done for places like Ballymoney, Keady and Fivemiletown. In all of these location programmes the BBC recording unit was used, and the latest technology would arrive on site. By means of suitable 'colour' description and the conversation of the inhabitants – encouraged to talk or reassuringly interviewed – a picture of the place would be realised. Bell did some of the interviews in person; his years of apprenticeship in many jobs made him an exemplary microphone sharer, matter-of-fact, unthreatening, witty and egalitarian.

Other portraits of places were more studied, scripted by local writers and some included dramatised 'scenes'. John Boyd depicted east Belfast in a series called *I Remember* which was broadcast intermittently after 23 November 1949. In the same series John O'Connor (1920–60) recalled the Armagh of his boyhood which he had used in his novel of the city *Come Day Go Day* (1947). Michael J. Murphy (1913–96) was an ideal laureate of south Armagh. Sam Thompson, who was one of Bell's more exciting discoveries, wrote 'The Long Back Street' which described a working-class childhood which ended with a paintbrush in the shipyard. Bell himself wrote *Strangford Lough Remembered*.

Another series, *Within Our Province*, began on 7 September 1949 with a programme by John O'Connor about the Armagh apple industry, and over the next four years dealt with such topics as the housing problem, rope-making, afforestation, the fight against tuberculosis (two programmes by Graeme Roberts) and student nurses (two programmes by the novelist Janet MacNeill). One broadcast dealt with the Ulster weather, a lively look at a dull topic, and Anne B. Latimer told what it was like 'To Be a Farmer's Girl'. The last programme was 'The Herring Fisherman', by Bill Everingham, broadcast on 23 October 1953.

Another lively series was *Country Profile* which painted portraits in sound of rural occupations. Among these was 'The Country Editor' (7 October 1949), and 'The Country Dressmaker' (9 October 1949) with a script by the engineer John D. Stewart. The young poet Roy McFadden, who had qualified as a solicitor in 1944, wrote about his profession (20 April 1950), though his own work was urban rather than rural. (He also contributed a feature, *Dear Mr Allingham*, on the nineteenth-century Ballyshannon poet William Allingham which was broadcast on 22 June 1951. A bus strike kept him away from rehearsals and communication was by telephone. Responding to some mild criticism by the author about interpretation Bell's brusque comment was, 'It's not in the script.') John O'Connor wrote 'The Postman' (23 December 1949), and collaborated with Gerald Rafferty on 'The Country Breadman' (6 April 1951 – probably the programme for which Bell and Gerry McCrudden went to such extremes to get the sound effect of a sliding drawer). 'The Cobbler' (18 November 1952) was written by Michael J. Murphy, who was the main ferreter of lore for another series, *Fairy Faith*, which ran weekly from 11 March until 8 April 1952. In an article called 'In Search of Fairy Lore' in the *Radio Times* for 7 March, Bell told how 'We met men and women who could hardly tell their stories for laughter, but we politely stared the laughter out of face and got the story.'

Recording methods were cumbersome in comparison with later techniques. The equipment was heavy and bulky, and the 'country microphone' could not be far away from the recording machine which held the large shellac discs. The machine used by Bell took up most of the back of the sturdy Humber car which came to know every loanen, boreen and *casán* in Northern Ireland. Pat Loughrey, the present controller of BBC Northern Ireland, summed it up in his contribution to *Broadcasting in A Divided Community* published by the Institute of Irish Studies at Queen's University Belfast. In an essay entitled 'Culture and Identity: The BBC's Role in Northern Ireland', Loughrey wrote: 'Sam Bell went to Queen's Island and to every glen in the Sperrins with his recording machine. By contemporary standards the material was rigidly scripted and stilted but in its time it was wonderfully innovative and enriching.'

The significance of sound recording as part of an archive had been well understood by the workers of the Irish Folklore Commission, which was set up by Seamus Delargy (1899–1980) in 1935. Delargy had used the even more cumbersome Ediphone to record priceless *seanchas* from the traditional storytellers both in Gaeltacht and other areas. As Bell records in his 'rough notes':

> Realising how much of the countryside was draining away I carried out a wide survey of the fairy lore and superstitions in Ulster in 1951–2. The subsequent programmes that I compiled from this recorded material were broadcast in the NIHS [Northern Ireland Home Service] and then in the Third Programme. This was the first serious investigation into this field for many years and copies of the recordings were given to the archives of the Irish Folklore Commission, Dublin, and, when it came into existence, the Ulster Folklife Association.

Michael J. Murphy was the main collector and worked closely with Delargy. Bríd Mahon mentions him in her memoir of her Irish Folklore Commission years, *While Green Grass Grows* (1998):

> When Delargy recruited Michael J. Murphy (1913–96) first as part-time and later as full-time folklore collector, or 'cultural intelligence officer' as Michael liked to put it, he was already popular as a broadcaster for the BBC in Belfast and had written books on the folklore of the northeast. Between 1949 and 1983 he covered most of the northeast, spending long periods on Rathlin Island, in the Antrim Glens, the Mournes, Fermanagh, Tyrone and Armagh. His informants were

of every class and creed, Protestant, Catholic and Dissenter, and were proud to have the folklore of their ancestors recorded. He helped us film and record the traditional Orange processions at the Field in Finaghy in the days before darkness descended on the six counties of the northeast. He wrote more than a dozen plays and books dealing with the Irish countryside and gathered what is probably the largest collection of oral tradition anywhere in the English-speaking world.

The first official move to record local folklore came from Cahir Healy, the Nationalist MP for Fermanagh, who was a member of the Northern Ireland Advisory Council, the committee of local worthies whose stated purpose was to give the local BBC management the benefit of a range of Northern Ireland opinion. He found it odd that Third Programme researchers based in London were being sent to 'record the folklore and music of the twenty-six counties and neglecting the six'. (Healy was later to be the subject of a television programme in Gerry McCrudden's *I Remember* series which was hosted by Bell. It was broadcast on 13 May 1969, and three days later Healy wrote to Bell in tiny handwriting nearly as elegant as that of the addressee: 'It was a delightful experience co-operating with one so distinguished in your own field.'

Bell recalled to Rex Cathcart the positive response made to Healy's suggestion by Andrew Stewart, who by now had replaced George Marshall as Controller:

> One day he called me into his office and said, 'I've got hold of some money and I want you to go out and look for the heroic tales and myths of Ulster.' We were lucky in having the folklorist Michael J. Murphy about and so went off to ask him about the suggestion. He said that the heroic myths were pretty dormant and what survived was so corrupted that they were not worth collecting. 'But,' he said, 'there are the fairies.'

Bell recalled the nature of that corruption in an interview by Terry McGeehan in the *Sunday Press* of 10 June 1984:

> There were no heroic myths; they were all corrupt as we soon learnt. One day we were recording an old fellow in the Mourne Mountains and he was telling us all about Finn McCool, Cuchulainn and Patrick, and the next thing he manages to drive a Cadillac into the story. He obviously had a son in New York or somewhere and he was mixing up myths with his letter home.

The work of finding the lore and recording it from the *seanchaithe* took months. (The Irish word is the only one that does justice to the age of the material that had been handed down orally. The word *sean* ('old') and the word *béaloideas*, used for folklore, literally means 'oral teaching'.) The old men and women from whom the lore was collected expressed relief that the old stories would not perish with them. As Cathcart puts it:

> A large reservoir of folklore was built up and from it was distilled the distinguished series, *Fairy Faith*. Professor Delargy of the Irish Folklore Commission was enthusiastic about the project and regarded it as 'the most important work in Irish Folklore in modern times'.

Andrew Stewart was extremely happy to include that comment in his quarterly report to the Board of Governors in May 1952.

Another important incidental work of conservation was in the field of music. Bell's 'rough notes' are again informative:

> It was evident that a great part of our folk music was also in danger of vanishing. The BBC gave me permission to send Sean O'Boyle, an authority on Irish folk music, with Peter Kennedy of the English Folksong Society on a number of exploratory surveys of the Ulster town and countryside. Over two hundred pieces of music were recorded and copies of these are now in the BBC Recordings Library, London, and the Irish folklore societies. For some time I had been drawing from my programmes on the Sam Henry *Songs of the People* series which had been appearing in the *Northern Constitution* newspaper, Coleraine. I had this vast collection, nearly nine hundred items, photostated and indexed. Copies are now in the Belfast Public Library and available to a much wider public. A small but valuable collection of Belfast street songs had been gathered by Hugh Quinn, the dramatist. Working with Mr Quinn I compiled broadcast programmes from this material and several of the songs have now passed into the repertory of Ulster choirs and singers. The Midland Region of the BBC were so delighted with one of the programmes that they sent for the recordings and broadcast a selection of Belfast street songs from Birmingham!

Sean O'Boyle (1908–79) had been born in Belfast and had already a considerable reputation as a Gaelic scholar. On graduation from Queen's he was appointed to the staff of St Patrick's College, Armagh, where he taught until his retirement in 1973. His work on Irish music includes *Cnuasacht de Cheoltaí Ulaidh* (a collection of Ulster music) and *The Irish Song Tradition*. Between 1952 and 1954 he, Kennedy and Seamus Ennis (1919–82) gathered enough material for two major series on Ulster song: *As I Roved Out* and *Music on the Hearth*. The latter, introduced by O'Boyle and produced by Bell, was broadcast from 30 October 1953 until 14 September 1956. Bell went with O'Boyle on the earliest song-seeking expeditions, but soon O'Boyle flew solo and another precious archive was safely secured. O'Boyle continued to make programmes, writing scripts and using music from his own collection. The Sam Henry songs were eventually published by Blackstaff Press, most of the preliminary editing having already been done by Bell's department.

Bell was appointed Features Producer and writer, and it was he himself who gradually defined what his job was. He had before him the example of the Features Department in Portland Place and the variety of the programmes that he devised was an index of the elastic definition of 'feature' and of his own inventiveness. He was conscious of the need to give Northern Ireland a voice but he was also aware of the virtue of excellent writing. His own wide reading and deep and ever-growing knowledge of the region led him to realise that there were many stories still to be told. And he presumed, as it turned out correctly, that there were new writers to be discovered. There were also, of course, the friends from the past, the companions of Campbell's Coffee House, Murlough Bay and *Lagan*. The number of individual programmes originated by Bell, and requiring a script (as opposed to those rendered from outside broadcasts), runs into hundreds. The list of programmes written by Bell himself includes some of the finest ever devised for radio, as the uptake by other networks clearly indicates. He wrote at least forty scripts himself, and probably many more – the easiest way to rescue a poor script by someone else was quietly to 'rework' it.

If one were forced to choose the finest of his own scripts for an *The Essential Sam Hanna Bell*, there are six features that would have to be included: *This Is Northern Ireland* (26 October 1949), *Rathlin Island* (6 October 1950), *In Praise of Ulster* (1951), *The Islandmen* (28 January 1953), *Kist o' Whistles* (17 November 1954), *Johnston of Ballykilbeg* (8 November 1960) and *The Orangemen* (11 July 1967). The best programmes produced but not written by him would include *Return to Northern Ireland*

(27 October 1950) by Bertie Rodgers, *Dove over the Water* (24 March 1954) by J.J. Campbell, *The Return Room* (23 December 1955) and *City Set on a Hill* (1957) by Bertie Rodgers, and *Wee Joe* (24 November 1959) by J.J. Campbell.

This excellence was appreciated in London if not always in Belfast. But even the begrudgers in Ormeau Avenue had to admit (as Fergus, Bell's son recalls) that reviews of the programmes were universally favourable. The begrudgers basked in reflected glory when many of the features were networked. Bell was protected by his anomalous position as a member of the London Features Department, though located in Belfast. But Fergus emphasises that his father was conscious of animus if not actual enmity from Henry McMullan, who was Head of Programmes for most of his career. McMullan was regarded by Glengall Street as a safe pair of hands (not only did he seem to disavow any Irish connection but was unconvinced of the existence of an Ulster identity separate from that of what he would have referred to as the 'mainland'). The young Fergus could not help but be conscious that relations between the two were watchful and mutually frustrating; as he grew to manhood he heard many complaints of obstruction and discouragement. Bell was convinced that it was McMullan who thwarted his attempts to secure promotion, and who kept him at a distance from television.

Perhaps the most judicious summary of Bell's time at the BBC is that of his friend Douglas Carson who commissioned and produced many of the programmes Bell wrote in his retirement. It is the peroration of an 'obituary' piece entitled 'The Antiphon, the Banderol and The Hollow Ball: Sam Hanna Bell, 1909–1990' and printed in the *Irish Review* (No. 9, Autumn 1990):

> The local management in Ormeau Avenue was frequently uncomfortable with his initiatives; and unionists at Stormont were alarmed. He fought his corner with determination. He frightened bureaucrats with his achievements. They feared his reputation and his wit. And always they were conscious of MacNeice and Gilliam, the network of associates in Portland Place. Effectively he used the strength of London to undermine officialdom at home.
>
> As an octogenerian, Sam went back to the microphone. 'How would you like to be remembered?' they asked him. 'Most certainly,' he replied, 'not by broadcasting! You're not going to be remembered

by the fact that you played rugby for Donaghadee!' The BBC was still the hollow ball, and a last kick at it was a birthday treat. But football needs more than exceptional strikers, and his problem, in Belfast, had been the lack of a team. For most of his twenty-five years in the Region, the only active athletes were himself and John Boyd: and both of them were playing outside left. Despite that, they kicked with skill and scored goals. And Sam became a local institution. In the creative life of Ulster he carried the banderol. As well, his voice was known in every home. He introduced his neighbours to themselves – an antiphon of voices round the hearth.

6

MISS RESIDE

S AM HANNA BELL was thirty-seven years of age in 1946 when he settled into the job of features producer. With his intellectual, political and literary background he had many friends and undoubtedly had had some love affairs. From the information that can be gleaned from letters, testimony of friends, and occasional lapses in reticence, it is clear that the war years were an exciting time. Belfast had been shaken out of its provincial doldrums by the influx of allied forces, with Lisburn full of soldiers, the city surrounded by heavy anti-aircraft batteries, and navy and air-force types thronging the city's dance halls and clubs. This was to say nothing of the Americans who, in John Boyd's words, 'appeared on the streets of Belfast looking too well dressed, too well fed, and becoming too popular with the girls'. There was *Lagan* to edit and an apprenticeship to be served in the business of writing. There were also young women.

One of the documents that throw light on these years is David Millar's diary. It was not intended for publication and its brief glimpses of Bell have the virtues of contemporaneity and a total lack of wisdom after the event. There was a sense during the war years, only briefly shattered by the 1941 air raids, that the hostilities were far distant. Food was rationed but butter, meat and eggs – and drink – were plentiful across the border; and tea, banned books and contraceptives were happily received there in exchange. Travel restrictions meant that use was made of local amenities, and the Youth Hostel movement was fully supported. Millar recalls a weekend in April 1940 spent at the Slievenaman hostel in the Mournes where members of the left-wing International Club were holding an informal seminar. The list of people present shows how lively and international the gathering was with academics, civil servants, and European refugees present. Bell gave a talk to the club on 14 September 1941 on 'Ulster Protestants' which, as the diarist says, was 'really a short history of Protestant Republicans – the United Irishmen & co'. A party on Boxing Day 1942 in the flat shared by Bell and Bob Davidson had a dazzling (by Belfast standards) array of talent: the journalist Ray Rosenfield, who was to write a feature for Bell on a kibbutz called *Nachlat Belfast* (29 June 1953), Tom Carr the painter, Joe Tomelty the novelist and playwright, Richard Rowley, Robert Greacen, Denis Ireland and John Boyd. It was in the cold light of the next day that *Lagan* was born.

Bell was a senior figure in this company. He bore a striking resemblance to Bernard Shaw, and it was his custom to go to the annual Arts Ball as the Sage of Synge Street, while his friend John D. Stewart capitalised upon his likeness to Robert Louis Stevenson. Especially when the drink was flowing, Bell was likely to make sober pronouncements on life and literature. At times the conversation became ribald, as when Bell suggested that Millar should write a novel called *Rumple Foreskin*. (Millar declined, claiming that Bell was better qualified in this matter than he.)

Millar's diary entry for Saturday 11 September 1943 records that the name of Mildred Reside came up in the course of a conversation before tea in Bell's flat. John Boyd talked about the girl he was courting, while 'Sam attended to the pan'. Millar noted:

She's a kindergarten teacher in Jack's school [Wallace High School in Lisburn]. She is attractive, intelligent, well-bred, has personality and is a little shy.

Boyd took the credit for introducing the pair at a time when Bell was 'recovering from an unhappy love affair':

Still, I had some colleagues [at the BBC] whose company I enjoyed and who enjoyed my company. Sam Hanna Bell was the one I was closest to. . . . I had introduced him to Mildred, the golden-haired schoolteacher who later became his wife. We had in common those holidays spent at Murlough Bay long before we had joined the BBC, and during my twenty-five years as a producer he and I often spent our lunch-times together, buying second-hand books in Smithfield, borrowing books from the Linen Hall Library, or just wandering around the town gossiping. We shared an enthusiasm for Thomas Hardy, but perhaps taking our cue from MacNeice and Rodgers we usually avoided literary discussion; we were the two members of staff most interested in politics, both of us left-wingers.

The kindergarten teacher and Bell were married on 31 October 1946, and the honeymoon was spent in Cork with a few days in Ballybunion, County Kerry, where they had excellent poached salmon (probably in both senses!). Sam was not quite thirty-seven and Mildred was a year and a half younger. She had been born in Newry on 20 April 1911 and christened Mildred Ferguson Reside. She was educated at Newry Intermediate School and later as a boarder at Ashleigh House in Belfast, where she afterwards did a fair amount of teaching. In 1929 she became a student at Alexandra College in Dublin, which in those years had an education branch for Froebel training. The option of reading French at Trinity was rejected in favour of infant teaching. She was appointed to the French School at Bray, where the pupils were taught all subjects through that medium, and taught happily there until the outbreak of World War Two.

The Reside family were unionists and though Mildred was rather more liberal she seems to have felt uncomfortable at the idea of staying in the neutral South while Northern Ireland was at war. During August 1940 she charted almost fifty-eight hours of ward work at Newry General Hospital as a member of the Civil Nursing Reserve. She began teaching in the preparatory department of Wallace High School in Lisburn, where John Boyd and David Millar were colleagues. A letter thanking her for a 'splendid contribution of £50', the proceeds of a dance that she organised for the Duke of Gloucester's Red Cross and St John Prisoners of War Fund, was sent to the school on 15 January 1943. She continued to teach there after marriage, travelling each day from 3 Crescent Gardens, an address considerably more convenient for the features producer than for the teacher.

Her letter of resignation from the school was accepted regretfully by the board of governors on 30 September 1947, and Fergus Hanna Bell was born on 12 February 1948. Among the papers of that year are letters from Mildred to Sam addressing him as Sorley. (The Irish name Somhairle is borrowed from Old Norse and means 'summer-journeyer' and also 'Viking'. It was anglicised in Ulster as Charlie but in Scotland it became Samuel.) In one letter postmarked 13 May she says: 'Fergus was inspected by the entire family from Grandmother to grandchild and seemed to stand up to the test with great calm and aplomb.' Postcards arriving about the same time were signed 'Mildred and Baby Fergus'. On 26 April 1950 Mildred writes from a 'snowbound Belfast to Dada who has gone to Ballycastle by car'.

The family moved to the country, renting Chrome Hill Cottage, near Lambeg, County Antrim, which was part of the property of the Misses Downer who owned Chrome Hill House. Always a keen gardener, Mildred worked happily in the Downers' vegetable patches, 'helped' by her growing son, who had his first taste of school at Holly Lodge. The move back to Belfast in December 1953 was motivated partly by the need to find appropriate education for Fergus and partly by the sadly sudden availability of money to buy a house. Both the Reside parents had died earlier that year, and Mildred's legacy of £3,000 enabled her, Sam and Fergus to move to 160 King's Road, which was their home from then on. Mildred's diabetes was first noted at the time of Fergus's birth and it remained at first an intermittent but later an increasing source of disability. The condition was known colloquially as 'brittle' and was notably hard to stabilise. This required occasional trips to the Royal Victoria Hospital but it was not until the last fifteen years of her life that she could have been described as an invalid. She taught regularly but not permanently in the preparatory department of Ashleigh House and for the rest ran her home, cultivated her garden and cared for her husband and son.

As his friends noted (with varying degrees of laddishness), once married Bell led the life of a devoted and respectable middle-class husband; he and Mildred were clearly happy together. His job required his occasional presence in Portland Place and he spent many hours writing, travelling, recording and producing. In spite of all this, his home and family were very important to Sam and in those days before universal phones, letters to and from home were regular.

A significant part of his time was spent upstairs in the room that was his study. The ceiling, which was originally off-white, acquired over the years a tobacco-coloured patina. The study was shelved in mahogany and a converted washstand served for a desk on which rested a series of typewriters. Bell's prodigious correspondence was usually typed, sometimes on fairly flimsy paper. Drafts of replies to letters received were normally written in pencil in the flawless hand that was his hallmark. Drafts, notes, writings in the early stages of their genesis, were usually done in an armchair with a piece of plywood laid across the writer's knee to act as a desktop. The room smelled of tobacco smoke and the books that weighed down the shelving still have a whiff of old Virginia.

Fergus, though an only child, was loved but not indulged. He had a term in Fullerton House, the preparatory branch of Methodist College, then moved to Cabin Hill, which was similarly connected to Campbell College, in January 1957. A letter written on 31 January 1957 to May Reside (Mildred's cousin in Halifax), and accompanying a copy of *Erin's Orange Lily*, contained the news that 'Fergus has started Cabin Hill. His two main enthusiasms at the moment seem to be football and stamp collecting – both of which are very good for him.' Attendance at the senior school (from 1961 to 1968) was a natural progression. Among the Bell papers are many birthday cards from mother and child and an early and brief attempt at an exciting adventure play by the son. Fergus knew his father was a writer, and from an early age the boy was allowed to visit the Ormeau Avenue studios, sit silently in the control booths during rehearsals and transmissions, and have goodies in the canteen. Though Bell worked relentlessly in his study and studio, weekends were as far as possible kept free. Father and son were keen rugby fans and there were school matches, concerts, plays, which Sam attended religiously.

Bell was an interested gardener, if not in Mildred's class, and his diary has regular entries about the purchase of flowers, shrubs and vegetables.

A small car originally belonging to Mildred's older brother Gerald was acquired shortly after the move to King's Road. It was a Wolseley Hornet, registration number BZ 3290, and when it was loaded down with luggage on the old Newry road to Killowen *en route* for the Resides' cottage for summer holidays there was always the terror that it might not be fit for the gradient at Hillsborough. In the summer of 1955 Fergus had his first visit to the theatre, being taken to the Grand Opera House on 12 June to see a production of *As You Like It* with Virginia McKenna as Rosalind, John Neville as Orlando, Eric Porter as Jacques and Paul Rogers as Touchstone. (His introduction to opera came four years later when he was taken to *The Barber of Seville*. According to a paternal note on the programme, 'This was Fergus's first visit to the opera. He enjoyed it.') Bell maintained a strong interest in theatre, especially Ulster drama, though the gradual deterioration in his hearing as he grew older meant that he made fewer visits to performances. His papers include tickets for the Royal Court Theatre, London, for 5 May 1956, the opening night of *Look Back in Anger* by John Osborne. Records of visits to the theatre hold equal place with the accounts of books read in a diary that Bell kept intermittently throughout the years of his marriage. He kept copies of all his typewritten correspondence and many old bills, but was personally reticent. The diary was as much commonplace book as personal record and references to his wife and child are sparse. The entry for 26 April 1957 reads: 'M. and I saw the comet.' On 15 April he records a quotation about the writer's need to be 'a psychologist but a secret one'.

On 8 November 1957 Sam and Fergus were involved in a car accident:

> Black treacherous ice this morning. Car skidded after two preliminary wiggles on the hill, went into a long slide and crashed into the sandstone wall at the garden next to Gilnahirk burn. Last thing I remember was the wall crumbling before the car. By great good fortune neither Fergus nor I badly hurt. He had the lens of his glasses cracked, I had right leg fractured and knee bashed up. When I recovered consciousness, M., police and ambulance had arrived. Great relief when I saw Fergus coming from a neighbour's house. We were popped into a hosp. ambulance and whipped off to the RVH [the Royal Victoria Hospital, Belfast]. After a long wait Fergus was allowed home and I was put into a ward bed.

He was moved to the Musgrave Clinic on 11 November and allowed home on 24 November, full of praise for the friends who had brought him 'books, cigs. etc'. The damage may have aggravated an old rugby injury which led to arthritis in later life, a condition alleviated for a time by the drug Opren, until its dire side effects were realised.

Bell did not return to work until 13 January 1958, having spent some of his convalescence doing a little work on *The Hollow Ball*. (The working title for this second novel had been 'The Dazzler' but the better title came in a sudden inspiration on 2 April 1957.) During the Christmas period he hosted two dinner parties, one for a legal friend, Martin McBirney, his wife and son Ross, the other for Ronnie Mason the BBC Northern Ireland drama producer, John Boyd and Joe Tomelty. In March the family went to Cabin Hill to see a school production of *Rory Aforesaid.*

Fergus got a camera and an atlas for his thirteenth birthday. ('Bless him. I hope he sees as many happy days.') Two months later, in April 1961, the child developed an inflammation behind his right eye which required a stay at the Clarke Clinic. ('House a bit lonely without Fergus. We go up every afternoon and evening and see him in Room 25. Have played several games of chess with him.') Fergus was home by the end of the month, 'no worse for his stay in the clinic'.

Fergus graduated LL B in July 1972 and after apprenticeship in his aunt's firm, Fisher and Fisher of Newry, was successful in his Law Society final examination. Sam records that 25 June 1975 was a 'wonderful day'.

> Following the examination he had been very pessimistic about the outcome. Everyone delighted and he fully deserves his success after all his hard work and his unflagging study. I feel rather smug because I felt from the start that he had made it. The main thing is that he is now really started on his career. All good fortune to the dear fellow.

7

THE FESTIVAL OF BRITAIN

A N EARLY PROOF of Sam Hanna Bell's position in the artistic establishment in Northern Ireland was his commission in 1951 as editor of an anthology, *The Arts in Ulster*. This was intended to be a significant local contribution to the general jubilation of the Festival of Britain. The festival had been organised as a centenary celebration of the great Victorian exhibition of 1851 initiated by Prince Albert to demonstrate the world supremacy of British industry. Herbert Morrison, Leader of the House of Commons in Attlee's postwar Labour government, also intended the 1951 festival as a gift to the British people who had suffered six years of austerity, in social and economic conditions often worse than those of the six years of war. Northern Ireland was expected to take part, as a brochure written by Tyrone Guthrie, a Cavan man and then in the ascendant as an innovative theatre director, reminded local people. Among the festival's products were to be a farm and factory exhibition at Castlereagh, a season of plays at the Opera House, and *The Arts in Ulster*, an elegant volume about all aspects of local artistic life. It was sponsored by the Council for the Encouragement of Music and the Arts (Northern Ireland) – CEMA, the forerunner of the Arts Council of Northern Ireland. The plays included *The Passing Day* by George Shiels, *Danger, Men Working!* by Bell's friend John D. Stewart, and a Belfast version of *The Sham Prince* (1718) by Charles Shadwell (?1675–1726) by the Armagh playwright

Jack Loudan. They were directed by Tyrone Guthrie. *The Passing Day* transferred to London and was the origin of Joe Tomelty's successful if sadly brief film career.

The commissioning letter to Bell arrived from W.H.N. Downer, then CEMA's general and financial secretary, on 4 February 1950 and specified the nature of the publication. It was to be of around 50,000 words with 'perhaps 20 pages of illustrations' and the letter listed the various experts who were to contribute and their fields. They included John Boyd on prose and the novel and John Hewitt (then Keeper of Art at the Ulster Museum) on painting and sculpture. The section on drama was to be done by David Kennedy who was later to write *Enter Robbie John . . .*, the definitive radio feature on the Ulster Literary Theatre, for Bell. It is likely that Bell had been sounded out and consulted beforehand as to who would be appropriate people to write the essays, for each of which the fee was to be twenty guineas. Joining Bell as editors were to be George Buchanan (1904–89), the novelist from south Antrim, John Hewitt and the wealthy scholar Nesca Robb (1905–76). (In fact George Buchanan seems to have played no part in the production of the book, though his work was given considerable coverage in John Boyd's essay.) A preliminary meeting of the editorial board was arranged for 8 February at CEMA headquarters in Tyrone House. The correspondence, filed meticulously by Bell, shows that on 4 March official approval for the necessary expenditure had been received and that Ian Harrap, the representative of the publisher George G. Harrap, came to Belfast on 6 April to meet the editors.

The complicated process of producing a book with many contributors may be traced in the correspondence, with apologies, disappointments, disagreements and points of political correctness figuring in the discussion. A report of the committee meeting of 13 May 1950 notes that in answer to John Boyd's probably mischievous question as to what region the term 'Ulster' covered, A.A.K. Arnold (who was in charge of the festival in Northern Ireland) had had word from London that references up to 1921 should refer to the historical nine-county province of Ulster, but that after that date the word should signify the six counties of Northern Ireland only. A letter of 12 June 1950 from Bell to Jack Loudan (then CEMA organiser and responsible for the progress of the book) asks for 'another month's grace' owing to revision of the manuscripts and other 'delays'. On 16 June Nesca Robb sent a twelve-page handwritten document commenting upon the material received. In it she admits her attitude is donnish but makes no apology: 'in a case like this I think it is an editor's duty to *be* donnish'. She is anxious to keep politics out of it 'as far as is humanly possible' – 'This is a book on the Arts in Ulster – not a disquisition on the Irish question' – an attitude very prevalent at the time but not one held by either Hewitt or Bell. She also wishes that some of the contributors 'could be persuaded to adopt a more cheerful and less scolding tone'. In true unionist form she deprecates David Kennedy's suggestion that 'the Gaelic springs of speech and action' play a part in the work of such Irish playwrights as Charles Macklin: 'All this stuff about Gaels seems a bit dubious.' In her criticism of Nelson Brown's essay on 'Poetry in Ulster', she finds the style a little lush and is at pains to contradict Brown's suggestion that the Irish were the keepers of the poetic flame in the Dark Ages. She succeeded in having changed a portion of his text that suggested that the political separation of Northern Ireland had caused 'a breach of mind and spirit'.

This partitionism would not have represented Bell's attitude. Indeed in a letter to John Hewitt on 12 July 1950 he makes a wry reference to 'the foreign bodies' having 'been removed from the honey-pot' in Nelson Browne's poetry survey. At some later stage Nesca Robb must have objected to John Boyd's article on 'Ulster Prose' but Bell was not moved to change it, as the letter to Hewitt makes clear:

> J.B. is to add a reference to O'Donnell and let you see it. I don't give a damn if Nesca Robb likes this contribution or not. I do, and I know as much and probably more of this aspect than she does. After all, it has taken quite a lot of courage on J.B.'s part to say what he has said. I back him in his 'waspishness'. We could do with a lot less fustian in our comment.

It is interesting that Bell wanted some notice taken of the work of Peadar O'Donnell (1893–1986), who in addition to being a fine novelist with a spare sinewy style was at the time editor of *The Bell* and perhaps notorious for his active left-wing politics. It is worth noting that he is not mentioned in the final text although his fellow Donegal man Patrick MacGill (1889–1963), referred to in the piece as 'Magill' and only nine years older, is. Perhaps this was an example of the festival definition of 'Ulster' in action, in that MacGill's best-known books were written before the Government of Ireland Act of 1920, whilst

Islanders, O'Donnell's finest novel, did not appear until 1928.

A committee meeting held on 2 August 1950 decided that a quotation from St John Ervine should be deleted from John Boyd's essay and that several deletions should be made in David Kennedy's account of Ulster drama. These included 'criticisms' of CEMA drama tours, references to the BBC, Louis MacNeice and W.R. Rodgers, and a quotation from James Connolly (1868–1916), one of the leaders of the Easter Rising. The inclusion of such material in a symposium associated with a government that execrated everything Connolly stood for must have been intended as a piece of deliberate impudence by the nationalist and Catholic Kennedy. In fact, the quotation was a mild and unexceptionable response by Connolly to what he saw as a too regionalist attitude on the part of Hobson and the other founders of the Ulster Literary Theatre:

> Until Ulster has absorbed the same genetic spirit that to-day is moving the rest of Ireland, until she has acquired the more notable marks of national homogeneity, all merely provincial development will run to seed.

Time has proved Connolly correct but the comment was too much for the Stormont government's representatives to take (Dame Dehra Parker, the Minister of Health, was president of CEMA), even at the zenith of Stormont's apparent permanence.

On the whole, however, there was considerably less acrimony in the generation of the book than might have been expected. As the final paragraph of Bell's letter to John Hewitt, referred to above, put it: 'I feel that when all the contributions appear cheek by jowl, they will give a more or less consistent picture of the province.' The cheque for twenty guineas which arrived on 15 August was very well earned, but the work continued. Bibliographies had to be garnered, appropriate illustrations chosen. Eighteen of the pictures, mostly in half- or quarter-plate, were of buildings, chosen to illustrate Denis O'D Hanna's section on architecture, but a number of writers and composers were given full-page portraits. These were: Joseph Campbell (1879–1944), William Carleton (1794–1869), Sir Samuel Ferguson (1810–86), Stephen Gilbert (b. 1912), Forrest Reid (1875–1947), W.R. Rodgers, St John Ervine (1883–1971), Joseph Tomelty, Edward Bunting (1773–1843) and Sir Hamilton Harty (1880–41). Michael McLaverty did not wish his photograph to appear and that of Stephen Gilbert was substituted. McLaverty had written to Bell on 29 September 1950: 'Surely you don't expect an Irish nationalist like myself to subscribe, implicitly or explicitly, to Festival activities. I couldn't do so until our broken country is healed.'

There was a witty frontispiece by Bell's friend Rowel Friers in the form of what was literally a sketch map. It showed the territory of Northern Ireland with just a hint of Inishowen so that the picture of the walled city of Derry could be sited correctly on the west bank of the Foyle. There were no words or other cartological devices, but in a design measuring four inches by four the artist succeeded in illustrating a bleach green, a linen mill, the Belfast shipyard, the Mourne Mountains, the apple orchards and archiepiscopal grandeur of Armagh, the fishy lakes of Fermanagh, and the potato drills of Tyrone. Bell's primacy as editor was established in a letter on 20 October from Downer which advised that 'the name of Sam Hanna Bell only may appear on the spine, though Mr Bell wishes Nesca A. Robb and John Hewitt associated with him on the title page'.

Throughout the winter of 1950–51, 'tweaking' of the text continued: at a meeting of the committee held on 2 November Dame Dehra Parker suggested that Sir Shane Leslie (1885–1971) should be mentioned in both the poetry and prose sections. He made it to the poetry essay but Boyd refused to include him. (Boyd did accede to the suggestion that mention should be made of Amanda McKittrick Ros [1860–1939] and Agnes Romilly White [1872–1945], author of *Gape Row* [1934], a novel set in Dundonald village – but only in a list headed by the legend 'I have not space to discuss such writers as' which included Bell as author of *Summer Loanen* and *December Bride*.) Dame Dehra had earlier suggested that there be a reference to Cyril Falls (1888–1971), the military historian, 'either in the introduction or in the section on prose'. Bell agreeably added his name to a list of 'Ulster historians who have been reassessing, and, indeed, so far as the layman is concerned, discovering the history of our country and our people'. It was agreed to ask David Kennedy whether James Cousins (1873–1956), who had written two plays for the Ulster Literary Theatre, should be referred to as Séamus Ó Cúisín. (He was.) Another suggestion (rejected) was that Tyrone Guthrie be included in the drama section.

On 23 January 1951 Bell wrote to Mrs S.E. Capper, secretary to

CEMA, enclosing a draft blurb for the back cover of the book. Its author is not very enthusiastic about it but suggested 'it may give a lead to the publishers'. A cheque for ten guineas arrived on 20 February and on 19 March Bell wrote thanking Downer for his copy of *The Arts in Ulster* with the hope 'that it will get a good reception'. In fact, considering the political aspects of such an undertaking and the limited area under consideration, it was an impressive and useful publication. The literary sections showed that 'Ulster' had its share of the 'writin' Irish. The art and architecture sections came as a revelation to many. Kennedy's drama section was also impressive, and the poetry essay could include among its writers Sir Samuel Ferguson (1810–86), William Allingham (1824–89), Joseph Campbell, John Hewitt, Louis MacNeice and Bertie Rodgers. Nobody thought to include Paddy Kavanagh in the list of Ulster poets, an omission impossible today.

Nevin Foster, who had written the music section, died soon after the book was published. A letter written on 18 April 1952 by John Bebbington, the Belfast city librarian, thanks Bell for Foster's manuscript and notes that Bell himself had joined the ranks of the famous by the recent decision of the censorship board in the South – a reference to the banning of *December Bride*.

Bell's introduction, which he christened a 'banderol', survived unscathed from the attentions of his fellow editors. Indeed it deviates hardly at all from the first draft, written like most of Bell's drafts in meticulous handwriting on the backs of old radio scripts. A few overripe metaphors were excised: 'I should be more profitably employed in trying to steady and hold up for inspection the currents in the sea of Moyle.' And the words 'Catholic or Protestant' were removed from the sentence, 'There is nothing, I should say, more distasteful to an Ulsterman, Catholic or Protestant, than to be hugged by a myth, unless, of course, he has had the privilege of creating it.' Nesca Robb wrote on 11 August 1950:

> Many thanks for the 'banderol'. It seems to me to fulfil its function admirably, both as an essay that is interesting and pleasant to read in its own right & as an appetiser for the other six courses. Also it does pull the book together – very necessary with a composite work. I haven't any alterations to suggest.

In fact the essay is a brilliant piece of political tightrope-walking while serving its purpose as an introduction to the state of the arts. As Nesca Robb says, it is a most compelling essay. 'We have with us still in Northern Ireland,' Bell says, 'an antique conflict, resolved long ago in Western Europe – the conflict of religious dogmas, encrusted with loyalties, prejudices, and racial aspirations.' Yet with an apt quotation from W.R. Rodgers he turns this to his argument's advantage: 'It is this diversity and interplay of opposites that makes Ulster life such a rich and fascinating one.' Something of the tone of the first editorial of *Lagan* is repeated as he chides Ulster writers for being so dainty about facing the facts of 'the troubled surface' of Ulster life:

> What has been done to set down those tensions and loyalties and swift angers that agitate us? Again, little enough. A few stories by Shan Bullock, a few plays such as Jack Loudan's *Henry Joy McCracken* and Joseph Tomelty's *The End House*, and a plethora of others that start off boldly enough, lose their nerve, and plunge up to their oxters in sentimentality. We have had to wait until as recently as two years ago for our first historical novel of importance, W.F. Marshall's *Planted by a River* [1948].

He is clearly confident, not to say magisterial, when speaking of literature and drama, about the need to appreciate the 'rich store of folklore in story, ballad, and custom' and the real possibility of its leaching away in the tide of modern life. His account of the changes brought to the Ulster countryside when 'a pattern of life that had shifted little in three hundred years became suddenly, and not too silently, transformed' is an old melancholy song. His 'amateurish' enthusiasm for the other arts of music, art and architecture seems to equate him with the common reader, but his work for the collection of Ulster song, his crisscrossing of Northern Ireland for his radio features, which gave him more than an acquaintance with the buildings mentioned in Hanna's architectural essay, and his early training in art, to say nothing of his admitted first ambition to be a painter, all belie his claimed 'ignorance'. As with all the work that Bell undertook, native talent combined with painstaking effort and patience meant that like Oliver Goldsmith, in Dr Johnson's famous encomium, he touched nothing that he did not adorn: *Nullum quod tetigit non ornavit.*

8
DECEMBER BRIDE

D*ECEMBER BRIDE* was published by Denis Dobson in London in 1951 and by E.P. Dutton Inc. in New York the same year, but like all Sam Hanna Bell's work it had been a long time a-growing. David Millar's diary records that Bell regularly borrowed a house called Laurel Cottage on the Braniel Road in Hillhall to work on the book. The entry for 13 May 1944 recalls a trip to Laurel Hill with Martin McBirney:

> Sam who came late in the evening is staying for a week to write. He brought with him the first draft of his novel 'December Bride'. He outlined the plot but did not read any of it to us.

A finished section called 'The Green Springcart' appeared in the third number of *Lagan* (1944), corresponding to pages 83–108 of the published book. The completed novel (299 pages) gives the impression of so much working and revision as to have become a kind of distillation, an irreducible minimum. Of Bell's novels it is the one in which the writing is sparest, with few passages of lyricism except that the year in its turning, with its seasonal change and associated labour, is a kind of extra character. The life of Rathard, the hill farm where the Echlin family lives, is given in almost statistical detail. It is here that Sarah Gomartin comes, with her mother, to keep house for the Echlin brothers.

The epithet 'Hardyean' has been freely applied by critics to *December Bride*. It is applicable only in the sense of a bountiful but exacting nature which is at once benefactor and adversary. There is no sense in Bell's novel of a President of the Immortals having sport with the characters. In fact, apart from *Tess of the D'Urbervilles* and *Jude the Obscure*, the novels of Hardy are by comparison with the sociological and psychological accuracy of *December Bride* romantic Victorian melodramas. Perhaps, however, Sarah Gomartin is the kind of character who would have interested Hardy since he created so many strong and wilful women himself, from Fancy Day to Bathsheba Everdene. The persistent enigma, the unresolved mystery in a story that has the new generation expiate the sins of the old, is how to interpret Sarah's character: is she instinctively manipulative or an independent woman born out of her time?

The kernel of the plot was an actual *ménage à trois* that Bell's mother's family, the McIlveens, knew about, perhaps involving distant relations of their own. The story was an occasion for mildly ribald mirth rather than censoriousness but Seán O'Faoláin, who acted as a distant literary mentor to Bell, persuaded him to consider it as the basis for a novel. There is a sense of the nemesis that might follow on the disruption of Shakespearean order as described by Ulysses in *Troilus and Cressida*, I. iii. 85–8:

> The heavens themselves, the planets, and this centre
> Observe degree, priority and place,
> Insisture, course, proportion, season, form,
> Office and custom, in all line of order.

The effect disregarding this is that 'right and wrong . . . should lose their names.' The sin associated with the Echlin household is not so much the breaking of sexual taboos (the rural community knew the facts of life) but that the quibble over the paternity of the Echlin children and the subsequent withdrawal into social isolation was a break in the normal workings of the society. This is an offence against a god of society who has only a remote connection with the Biblical Jehovah who is worshipped formally at the Sabbath meeting-house.

Bell was reared in Rathard in a sense, since his grandparents' community at Raffrey with its isolation, its neighbourly interdependence and its religion is a model for the novel's location. The religion was Presbyterianism, which Bell's ancestors had brought with them from Scotland in the seventeenth century, and which stressed predestination, particular election, Biblical authority, the essential depravity of man and, significantly in this case, the obligation upon the community to enforce the Church's discipline. The harsher aspects of Calvinism had been modified by time, so that, by the early 1900s, the period of the novel's action, for many country people Presbyterianism was more social than theological, and its demands had sometimes to take second place to the agricultural lives they led. As the author's voice puts it in the novel:

> In a drought the peasants might flock to church with every mark of fervour to pray for rain, but they knew that when the rain did come, it would come fast, rolling, drenching the world from horizon to horizon and not seeking out, with scrupulous justice, the meadows of the pious.

The Echlins are hardworking and prosperous farmers with a holding above the northwest shore of Strangford Lough. On the death of Margaret Echlin, her bereaved husband, Andrew, invites Martha Gomartin and her thirty-year-old daughter Sarah to do the work of the dead woman. ('It was as if the whole framework of the farm's daily life had been withdrawn. Hardly a task about the kitchen or the fields but now lacked some essential part.') Or as it is put more tersely by Andrew: 'Ye can see, Martha. There's hands wanted here.' Martha's response is equally economical: 'Things might be redd up a wee-thing, Andra.' Her husband, Charlie Gomartin, had been a thatcher, and like all of his kind was required to travel to ply his trade. After longer and longer absences from home he disappeared altogether. The sons of the Echlin house, Hamilton and Frank, are notably different in character and skills. Hamilton, the elder, is laconic, phlegmatic, and a prodigious worker. The running of the farm is in his charge, the determining and allocation of the year's work, from sowing to harvest, from insemination to calving, is instinctively planned and efficiently contrived. Frank, his younger brother, is more skilled, more adept at mending and building, more conscious of the beauty of the place and its flora and fauna, and more of the artist.

Sarah is a good worker, systematic and quiet, and soon a favourite with Andrew, to whom she responds as to a father. She gradually establishes herself in the life of Rathard, independent of and largely disregarding Martha. Hamilton (Hami) in his phlegmatic way appreciates her virtues but finds her presence no strain; Frank is much more aware of her as a woman and finds her unselfconscious sensuality disturbing. The sudden death of Andrew (by drowning, as the party returns by boat from a visit to a cousin's island farm) removes the authority figure from the household; Sarah has sexual relations with both brothers and, more significantly, becomes the mistress of the house. The novel begins, however, more than twenty years later. By then the Echlin brothers have been labelled 'bad blood', with an implicit need for expiation. It is by Frank, the softest and most reckless of the three, that the price for the deviation from the prevailing *mores* is paid. He attempts to break out of the Rathard isolation and courts Molly McFirbis, a local girl, but he is so badly beaten by the men of her family that he is left a cripple.

The tone of the book as a whole is set by its opening sentence, which contains images not only of death and sterility but also of disapproval and social control: 'Ravara meeting-house mouldered among its grave-stones like a mother surrounded by her spinster children.' A winter wedding takes place. But the reasons for this are not explained, and the mature bride has symbolic difficulty in sliding the wedding ring over her work-gnarled knuckle. The mood is quiet and there is little in the way of celebration. The young minister who presides at the uneasy rites thinks it 'no irreverent fancy to interpret as the Divine Will that he should be instrumental in bringing back to the paths of propriety these two souls that must have caused his father so much sorrow'. But his second thought is, 'Yes, I trapped her into it. I failed just as my predecessors failed; as much as my father failed.' Later, in conversation, his father consoles him thus: 'If the reasons for most marriages were stated you would be astounded at the ingenuity of your fellow-men – and perhaps appalled at their courage.' Almost before the reader has time to consider this the chapter ends. The witness to the marriage was a 'youth of about nineteen years of age' and some of the few spectators suppose that the boy is the couple's son:

> 'making his own son follow him as best man – it's a crying shame!' . . .
> The man with the billhook shot a lance of tobacco spittle into a cluster
> of porcelain flowers. 'Whose son?' he asked.

The last chapter in the book describes the success of the minister, Sorleyson, in persuading Sarah to marry so that her daughter, Martha, can wed her fiancé, Joe Skillen. Sarah explains this to Hami:

'He says we'll have to get married before Martha can get married.'

'Ah,' said Hamilton, gazing into the fire. 'And when's this tae be done?'

'On Wednesday's-a-week.'

The man raised his head. 'Wednesday? Then I maun go tae Killy-leagh for coals on the Thursday?'

The book ends on a note of exhausted peace:

> Hamilton pulled off his socks and hung them on the crane. He held out his naked soles to the glowing embers and sighed with pleasure. Then he got up and turned out the lamp and ran it up to the roof. A nimbus of flame danced for a moment in the globe, flickered and vanished, and from all the corners of the kitchen, ancient shadows crept out, silent-footed, to sit by the dying fire.

The character of Sarah aside, the most striking thing about the book is the realisation of place and community. Bell was one of the best delineators of the Ulster-Scots and their descendants, but his empathy with the northern province is ages older than the relatively recent Plantation. It was important for him to remind his readers of the rath behind the Echlin house, 'where an earlier people had looked down on the sinuous waters of the lough'. (Raffrey ['heather fort'] and Rathard ['high fort'] both have the Irish word *ráth* in them.) Bell records that one of the competitors in the scarf game at Ravara fête is nicknamed Moiley, 'because of his high bald forehead'. The word is an interesting survival of the Gaelic word *maol* which means 'smooth' or 'bald' (and is also applied to a hornless cow). Another dialect word, 'mealy-creeshy', is used to describe the supper of fried oatmeal, the expression being Scots and still in use in Wigtonshire, the 'creeshy' coming from the old French word *craisse* meaning 'fat'. Phrases such as 'my mouth's as grummly as a puddle' draw on the rich vocabulary of Ulster-Scots speech.

The politics of the period, when Home Rule agitation was stilled after the fall of Parnell, hardly impinge upon the lives of the people at all. True, the Orange Order is mentioned. But none of the Echlins have ever been members. Andrew has gone once to the Field with his neighbours but was revolted by the speechmakers who were 'landlords, politicians and clergymen'. He has been to dances in the Orange Hall and it was there he met his wife. 'But he left to his neighbours the July walk, the bouncing fife and the braggadocio of the belly-drum'. The Echlins' closest neighbour, Petie Sampson (whose wife Agnes is a kind of spae-wife with a knowledge of healing herbs) was the pride of Ravara's Loyal Sons because of his fife-playing.

> and the little man had led his Lodge to the Field and back for many years. Now as they marched and counter-marched on the country road to the patterned thunder of their drum, Petie skipped ahead of them blowing vigorously on his instrument. For years the drumming had been held some distance from Knocknadreemally, at Petie's re-quest, because of his regard for his neighbour, Owen Dineen.

This freedom from atavistic fear of the age-old enemy (remarkable by today's standards) is shared by the Echlins but not by Sarah. In a sig-nificant scene Sarah's insensitivity towards Catholic belief is revealed and chided by the normally taciturn Hamilton. At times even the best-run farm needs outside workers and Bridie Dineen, Owen's wife, is brought along to Rathard to help with the potato picking. She is de-scribed as having a henlike quality:

> even when she was alone, she walked with a short hesitant step as if she were afraid of trampling one of her many children. Outside her own house she spoke to her neighbours with that courteous but evasive briefness that marks the Catholic in a Protestant district. Before she had set her foot in the kitchen of Rathard Sarah disliked her.

In those years Catholics were obliged to refrain from flesh meat on Fridays. It is therefore an act of refined cruelty for Sarah on a Friday to place bacon before Bridie, hungry after a morning of back-breaking work, at the meal that is an accepted part of the payment. Her friend Agnes Sampson quickly transfers the meat on to Hamilton's plate. Hamilton apologises profusely and requires Sarah to cook fish. Later he chides her:

> When the others had trooped out of the kitchen Hamilton spoke to her before he left for the field. 'That was a sore way ye had wi' that woman,' he said abruptly.
>
> Sarah turned her back on him and went on scraping dishes.
>
> 'Are ye heeding me?'
>
> 'Aye, I'm heeding ye.'
>
> 'Well, listen to what I'm saying.' He put his hand under her chin and drew her round, and at the touch of her face in his fingers, his resentment weakened. 'There's been a power o' harvesters come and

gone here in my father's and his father's time. Not one of them but couldn't say he got good kitchen and the right money in his hand at the end o' the day. It'll be the same in our time. Heed that now, like a good woman.' Her soft petulant face was framed in his fingers. He bent and kissed her on the mouth.

She stood motionless in the kitchen, watching him through the window as he crossed to the stable. The dishcloth had fallen from her hand to the floor. The words 'in our time' went singing through her like strong wine. But the image of Bridie Dineen came back to her mind, and she hardened her heart in anger against the red-haired woman.

Sarah's dislike of Bridie is, as I have said, partly atavistic but there is also the element of a strong woman hating a weaker. Another deeper instinct at work is a kind of social envy: this poor cottier's wife with her imprudently large family has a higher local reputation than Sarah, who is so much superior in all the virtues save conformity. So, though Hamilton's words confirm her position as woman of the house, she still cannot purge her anger. Later, when the Echlins are able to extend their holdings and they need to use one of the tenant cottages as a 'pratie-house' (another Gaelic survival, from *práta*, potato) it is the Dineens who are forcibly rehoused. It is Sarah who suggests it but the brothers acquiesce: 'deep down in all three the centuries-old enmity against the papist stirred, and neighbourliness and a more ancient kinship were forgotten'.

The Orange Order is the only overt indication of the old atavism in the almost totally Protestant community. The only other Catholics mentioned are the Ogle brothers, Hugh and Peter, whose kindness to Petie Sampson comes undone in a setpiece describing a visit to Edwardian Belfast. Apart from references to what Louis MacNeice called 'the voodoo of the Orange drums', the Orange Order is seen as a social club. The fête at which Frank Echlin has the misfortune to meet Molly McFirbis is described with anthropological accuracy as 'a puritan propitiation to amorous merrymaking', and is exactly like the *feis* or *aeraíocht* in Catholic areas. There are cultural differences, of course: 'There was no country dancing. Long ago they had lost the arts of the ballad and the dance, which as kin, they had once shared with the ancient people of Ireland.' But the *ad hoc* sporting events (field races, the throwing of small logs at targets, the barefoot high jumps over willow wands resting on the shoulder of two volunteers, the scarf race described with researcher's accuracy) would have been common to both tribes.

The public practice of religion is important to the Ravara community but it is not an absolute essential. The egalitarian nature of Presbyterianism emphasises the individual and his righteous conscience. Andrew Echlin finds no inconsistency in his deeply held faith and his principled abstention from public worship:

> A few years before his death, when he was an elder of the congregation, the minister had installed an organ in the church. Andrew had protested. His protest had been unheeded. The organ had been installed and the precentor, whose bass voice had led the praise as long as anyone could remember, had been driven out to a pew in the church. That Sunday morning, on the first note of the instrument, Andrew and several of the elders had risen and left the building.

(The business of the coming of the organ to Presbyterian churches in Northern Ireland and the downgrading of vocal praise was to be the subject of one of Bell's most entertaining and successful features, *A Kist o' Whistles*, which was first broadcast on 17 November 1954 and repeated a year later.)

The place of religious practice is understood well by the various ministers who have the care of the souls of the Ravara community. The vast majority of the people led lives of Sabbath piety: the stories of Sunday as a stretch of joyless immobility except for Sabbath journeys to kirk and conning of texts that have come down from the time suggest stoicism and fear of the Lord rather than joy. Justification before that Lord would normally be seen in the material prosperity of the faithful; being poor or unsuccessful, indeed any misfortune, could well be interpreted as the work of God, as expiation for some sin of the sufferers or of their progenitors. Yet the final arbitrator was the personal conscience, which could in people of a particular psychological bent approach autonomy. If any of the trio at the heart of the Rathard scandal had been questioned about the moral aspect of their actions or attitudes they might well have been shocked at the suggestion of wrongdoing.

When Frank is crippled by the McFirbis men for trying to spread 'the bad blood' into their homestead, he accepts the dreadful visitation as his due: 'I sinned onct, and God chastised me.' He can no longer accept Hamilton's reassurance:

'The three o' us, Frankie,' Hamilton mumbled. 'The three o' us woven throughother.' He felt Frank draw away from him and saw the furtive sidelong glance of his eyes.

'That's a lie. I'm no part of ye now. I'm not woven intae this place. I'm the broken reed wi' the withered pith.'

His remorse makes his isolation more complete, and in a poignant scene he attempts some explanation to Andrew, Sarah's first child, but fails and breaks into frustrated tears.

In such a moral structure the minister of religion is relegated almost to the noncommital role of psychotherapist: 'What do *you* think it means?' The elder Sorleyson capitulates to his own desire when he touches Sarah's breast, and the incident has all the greater charge in that it happens when the minister is visiting Rathard to impress upon Sarah the need to have her problematic child baptised. His son achieves a victory years later by means of the winter wedding but it seems hollow to him. The only basis for the 'most remarkable wedding-service' is not morality, or religion, but provision of the gift of respectability to the young Martha, who can now marry her Joe.

The irrelevance of preacher and prayer to these Echlins (and effectively to any of their neighbours in equivalent situations) is connected with the primal force behind all their lives: the insistent demands on those who, like Patrick Maguire, have made their fields their brides. Much of *December Bride* is devoted not to the people, but to the country year, its changing moods and its insistent demands. Satisfying as the story and characterisation undoubtedly are, one remembers with a kind of awe the descriptions of winter storms, spring quickening, and summer lushness.

> They were now passing through the short glimmering days of the year, days of drenched storm-driven twilight. Every day from horizon to horizon the sky was filled with matted clouds creeping to the east. At noon for an hour, an unearthly pearly light fell on the walls and fields, a light that pressed on the head and hurt the brain, and those who had to be out did so with averted heads, hurrying quickly from doorway to doorway. Then the baffled sun drew away and the countryside slid back again into dripping icy darkness.

December Bride leaves the reader with the impression of wisdom, poetic precision, sociological accuracy, and a great understanding of human nature. It is widely recognised to be Bell's best novel, an assessment reflected in its inclusion by Carmen Callil and Colm Tóibín in their *The Modern Library* as one of the best 200 novels in the English language since 1950. None of the later novels has its terseness or clarity of prose.

The *Belfast News-Letter* published a review by 'R.M.' on 10 December 1951. Under the subhead: 'Ulster writer's debut as novelist', the author predicted that the 'eagerly awaited' novel from one who had 'already proved his worth as a short-story writer and is, of course, an outstanding exponent of the radio medium in Ulster . . . will not be welcomed by everyone in his native Province'. R.M. observed that the subject of doubtful parentage is 'dealt with in a masterly – and delicate – manner'. The idiom too 'is absolutely authentic, and odd dialect words constantly brighten the pages'. The review closes with a warning: 'Those who live in an airy fairyland of the mind, where all hearts are kind and everyone is gentle, had better leave it alone.'

R.M. was Ruddick Millar (1907–1952), a Belfast playwright and friend. He took the precaution of sending Bell a copy of the review 'so that you'll know if there is any difference between it and what actually appears'. (In fact the review was printed in full and did not suffer from the editor's blue pencil.) Millar included a review written by Norah Meade Corcoran in *The Sign,* an important American Catholic journal; the review admired the novel and concluded: 'It is a spare, well-told tale, into which creeps an occasional note of tenderness and a hint that his people are not as grim as they appear. There is violence aplenty and bigotry, too, but the author is consolingly objective.' In a shorter unsigned piece in the *Belfast Telegraph* on the same day the plot is discreetly summarised and the potential reader is advised: 'True to life and character, this is a book which should establish the author as a writer of serious purpose.'

In the *Northern Whig* it was discussed in a composite review by Rachel B. Field of 'an Ulster selection'. The other books treated were *Final Harvest,* a collection of poems by Richard Rowley, Bell's first publisher, and a reissue of *Gape Row* by Agnes Romilly White. *December Bride* is by comparison described as 'rather sterner stuff', and much is made of the perceived Hardyean similarities, including a grotesque comparison of Sarah with Arabella, Jude Frawley's wife. The review neatly avoids any mention of the Echlin *ménage à trois,* talking unspecifically of 'a pattern of elemental passion and its battle with half-assimilated conventions of civilization'. Field's conclusion seems strangely out of sympathy with the novel's intention:

> Mr Bell writes of passions, but his prose is cool; his metaphors, striking and measured, mirror a scene or a mood, but do not recreate them vividly, searingly; it is cruelly, not persuasively, evocative and herein lies the real difference between the climate of this novel and of Hardy's 'Tess'.

Outside the book's native province the reviews were generally favourable. Ann F. Wolfe talked of 'a welcome new poetry to his cycle of Irish farm life as lived to the strict rhythm of the Northern seasons' in the New York *Saturday Review of Literature* (1 September); Robert Lowry noted the 'fatalistic certainty of a folk tale, brightening [the] scene with that gift for earthly simile which readers have come to expect in Irish writers from Dingle Bay to Belfast Lough' (*New York Times*, 12 August). It was chosen by the Club du Livre Français and had a subsequent Gallic life as *Noces d'Hiver*. To the reviewer in the *Irish Times* (15 December) it was 'perhaps, the best novel about Northern Irish life which has yet appeared'; Elizabeth Jenkins noted in the *Manchester Guardian* (21 December) how well Bell conveyed 'the beauty and remoteness of the scene' and described 'his subsidiary characters, in particular Sarah's old peasant mother', as 'excellent'. Richard Church in the soon-to-be-defunct *John O'London's Weekly* (21 December 1951) asserted that:

> Sarah's calm, deep and passionate nature will provoke obvious comparison with some of Hardy's women. So will the sureness of the setting, and the Greek sense of fatality in the clash of character and circumstance. A most remarkable first novel . . .

When the book was reissued by Blackstaff Press in 1974 the reviews were universally good. As a diary entry for November of that year puts it: 'very favourable reviews of *December Bride* in *Hibernia*, *Irish Press*, *Honest Ulsterman* etc.'

The last word on *December Bride* must be its author's. In a draft of a note to an unidentified 'Paddy' (perhaps his friend Paddy Lennon of Saul), characteristically written on the back of an envelope, Bell wrote:

> You really are very generous about *December Bride*. And of course you're right about the autobiographical bit. I think I told you years

ago about meeting, one evening, in Mooney's bar, a childhood pal, Frank Shaw, a blacksmith from Derryboy. Frank told us the tale about the two brothers and the servant girl. We fell about with laughter. But that story stuck to my memory like a burr. I tried it first as a short story. It ran all over the edges. It had to be something longer. So it became a novel into which I poured all my nostalgic memories of a vanishing way of country life. It's interesting that I was never moved to write a sequel or anything similar. In other words I had exhausted that vein of ore.

9
PLAYS AND FEATURES

S AM HANNA BELL wrote about forty radio scripts for the BBC and several for television while he was on the permanent staff. Dramatisation was a normal part of these programmes – indeed a necessary part if interest in often complicated stories was to be maintained. Moreover, the dramatised or semi-dramatised script was the normal format in Gilliam's Features Department. It was natural, then, that a writer so interested in the theatre should turn to the writing of imaginative drama. Among the list of programmes attributed to Bell is *The Sliddry Dove*, 'a comedy' by Sam Hanna Bell and G.P. (Gerry) McCrudden, then a studio manager in Belfast. It was broadcast on Thursday, 17 April 1958, with a full hand of the best Ulster actors of the time – Harold Goldblatt, Margaret D'Arcy, Elizabeth Begley, James Ellis, J.G. Devlin – all of whom made reputations beyond the confines of Northern Ireland. The script was very much of its time, set in the peaceful rural Ulster of the 1950s, with the sharp and effective dialogue that one expects from two professional broadcasters.

The Sliddry Dove was meant for the stage but never quite made it. The authors' original idea was a light-hearted, even farcical, Christmas show for the Ulster Group Theatre. Written in 1955 it was not intended to compete with the professional pantomimes showing in the Grand Opera House or the Empire; rather, it was to be a seasonal alternative to *Cinderella*. The original idea came from Bell and the co-authors developed the storyline during regular meetings. At intervals they would compare their versions and generate a final agreed text. As Gerry McCrudden remembers it, the play as they wrote it became more serious, with more matter and more developed comedy. It was offered to the Group Theatre but not accepted. A diary entry by Bell for February 1957 reads thus:

> Last week J.E. [James Ellis] gave me back *The Sliddry Dove*. Feel he didn't like it. Don't blame him although it seemed amusing when G.McC. and I were writing it. Lost all interest in writing plays.

On 28 August Bell sent the play to Hubert Wilmot with a view to its being staged at the Arts Theatre, but it was returned on 20 September:

> *Sliddry Dove* returned by Wilmot. 'Liked it – but etc., etc.' His criticisms quite useless. Depressing how ill-informed and helpless our theatre people are when asked for constructive comment. This sounds uncharitable but is, unfortunately, true!

Finally the script was sent to Ronnie Mason, the head of drama at Ormeau Avenue, on 22 January 1958 to be adapted as a radio play. The diary entry which records this also has the observation: 'Feel this story would make quite an amusing short novel.' The accounts department offered £50 8s (48 guineas) to Bell as part-author.

The story had to be squeezed to fit into the magical fifty-eight minutes before Big Ben and the main evening news, and it shows signs of that compression. The actors seem to have too many words to get through in the time, and the Shavian elements of the comedy tend to become lost in the rush of dialogue. With hindsight McCrudden feels it would have been better for Bell to reconstitute it as a radio play to suit the time available. (McCrudden had by now gone to work in television in London.) In spite of this it works very well. It has humour and tolerance, and the tensions of a divided society are cosily muted.

The title, as is explained during the course of the action, is the name of a new and independent newspaper to be published in the village of Sliddry (not the most unlikely Ulster placename), a newspaper that will be 'wise as the serpent; peaceful as the dove'. As its owner/editor Theodore Birch (played with stern avuncularity by Goldblatt) puts it:

> unlike the immortal Skibbereen Eagle I have no desire to fix my eye on the Czar of all the Russias, but I consider myself free to comment on the petty czars and czarinas that appear occasionally in our public

life, regardless of the party or faction to which they belong . . .

It is all fine liberal stuff and rather like Miss Prism's description of fiction as books in which the good end happily and the bad unhappily.

The necessary love interest is between Birch's secretary and the vain, silly but agreeable young reporter Harry Teacey, played by James Ellis, whose exposure of a 'scandal' about the water supply, nearly finishes the *Dove* after seven months of peaceful wise life. There is also the suggestion of a possible understanding between Birch and his distant relative Amelia Kellet-Birch, but she ends up engaged to the editor of the *Newtowndullard Chronicle*. The play concludes with the staff's decision to fight the Apex Construction Company's libel action, Birch having accepted the large honorarium due him as the trustee of the SPCPNI (Society for the Propagation of Culture among the People of Northern Ireland), a neat satiric touch.

There are many similar flourishes. McComb, the extremely well-read mechanic who maintains the printing machine, swears 'Great Gutenberg!' and apostrophises Caxton. The theatre review that Teacey offers as part of his portfolio suggests that the play lacks structure in the third act. When challenged by Birch he says, 'You see that's always said about the third act of an Ulster play – it's a sort of – of – . . . convention.' Sir Thomas McElderry, star of the *Newtowndullard Chronicle*'s correspondence columns, offers the *Dove* letters on the first cuckoo, 'modifications in the hat badges of the Royal Irish Constabulary 1897–1903', and the fact that the new Orange banner for the Sliddry lodge has Martin Luther as a Franciscan and not as an Augustinian. Teacey at one stage reminds Birch '. . . in this country a jumble-sale can be made to sound subversive'. McComb, speaking with the voice of the authors, criticises Teacey's style with, 'Every noun you use is as dead as Brian Boru – and it gets four adjectives as coffin-bearers.' Janet, the secretary, also echoes their beliefs when towards the end of the play she announces, 'Mr Birch, in the past six months you have taught me to avoid the verbal cliché. But I'm forced to use one now – you are speaking of the man I love.'

The Sliddry Dove is a well-made, amusing piece of work and survived its treatment at the hands of the unknown adaptor. Typically Bell's work lived in his mind in an eternal present, and on 10 February 1960 he wrote to his co-author saying that he thought of turning *The Sliddry Dove* into a novel:

For some time now I have had a desire to re-write as a novel the story of Theodore Birch — his paper *The Sliddry Dove* and that remarkable organisation the Society for the Propagation of Culture among the People of Northern Ireland and all the other etceteras. Anyway before I start I feel that I should let you know my intention. I am eager to do this and know I could finish it off in a couple of years or so.

(For nearly any other writer with the plot and much of the dialogue already in existence the proposed time would have been 'a couple of months or so' but, as Bell admitted elsewhere, he wrote 'very laboriously'.)

Gerry's response came in the first paragraph of a letter written on 22 March:

I was delighted to hear that the *Dove* is to be remoulded in novel form. I've no doubt whatever you'll make a lovely job of it, and look forward to seeing it, one fine morning, 'plastered' all over Smiths at Waterloo Station.

After that *The Sliddry Dove* passes out of recorded history.

In the edition of the *Radio Times* for 11 April 1958 a piece about the play notes:

Sam Hanna Bell has been the author of many memorable programmes from Northern Ireland. His published work includes a successful novel, *December Bride*, which was published in America and France, and has since been adapted as a play and performed on stage and radio as *That Woman at Rathard*.

It was almost inevitable that someone would try to make a play out of the strong material of *December Bride*. The genesis of the adaptation (which was staged at the Group Theatre in February 1955 and again twelve years later by the Lyric Players Theatre) is not known. Certainly Bell's friend Martin McBirney had a hand in the adaptation and it may have been his suggestion that started the process; the extent of his actual contribution remains doubtful. The script reads well and it is interesting to see how the material of the novel was reconstituted for the stage. One of the means by which the plot of the novel is made more dramatic is the concentration of the time of the action; there are also a number of confrontational scenes between Sarah and her mother, Sarah and Frank, and Sarah and Hamilton. The weakest part of the work is an extended, almost Shavian debate in the third act between Sorleyson, the minister of Ravara, and an interpolated character, Dr Sproule, about the morality of prevailing upon Hamilton and Sarah to marry each other.

The death of the father, Andrew, one of the novel's climactic events, in the play is not as in the novel the result of a act of self-sacrifice to save the others from drowning. Instead Bell adapted an incident in 'The Broken Tree', one of the stories in *Summer Loanen*. Just as in that story Hans Gault's whole life is changed when a tree breaks as he is attempting to pull a fallen cow out of a deep ditch, so too in the play a broken tree causes mortal injury to Andrew. The death and the local focus on Rathard bring things to a climax. Martha, Sarah's mother, understands the changes that the death will bring to the household and her future. Sarah admits that she is pregnant but has already rejected Frank, the father of the child. His association with Mollie Crockart, the daughter of a local ne'er-do-well, results in his death at her father's hands. The play ends with a kind of weary peace as Sarah's demeanour implies an agreement to stay and heal the reputation of Rathard.

The play is considerably less subtle than the novel, with the relationships of the original *ménage à trois* made much simpler and cruder. The reputation of a cursed house that Rathard attained in the novel was not the result of the births of two children but rather of the community's doubt as to who the father was. What is lacking, too, in the play – in addition to the many ambivalences that make the novel so fascinating – is depth of feeling, and the sense of time passing. Even so, the new script is a powerful piece of drama with some memorable lines: 'I have neither the wit to explain, Sarah, nor you the heart to understand'; 'For all my father cared we might be sitting in the cottage accepting the thin farl of charity and the thick buttermilk of neighbourliness'; 'In two years the sod has never healed over our burying-place in Ravara churchyard.'

There were opening-night telegrams from such friends as Rowel Friers, Joe and Lena Tomelty and her mother Min Milligan, who was a leading actress with the Group Theatre. Letters of appreciation came from A.R. Foster who hoped it would be taken abroad 'into an ampler ether', and from the artist Mercy MacCann who also felt that it 'should reflect Ulster on a London stage sometime, as it would have a universal instead of a local appeal'. In his reply Bell reminded her that it was his 'first shot at a play and I learnt a lot just sitting watching it. I am not very happy about the construction of the third act.' The play was broadcast on 17 October 1963 as a BBC drama department offering.

In an edition of *The Arts in Ulster* broadcast on 4 March 1965, Bell talked to John Boyd on the subject 'My Approach to Writing'. In it he mentioned the play: 'It was done in the Group Theatre and pleased the critics but the public stayed away.' The public reaction to the Lyric production was rather more positive and though there is no account of that production in any of the Bell papers, except for a flyer from the Lyric Players Theatre, 11 Derryvolgie Avenue, indicating that the third act had been rewritten by the author, the entry in the diary for 15 February 1967 reads:

> Informed that I hadn't been shortlisted for AHP [Assistant Head of Programmes] job. Had tried not to bank upon it but v. depressing nevertheless. This evening went over to Lyric Theatre to watch run-through rehearsal of *That Woman at Rathard*. All in all, v. promising and gave me a bit of a lift.

John D. Stewart, reviewing the Lyric production for the *News Letter*, found it a masterpiece: 'I had forgotten with all the theatrical rubbish I have seen here in the past few years, that we had men who could write so well.'

The play had another manifestation as *A Roof Is Not Enough*. This was prepared by Bell as a television script in February 1961 and sent to the Abbey Theatre in Dublin in its original form on 26 June. A letter written on 11 October by Ernest Blythe (1889–1975), who was then managing director, regretted that the two independent and unnamed readers were 'strongly against acceptance . . . their objection being mainly to the plot.' The language of rejection is seldom appreciative, but Reader B's report shows a remarkable insensitivity to the play's essence:

> A far from satisfactory play even though written with a fair amount of technical competence. Its biggest fault lies in the story which is not only unreal from the point of view of life, but what is worse, from the point of view of the theatre. The author faces us, and himself, with a situation in which two brothers lie with a servant girl who is eventually with child. Brother A loves girl; girl loves brother B; girl also loves security representing brother A. Suspense consists of doubt concerning paternity. Strindberg might have made something of the situation but here it amounts to three incredible and rather dull acts, in which the reader's interest is held merely by Mr Bell's flair for

sustaining local colour, which makes his plot, as well as his handling of it, seem unnecessarily outlandish.

It is clear from Reader A's remarks that the plot had undergone another change: there is no indication of any injury done to Frank, who heads for Canada leaving Hamilton free to

> propose marriage in flowery language worthy of East Lynne. Heroine hums and haws but finally makes for Belfast after her man, telling her mother in response to her query 'Where will your journey take ye?', 'Wherever my husband says.' (Collapse of elder brother, followed by collapse of curtain.)

It is hard to understand such inability to see the potential of the play on the part of professional play readers. The stage versions have not the passion or sureness of touch of *December Bride* but the successful 1990 film version of the novel demonstrates powerfully what was possible. Perhaps the novel could not be rendered with the same intensity into the inflexible shape of the old three-act stage play.

That Woman at Rathard had another run in 1985 when Theatre Ulster produced it at the Riverside Theatre, Coleraine, directed by the playwright Frank McGuinness; it opened at the Arts Theatre in Belfast on 22 April. Invited to the opening, Bell replied that he would accept: 'There will be four in my party. As my hearing is not all it should be I would appreciate it if the management could find us seats near the middle front on the right.' (A receipt from Interflora records that £22.50 was paid for flowers for the cast.)

Bell's contract with the BBC required that he write as well as produce scripts. Some were about places: one of these, the early *This Is Northern Ireland*, was first broadcast on 6 October 1949 and was repeated on the following St Patrick's Day on both the network Home Service and the General Overseas Service; it was given another hearing seventeen years later. Other places that made fascinating features when viewed through Bell's eyes were Rathlin Island, the Lagan (in *The Three-leafed River* which was broadcast on 6 October 1951 and reconstituted as a television feature, *The Trident Port*, fourteen years later) and the Silent Valley reservoir (in a television film, *Water from the Rock*, 30 September 1964). There were also several portraits of counties. Other rich sources were strange stories from Ulster's past, accounts of dark deeds, unhappy love affairs, missing heiresses, and dramatic court cases, material which would later prove a staple for his articles in the *Ulster Tatler*. The feature programmes that resulted included *The Lady of the Manse* (9 May 1956) and *The Clue of the Four Soldiers* (19 February 1957). Some, like the regular anthology programmes such as *A Christmas Garland* (27 December 1946), *The Warm Side of the Stone* (19 March 1957), *Autumn Anthology* (4 October 1963), and '. . . *and Good Wishes for the New Year*' (19 December 1964) and several editions of *Irish Voices*, were created with deceptive ease, their mix of song, verse and story evidence of their compiler's wide reading, sense of humour and flair for choosing performers.

Two programmes that are particularly memorable are *A Kist o' Whistles* (which was broadcast on 17 November 1954) and *The Orangemen* (11 July 1967). Each required expert research, the first was researched by the Rev. John M. Barkley DD (d. 1997), who was professor of Ecclesiastical History in the Presbyterian College, Belfast. The second was prepared by Aiken McClelland (d. 1981), who at the time was a teacher but later in 1967 joined the staff of the Ulster Folk and Transport Museum at Cultra. The 'kist o'whistles' – the word 'kist' is Lallans for 'chest' – was the organ or harmonium that a certain faction of the Presbyterian Church resisted as an inappropriate instrument for public worship. The script contained a mixture of material for narrators' and actors' voices, organ music, dramatised sessions of the Assembly and such like. The actors who took part included many whom Bell used regularly, including some talented amateurs. Many became his close friends. Jack McQuoid, James Ellis, James Boyce and John McBride were to figure in many productions – and such giants of the BBCNI unofficial repertory company as R.H. McCandless were still about in those years.

The theme of a long–dead controversy that exercised clergy and laity alike from 1868 until 1892 may not now seem suitable material for an entertaining feature, yet even in script form it is full of life. Bell was a master of the radio script: his balance of different forms of aural stimulus – narrators' voices (in this case such sound anchormen as Michael Baguley and Charles Witherspoon), dramatised scenes, interpolated verse, music and song – was masterly, and he was famous – at times infamous, as his hearing deteriorated – for the precision of his sound effects. As Denys Hawthorne, one of his regular actors from 1951 to 1958, told me, 'If a feature called for the sound of a particular bell in a church in Aughnacloy then that was the sound that was recorded.'

What comes across with humour and satisfactory suspense in *A Kist o'
Whistles* is a sense that the controversy was not a trivial affair (though
the High Anglican author of *Gulliver's Travels* might have enjoyed
satirising it) but a matter of vital importance to the parties. One of the
neater aspects of the programme was the incorporation of contemporary verses by a satirist who used the unimpeachable name
Veritas:

> The Kirk is in a sorry plight
> Brimful of disorder;
> For speakers speak, and writers write
> Regardless of all order.
> How fond some are to raise a rout,
> Is it not most amazing
> That such a fuss is all about
> A huge machine for praising?
> – Or what is better far expressed
> Syne in the land of thistles:
> But whole in earnest, half in jest
> The 'Auld Wife's Kist o' Whistles'.

The Orangemen was considerably more complicated; it covered the
history of Orangeism from its earliest appearance after the victories of
William III and the catastrophe of Limerick in 1690 up to its implicit
position of political power in the state of Northern Ireland. It was appropriate that McClelland, who was the librarian of the Grand Orange
Lodge of Ireland and founder of the Orange Lodge of Research, should
provide the historical facts. A file of documents that Bell kept during
the writing and researching of the programme contains clippings from
the *Belfast News-Letter* of articles by Stewart Mackay about such famous
conflicts between Orangemen and Ribbonmen as the battles of Clonoe
(13 July 1829) near Stewartstown in Tyrone; Derrylin on the same day;
Maghera (1830) and Garvagh (1813); there was also correspondence
with McClelland, and a 32-foolscap-page account of the history of the
Orange Order and other material researched by McClelland (for which
he was paid £63), a chronology, and typescript and manuscript versions of contemporary pro- and anti-Orange ballads. These were sung
in the programme by Tony McAuley, James Shaw and Maurice
O'Callaghan.

The programme began with a somewhat cleaned-up version of the

Orange toast as devised by the members of the Skinner's Alley aldermen who had been removed from Dublin Corporation in 1688 by James II:

> To the glorious pious and immortal memory of the great and good King William who assisted in redeeming us from popery, slavery, arbitrary power, brass money and wooden shoes. May we never want a Williamite to kick the arse of a Jacobite! And he that won't drink this, whether he be priest, bishop, deacon, bellows-blower, gravedigger, or any of the fraternity of the clergy; may the Devil jump down his throat with a red hot harrow, with every pin tear out a gut, and blow him with a clean carcase to hell! Amen.

The date of broadcast, 13 July 1967, was significant not only for its day but also its year, which was effectively the last full year of 'peace' in the troubled North. The yearly marches had become low-key and, if not actually folksy, as some supporters have argued, then less gratuitously sectarian than they had been in the past and were to become again with the Troubles. The various affrays, including the 'founding' Battle of the Diamond at Loughgall in 1795 and the notorious Dolly's Brae (1849), were rendered by contemporary or near-contemporary ballads with Orange band tunes and Lambeg drums acting as fearsome punctuation. Notable characters from the history of the Orange Order who featured in the programme included William Blacker, James Sloan and William Johnston – 'of Ballykilbeg' (1829–1902) – who had been the subject of an earlier feature written by Bell which was broadcast on 8 November 1960. (A weary note in the diary written on that date reads: 'Produced this evening my feature Johnston of Ballykilbeg. Took me over a year to write, off and on.') One fine moment of drama in *The Orangemen* was a memory of the Somme and the Ulster Division's heroism at Thiepval on 1 July 1916, the anniversary of the Battle of the Boyne, when the troops charged wearing their Orange collarettes and shouting, 'Remember the Boyne!'

It was a magnificent feature. Even those on high showed their satisfaction: on 27 February the following year the writer/producer was given a bonus of £100 for 'your outstanding work in connection with the historical programme "The Orangemen"'. He was similarly rewarded for the television series *I Remember* (April–May 1969) produced by Gerry McCrudden in which he acted as host and subtle prompter to

R.H. McCandless, John Hewitt, Seamus Delargy, James Mageean, Peadar O'Donnell and Cahir Healy. He was the ideal man to stimulate recollection in these famous Ulstermen, mostly friends and colleagues, and the transcripts show that the unscripted programmes had the ease and fascination of the best conversations.

10
AN OLD ULSTER CUSTOM

AMONG SAM HANNA BELL'S PAPERS for the year 1950 is an agreement dated 3 December between him and Denis Dobson Ltd, the publisher of *December Bride,* for a book of 'folkways' in the north of Ireland. In earlier correspondence in the September of that year the working title 'An Old Ulster Custom' had been agreed. This was some months before the publication of the novel and may have been a kind of early response to the usual option clause in publishers' contracts which requires 'the first refusal of (including the first opportunity to read and consider for publication) the author's next two works . . .' or some such formula. The folkways book took six years to complete and in that time had several changes of title, including to 'Old Ulster Customs' (1953). In the end it became *Erin's Orange Lily,* which did not please the author. In a diary entry for 10 October 1956 noting the publication of the book, Bell described the title as 'not the happiest collaboration' and noted that it was chosen by the publishers to suit the US market. A letter written to the Rev. K.D. Harvey of Duncairn Presbyterian Church on 21 November 1956 went into more detail:

> This book was originally planned as 'It's an Old Ulster Custom' in a series of old customs books run by Dennis Dobson. Unfortunately Dobson failed and was eventually backed by the New York publishers Putnam. The manuscript had got as far as galley proofs and the

blocks were cut, so Putnam revived the idea of publication. If you suspected a rather Yanky flavour about its title this explains why!

The very word 'Erin' (the anglicisation of a dative case) reeks of the sentimental ballads and parlour verse of Tom Moore or Charlotte Alington Barnard.

The book was written in what spare time Bell had from the colossal workload demanded by his position as Features Producer. John Boyd notes in *The Middle of My Journey* that as talks producer he had little free time during the week and relished the weekends when he had time to spend with his wife and children. 'The conditions were serf-like.' He quotes a paragraph from the agreement he signed on his appointment in 1946:

> You agree to devote the whole of your time and attention to the service of the Corporation and to attend for duty at such hours of the day or night as shall from time to time be decided by the Corporation.

Bell had probably as great a workload as Boyd. In a scrap of handwritten manuscript found among miscellaneous papers Bell states:

> Features Department usually had one broadcast a week. And the time I was given would now be called 'prime time' – slap in the middle of the evening's listening. If you had a sixty-minute script then that ran from eight o'clock to nine. And a thirty-minute script from 8.30 to nine. But there was one strict stipulation – you had to be off the air thirty seconds before the first stroke of Big Ben.

The workload inevitably took its toll. One aspect noted by John Boyd was the necessary isolation of the writer:

> Sam Hanna Bell . . . had an erratic streak that sometimes surfaced unexpectedly, when he would seek company to break the loneliness of writing his scripts. He would come into my office and suggest going across the road to the Elbow Room for a drink.

Bell's research for *Erin's Orange Lily* was extensive. Papers and tantalisingly intermittent and laconic diary entries indicate that, as with his series of radio features *Fairy Faith*, lore was sought from unofficial field officers who wrote back with information about local practices and beliefs. In 1950 Jack McBride gave information about 'fairies in the nine glens', particularly in Glenariff; the artist William Conor wrote on 11 July 1952 saying it was 'not easy to comment on Ulster customs while we still have to live here'; John MacNeill of Monkstown (known as the Railway Poet of Whiteabbey) wrote on 7 October with a ballad he made about a legendary occasion when an Orange march used sidestaffs (the wooden poles for carrying banners) belonging to a Foresters' hall. The publisher's editor had written on 25 March for chapter headings, and on 13 January 1954 there is correspondence about illustrations.

The illustrations that appear in the finished book are an eclectic trawl from such older classics as *Wild Sports of the West* (1832) by the Reverend W.H. Maxwell (1792–1850), Thackeray's *The Irish Sketchbook* (1842), and the well-known travel books of Anna Hall (1800–81) and her husband Samuel (1800–89). The only contemporary decoration is that at the head of the first chapter (on the Lambeg drum), a brilliant almost-doodle by Willie Conor showing two Orange drummers and a fifer. The jacket sported a nondescript lily. Yet in spite of the author's misgivings about the title the book is a remarkable and worthy performance. It probably benefited from its deliberate and extended genesis; the foreword has an air of relief, not that a troublesome chore is at last finished, but that essential knowledge has been written down for preservation. In it Bell disclaims all pretensions to being a folklorist, but admits that he brings to the pages 'a lively curiosity in what my fellow-citizens do and how they do it, and the good fortune that in my daily work as a BBC features producer this curiosity is encouraged'. His admiration for the professional folklorist is expressed perhaps fulsomely:

> he has to have the patience of Job, the persistence of Palissy [the sixteenth-century French Huguenot who spent sixteen years in experimentation on how to make enamels], the deductive powers of Sherlock Holmes, and if you have a pet definition of a sceptic you can throw that in too. Add to this a knowledge of shards and shreds, music and monoliths, an ability to converse with fellow-savants in a dozen languages and dialects . . .

(His friend Michael J. Murphy put it almost as strongly: 'The folklorist knows he has to spend months, even, years, with one mind.')

The foreword also refers to the foundation of the Ulster Folklore Committee and agrees that 'it is not before its time, for the old ways of our community are vanishing rapidly.' The epigraph is from Spenser's *View of the State of Ireland* (1595) and it is worth giving it in full because of its wry appositeness – and its handy disclaimers:

I do herein rely upon those bards or Irish chronicles . . . unto them besides I add mine own reading; and out of them both together, with comparison of times, likewise of manners and customs, affinity of words and names, properties of nature and uses, resemblances of rites and ceremonies, and many other like circumstances, I do gather a likelihood of truth, not certainly affirming anything, but by conferring of times, language, monuments and such like, I do hunt out a probability of things, which I leave to your judgement to believe or refuse.

The 'lively curiosity' and 'the daily work' combined to make a memorable book. The accounts of lambeg drumming, open-air *feiseanna*, shipyard traditions, Boxing Day shoots, illicit liquor distilling, of people gathering in particular houses for a night's crack, fair-day dealing (in people as well as animals), the making and performing of ballads, and the wary reverence for the wee folk, the good people or whatever respectful appellation might placate their variable moods, were also the material of some of Bell's most interesting radio features. (And as we have seen he was able to bring his own testimony about the life of the remote farm and the remarkable entertainment that its denizens were able to provide for themselves.) From a list of almost two hundred individual features originated, produced and in many cases written by Bell, it is possible to pick many that are related to *Erin's Orange Lily*, for example Hugh Quinn's *Songs of the Street* (9 January 1952), *The Feis in the Glens* (30 July 1952), *The Big Drum* (8 August 1952), *The Islandmen* (28 January 1953), Sean O'Boyle's *As I Roved Out* (14 February 1954), *Hired and Bound* (3 March 1954).

The opening lines of the chapter 'Respect the Good Neighbours' underlines the radio link:

In June 1951 the BBC in Northern Ireland decided to explore the region for any fairy lore that might still linger in the glens and mountainsides. Michael J. Murphy, the Ulster folklorist, was commissioned to carry out the preliminary survey. The amount of material that came from Murphy as he combed the countryside surpassed anything we had expected. It also became evident from the ages of the storytellers that the exploration had started none too early.

Then in November, when he had completed his last report we set out with recording equipment to retrace his journey. We worked over Northern Ireland district by district, the Mournes, the Sperrins, South Armagh, the Glens of Antrim, with sallies to the Braid valley, the Fintona district, the shores of Strangford and Lough Erne. Although such a short time had passed since Michael J. Murphy's first visit we were met here and there by a padlocked door or a slow shake of the head. Some old man or woman had taken a grandfather's stories to the graveyard.

This introduction is useful in that it gives an impression of how Bell's features were made. *Fairy Faith*, the project in question, provided material for five programmes which were broadcast in March/April 1952. The series was extremely popular, pleased even the management, and provided valuable information for Delargy's folklore archive. But many of the recordings are now as unrecoverable as the contributors. The great advantage of *Erin's Orange Lily* is that it contains a lasting distillation of many lost programmes. The chapter 'Respect the Good Neighbours' describes the persistence of belief in fairies; the debate about the origins of the fairy race, whether *Tuatha Dé Danann* or lukewarm fallen angels who did not deserve Hell and asked to be sent to Ireland 'as it was the neartherest place to Heaven'; the beliefs about stolen children, leprechauns, fairy bushes, May Eve (*Lá Bealtaine* in Irish and *Walpurgisnacht* in German) – the whole give-and-take relationship with *Na Daoine Beaga*.

In much the same way, the work done by Seán O'Boyle and Seamus Ennis on folksongs was commemorated in the chapter entitled 'Dancing at the Feis'. Many of the songs recovered by them now exist in independent recordings. It was the dances, the jigs, hornpipes and reels, none exclusively Irish, that made the *feiseanna*. Not every Irish person can sing, but many more can dance. As early as the fourteenth century tourists were being asked 'of saynte charity/come ant daunce wyt me/in irlaunde', and many took the anonymous author at his word. And there is no dance without music. Dance supplied two thirds of the Gaelic League's purpose in founding the *feis*: 'to encourage and revive interest in Irish music, Irish dancing and the Irish language'. 'Dancing at the Feis' noted that:

> The first Feis under the new dispensation was held in Belfast in 1900. It was enthusiastically supported by Protestants as well as Roman Catholics for this fresh flowering of Irish culture coincided with bright autumnal leaves of Irish Liberalism. The great political upheavals in the following years destroyed this concord, and the process was

hastened by the obtuse insistence on the part of the organisers to carry
over the festivals from Saturdays into Sundays; this innovation was no
less repugnant to Protestants fifty years ago than it would be to-day.

A later, very funny section discusses the often surreal names of dance
tunes. Bell questioned a *feis* fiddler who was playing a reel he knew:

'Who were the maids of Tulla?' I asked my friend.
    'I only know it as an air and I advise you not to go chasing relevance
through the titles of Irish dance music. What, for example, do you
make of Upstairs in a Tent or The Piper's Picnic or Saft Tam's Hornpipe or Fasten the Leggin'?'
    'Well, Saft Tam . . .'
    'Have you ever met him?'
    'Let me think . . .'
    'You haven't and you never will. He's a figment of a frenzied fid-
dler's imagination.'

The fiddler then goes on to suggest a possible origin of a reel's title:

'. . . A fiddler takes the floor. Suddenly his bow trots away in a quite
unpremeditated run of melody.
    " 'That's a new one!" somebody shouts.
    'He plays it again assisted by the memories of his fellow-musicians.
There's no doubt about it; it's a new one.
    'Now, country fiddlers are as notorious for their modesty as they
are for their geniality. The innovator's eye ranges round the company.
He sees the farmhand grinning at him out of the lamp's shadows.
"B'God!" he shouts, "I'll call it –" '
    'Saft Tam's Hornpipe?'
    'Exactly.'

'Give us a Bar', the chapter on country ballads and their makers, also
pays tribute to the work of O'Boyle and his collaborators. It reflects
the knowledge gained from such series as *Music on the Hearth* (30 October 1953–14 September 1956), *Folk Song Forum* (5 May 1955–13 March
1956) and other programmes.

The tone of the book is one of elegant writing, decorous curiosity
and fastidious egalitarianism. The language is genial, conversational,
almost humdrum, bent on message and not medium, but the writer,
the prose poet, cannot hold himself in check for ever. His purpose is to
record the life of the province and he does this with economy, humour

and tact; there are many good stories very well told but he can no more resist the startlingly apt phrase or sudden insight than the fiddler can prevent his fingers from discovering a new hornpipe tune. In 'Roaming the Fields on Boxing Day' he describes a cold Christmas thus: 'On Christmas Eve a sudden and bitter frost had grasped the countryside, and the following morning its whitened knuckles shone on the roofs and trees and rocks.'

(Bell's first solo appearance on television was the telling of one of the stories from that chapter, 'after laborious memorising', on 2 December 1959.) The darkness round an illegal still in 'The Way to Catch the Mountain Dew', Bell writes, was not broken 'until the second farm-hand let the light from the torch leak through the luminous crevices of his fingers.' Yet these minor and forgivable self-indulgences are rare. It is the people whose lives are pictured here that are the argument of his book: 'the daling-men/From Crossmaglen' who drive hard bargains with the help of 'split-the-differs'; the careful old man who 'trimmles' the chairs in a death house as a funeral leaves for the churchyard (on a day when 'the July sun was as bold as brass') in case the spirit of the departed might have gone to roost; the unknown graffitist who invented Big Aggie's Man and caused so many walls not only 'down the Island' where he worked but all over Belfast to bear witness to his ghostly presence. There are some who would argue that in spite of the excellence of the novels, stories and plays, Bell's greatest contribution to the culture of his country was the presentation of Ulster in all its aspects to those listeners who for twenty-five years lived in a golden age of radio. If this be true, then *Erin's Orange Lily*, which is the material counterpart of those many etherialised broadcasts, may well be his most important book.

The customs recorded in the book are now all but gone. The hiring fairs so graphically described in 'Travelling to the Fair' had disappeared even before the Second World War which, as these things do, changed everything. And in 1956, the year of the book's publication, the old customs were facing an even greater threat. Television in Northern Ireland was hardly three years old. A great spurt had been made in 1953 to have a transmitter built so that the coronation of Elizabeth II might be seen in Belfast. The Independent Television Authority was set up in 1954 (among the Bell papers is an invitation to the opening of the Divis transmitter) and by 1963 its coverage was extended to the west of the region. The neighbours who used to gather in to 'crack by the hearth' increasingly turned to face the box in the corner.

The great malignancy of present-day sectarian politics makes the drumming matches described in the chapter 'To Chap the Lambeg' seem to belong to a lost golden age when, whatever their triumphalist origins, the rituals were benign rather than offensive. The mid-1950s were years of relative peace and harmony in Northern Ireland. It was usual for Catholics to be among the crowds that watched the Orange processions in July and the Apprentice Boys' marches in August. Stories about 'the other side of the house' were sharp but not vicious, and were distinguished by genuine humour and respect for the other tradition. The chapter is written in this spirit. If the author had been questioned about Orangeism and its yearly manifestation he might, as many did, have argued that the old atavism was dead.

11
RODGERS, CAMPBELL AND THOMPSON

I<small>N THE</small> 'ROUGH NOTES' that Sam Hanna Bell wrote in 1962, the most extended piece of autobiography that this reserved writer ever produced, he states:

> Above all I consider my job is being properly fulfilled when I am successful in encouraging Ulster men and women to write for their region. I have produced the work of almost every Ulster writer of note, and the earliest radio scripts of John D. Stewart, Roy McFadden, John O'Connor, Nesca Robb, Norman Harrison and Sam Thompson were feature programmes. It was at my suggestion and invitation that Joseph Tomelty wrote his highly popular family series *The McCooeys*. Particularly I look back with pleasure on the outstanding programmes which authors have written for me or on which I have collaborated. *Return to Northern Ireland* and *The Return Room* by W.R. Rodgers, *Carleton of Tyrone* [broadcast as *The Poor Scholar*] by Benedict Kiely, *Dove over the Water* (the story of Columcille) by J.J. Campbell, *Enter Robbie John* (the history of the ULT) by David Kennedy, *Prisoner of State* (the story of William III and his Queen) by Nesca Robb, *Neither Wheel nor Hand* (James Larkin and the Belfast of 1911) by David Bleakley, *Ribbon Round the Coast* by Norman Harrison, *[My] Bundle on My Shoulder* by Jack McQuoid, *He Lies in Armagh Jail* and other scripts by John Kevin and P.S. Laughlin, *Mill Row* (in which the young author John O'Connor dramatised his novel *Come*

Day, Go Day), *Brush in Hand* and subsequent scripts (several of which were later on basic Home Service) by Sam Thompson.

One of the most fascinating accounts of the conception, genesis and difficult birth of a features programme is given in 'The Pursuit of the Fancy Man', an article written for the *Honest Ulsterman* (Summer 1991) by the BBC Northern Ireland producer Douglas Carson. It is subtitled 'Sam Hanna Bell and W.R. Rodgers, 1952–1955'. Bell and Carson were friends, and Bell had acted as best man at Carson's wedding to Marie Keenan at Saul parish church on 15 April 1971. In an introductory paragraph to the piece, Carson states that *The Return Room* by W.R. Rodgers was 'the finest radio feature produced in Northern Ireland after the War'. There is no doubt about its excellence: it is an example of the way by which 'sound can do many fine things which will never be possible on television', a sentence from an article Louis MacNeice wrote that is quoted in Carson's article.

In a way, Bell, MacNeice and Rodgers, three men born in the first decade of radio's century, produced the magic between them. They were contemporaries, (MacNeice was two years older than the others who were born in consecutive months in 1909), and they each played a part in making the twenty years after the Second World War a kind of golden age in BBC Northern Ireland. Carson's account of the making of *The Return Room*, an account that is often funny and always dramatic, shows Rodgers and Bell as *yin* and *yang*: the poet wayward, easily diverted, at times feckless; the producer – a writer himself but vastly different in method and procedure – patient, pragmatic, meticulous, as full of artistic integrity as his colleague and concealing anxiety under a bluff of mild bullying.

Rodgers had already, in 1950, written the feature *Return to Northern Ireland*, which Bell had produced. It was broadcast on 27 October 1950 and repeated, as was the practice, two days later. The programme was so successful that it went out on Basic (the general network) and Northern Ireland the following January and was repeated again on 20 November 1953. It seemed to Bell that some evocation of Rodgers's childhood in a strict and very respectable Presbyterian family in the Mount, a tentatively bourgeois enclave in proletarian east Belfast, might make a superlative feature. As Carson reports it: 'Rodgers was immediately enthusiastic ... The "working title" was *Return to Me*.' In time it became

'The Fancy Man' 'because ... fact is fancy and fancy fact', then 'Return to Belfast', a title with the virtue of specificity if little else, before it found a safe identity in *The Return Room*:

> The 'return' room in our house was an upstairs room at the end of the passage, a *cul-de-sac* room, in fact; it was never used by the family, but kept for visitors; it had a kind of foreignness about it.

By the time the final title was agreed, the deadline of 1 November 1954 had been missed by six months. The recording date had been, in the words of Rodgers's coaxing request, 'dis-placed' twice, but the reputation of the proposed programme was growing. It had come to the notice of Bell's old boss Andrew Stewart, now Controller of the national Home Service, and earmarked for Basic. The only copy of the working script had been tragically lost and magically restored to the BBC by a bus conductor. After much toil and trouble the final script arrived in the last week of August 1955. Bell liked 'every inch and line of it' and in response to Rodgers's request that he narrate it replied: 'It never occurred to me that anyone but you should narrate *The Return Room* – it would be no show without Punch!' Bell devised a description of the programme for the *Radio Times* which was as brilliant as the thing itself: 'A back-window on Belfast after forty years. This word's-eye view of Belfast is partly autobiographical, largely imaginary and wholly true.'

In spite of many warnings about the need to make travel arrangements in advance for December, a characteristically frantic telegram was sent: 'May I fly across 19th? Steamer berths unavailable.' What could the BBC do but say yes? Casting, arrangements for recording sound effects and the children's choirs went ahead, Bell staying at his desk all day on Sunday 18 December. The show was rehearsed for four days and then, apart from short inset recordings, it went out live on 23 December – and it was worth all the letters, threats and angst-filled hours that had characterised its course.

In a file of Rodgers's correspondence which the meticulous Bell kept, there is a memoir of the poet by him in radio talk format. It recalled their meeting as children 'when my family came on its annual pilgrimage from Scotland'. It also recalled MacNeice's 1945 invitation to 'a number of Ulster writers to submit radio scripts' of which, Bell wrote, by far the best was Rodgers's *A City Set on a Hill*, the story of Armagh through the centuries in which Cyril Cusack played all the bishops from St Patrick to Primate Alexander (the husband of the writer of the hymn 'All Things Bright and Beautiful'). Bell concluded the tribute thus:

> I had the good fortune to produce his last two feature scripts: *Return to Northern Ireland* and *The Return Room*. He was his own narrator. At the microphone he used what his friend George MacCann used to call his 'Presbyterian voice'. It may have lacked the organ stops of the professional actor. And yet what other voice and view could have wedded together so perfectly the biblical cadences of his boyhood and the city of his nativity?
>
> Son of Adam; Sin of Adam
> I was the heir of all that Adamnation
> And hand-me-down of doom: the old newcomer
> To the return room.
> The apple blushed for me below Bellevue;
> Grey Lagan was my Jordan, Connswater
> My washpot, and over Castlereagh
> I cast out my shoe.

A version of *The Return Room*, called *Sunday*, was prepared for broadcast to schools by Bell and Carson in 1971.

Later correspondence indicates that Rodgers and Bell intended a similar collaboration on a feature on the Battle of the Boyne. Bell wrote initially on 4 April 1957 suggesting two programmes broadcast within a week or so of each other, one on the 1798 rising in the north of Ireland, and the other on the Battle of the Boyne:

> I see them treated in a dramatic form; the declamatory voice; the special music; the historic exchanges; the ballad, etc. Here and there in a pecking sort of way I have gathered together some material on the '98 Rising which I think, if I get down to it, could be shaped into an hour. Would you consider writing the Boyne? Where in time one would enter the campaign would be a matter for thought – possibly at William's march south – possibly on the green grassy slopes themselves.

Rodgers had been in touch with Bell in March (writing appropriately on St Patrick's Day) to ask him to reconsider his refusal to contribute to a long-promised book, edited by MacNeice and Rodgers, to be called *The Character of Ireland*. The idea had first been broached by

MacNeice five years before. He wrote on 3 December 1952 describing the nature of the project – 'twenty chapters all by different writers, covering the more essential aspects of Irish life and Irish history'.

> Bertie and I are very much hoping that you will undertake to cover 'The Six Counties' (which should include an assessment of the Partition question!) I know this is a tricky one but we both feel that you are the man to cover it.

Bell replied a week later refusing the offer in spite of a 'fee of not less than forty pounds' for 8,000 to 10,000 words:

> Apart from the fuss (which would be considerable) if I were to assess the partition question, I am at the moment manacled by a book which I am writing for Denis Dobson for their 'It's an Old Custom' series and which is already a year behind. I put aside a half-written novel to start this intolerable job, so as it is I really have got too much on my plate at the moment.

(The novel was *The Dazzler*, the early version of *The Hollow Ball*.)

Rodgers's letter five years later was very persuasive; with most of the contributions in, he wrote, the pieces on Northern Ireland lacked any sense of the essential likeability of the place: 'the profile which emerges seems to me rather sketchy if not severe'. What was wanted was a general article conveying the feeling of the place and people, and no one could do that better than Bell. The latter, perhaps prescient that the book might never come to pass and still too busy with his own work, again said no. Even Rodgers's advice that the politics had 'been dealt with' did not persuade him. He replied on 4 April that he would have to decline again because 'after overcoming the inertia of a fresh start' he had 'got his novel moving again'.

> When I came back to it [after working on *Erin's Orange Lily*] it looked so bad that I threw it away in disgust. But I had 40,000 words written. I gave it to Martin [McBirney] to read and he convinced me that I had to go on with it. Now it's moving much better than ever before, and I know if I stop again it'll be the end of that novel.
>
> If I could have written the piece quickly – yes. But I write very laboriously and I need hardly say that I wouldn't offer you the broth and bones of old bits.

Rodgers wrote again on 11 April arranging to meet Bell and

understanding why he preferred not to accept:

> Of course you are right in deciding not to be diverted from the work
> in hand, the work that matters to you, and I'm glad to hear it's going
> well again and has got its second wind. It's more important by far that
> you should write a good novel than write a good essay or what-have-
> you for the Clarendon Press.

The letter also mentioned a scratch that had turned septic and was slow
to respond to antibiotics.

Rodgers's next letter (written on 26 June 1957) reported that he had
consulted T.W. Moody, Professor of Modern History in Trinity
College Dublin, who had introduced him to an authority on the Battle
of the Boyne. He had got a photostat of a contemporary engraving of
the battle from the National Library, 'and a long and highly relevant
Orange song which I hadn't known before'. Rodgers also claimed to
be about to start reading up the subject 'in the BM' [British Museum].
The letter concluded: 'So, could you let me know if the programme has
been officially agreed to, and, if so, is there an early possibility of getting
a contract for it.'

Bell wrote on 9 July that the contract would be issued and that 1
February 1958 would be the delivery date. After that there is no record
of the fate of the feature on the Battle of the Boyne nor of any
programme by Bell on the 1798 Rising. Rodgers wrote a letter of
sympathy on 5 January 1959 about the death of Bell's mother. Rodgers
died in a public ward in Los Angeles on 1 February 1969, a man of great
sensitivity, wit and intermittent personal dysfunction.

J.J. Campbell was a year younger than Bell and remained a close
friend until his death in 1979. His youth had been scarred by the sectarian violence of the early 1920s when his family were driven out of their
north Belfast home. He had been educated at St Malachy's College
(where he served as classics master for nearly twenty years) and Queen's
University Belfast (QUB). In 1950 he became lecturer in education at St
Mary's Training College and later head of the education department at
St Joseph's College. He was appointed director of the Institute of
Education at QUB in 1969. Campbell was a noted broadcaster and a
member of the BBC Advisory Council; he served on many committees,
notably the Cameron Commission on the Northern Ireland Troubles in
1969. He was an ardent nationalist, and in his twenties he wrote a

number of damning articles on sectarian crimes, which were first published anonymously in the *Capuchin Annual*, and later in book form as *Orange Terror*, but he had no time for republican paramilitary violence. He was bookish with the *gravitas* of a classicist, dryly funny, and a gifted writer.

In all Campbell wrote six radio features between 1951 and 1963 of which two, *Dove over the Water* (24 March 1954) and *Wee Joe* (24 November 1959) are remarkable. The first is the story of Saint Colum Cille, who was born in Tír Conaill and spent the last thirty-four years of his life as abbot of the monastery of Iona, which he founded in 563. (The distinction between feature and drama was at times problematic: Roy McFadden's verse play *The Angry Hound*, about the legendary Cúchulainn, was remitted to the Drama Department for production in 1952.) The name Colum Cille means 'dove of the Church' and the saint's canonical title, Columba, is the Latin for 'dove'. The title of Campbell's feature was therefore doubly apt, but it generated a perhaps apocryphal story that one BBC official with a fine sense of grammar suggested that the title should be *Dived over the Water*. In the feature, the stories of the saint's life, his piety, the copying of Finian's psalter, the judgement of King Dermot 'to every cow its calf', the bloody battle of Cul Dreimne that followed in 561, the sojourn in Iona as a *peregrinator pro Christo* ('exile for Christ') and Columba's settling of the dynastic affairs of the kingdom of Dál Riata and regularising of the position of the Irish poets at the convention of Druim Cett (near Limavady) in 575 are all dealt with in a language that, if not actually poetic, has an appropriate lyrical grandeur. The main part was taken by the Scots actor Tom Fleming (who afterwards played the saint once again in the television production of Brian Friel's *The Enemy Within*). Special music was composed by Havelock Nelson, who conducted the Northern Ireland Light Orchestra, and versions of the psalms were sung by the choir of St Mary's College.

Wee Joe was a portrait of Belfast's favourite politician, Joe Devlin, (1871–1934) who, though strongly nationalist and the head of the Ancient Order of Hibernians, cared for all the poor of west Belfast irrespective of creed. As one of the contributors put it:

> If one was in need from him – he was, so to speak, colour-blind. If one wanted his help – orange was green to him. If one did happen to be

Orange, as many of his suitors were, he did his best for you as he would have done if you happened to be green.

Wee Joe was a true feature with a narrator and a montage of recorded voices of people who had known and worked with Devlin. It was a fitting tribute to the tiny man who defeated de Valera in the election of 1918, worked tirelessly to improve working conditions in west Belfast, and impoverished himself in providing excursions for children and a holiday home in Bangor for the women of his beloved Falls Road. He was a true democrat and, in spite of endemic rancour in the city at the time of his death, many unionists walked in his funeral procession. He was part of the mythology of Campbell's childhood and it was entirely fitting that Campbell should paint the politician's radio portrait. As the narrator put it at the beginning of the programme:

> This is a programme, not a photograph: an image of a man based on the personal recollections of his contemporaries; a man dedicated to the service of working men and women as well as to the constitutional struggle for Home Rule; a politician whose influence in government circles became a legend.

Campbell remained a friend and correspondent of Bell. One letter from him (25 September 1959) contains a detailed account of the Clonard confraternity and the various exercises of the members. It was sent on request with a view to the writing of a feature about a remarkable part of the religious (and social) life of Catholic Belfast. As noted in Chapter 2, Campbell succeeded in wresting an autobiographical sketch from the reluctant Bell. Moreover, as Chairman of Convocation and a member of the Senate of QUB, Campbell undoubtedly played a part in the award of an MA (*honoris causa*) to Bell in 1970.

One of the notable qualities that Bell brought to his art whether as writer or producer was his experience of labour in both country and town. As he demonstrated in *Erin's Orange Lily*, the shipyard, foundries and mills of Belfast were as full of myths and folkways as the Sperrins and the Antrim Glens. In fact the much greater variety of town jobs made the urban radio features fascinating. In an article called 'The Microphone in the Countryside' published in the silver jubilee volume *The BBC in Northern Ireland – 1924–1949* (1949), Bell wrote that 'the voices of men and women describing their daily work, their recreations, their hopes and troubles, are the life and breath of regional broadcasting'. He continued to believe that the producers of the 1950s had been given a great opportunity to record working-class experience, as he told Rex Cathcart in conversation during the research for *The Most Contrary Region*:

> Up to this time [his postwar feature programmes] the working-class voice had never been heard in Broadcasting House, Belfast. Matt Mulcaghey and Mrs Rooney may have been supposed to reflect it in the 1930s but really that was a travesty. We now had a marvellous opportunity to go out into Queen's Island, to go down into the streets and have people talking about maybe innocuous things but the point is they were real people talking.

This change was reflected in the dramatic writings of Sam Thompson. He had been born on 21 May 1916 in east Belfast not all that far from John Boyd and had been apprenticed as a painter 'down the Island'. He was an active trades unionist – he once lost a job with Belfast Corporation because he had become a shop steward – and it was not inappropriate, since he had so actively campaigned against sectarianism, that his terminal collapse before his forty-ninth birthday on 15 February 1965 should have occurred in the offices of the Northern Ireland Labour Party.

One of the files among the Bell papers contains correspondence about a memorial fund that he helped set up to aid Thompson's widow, May, and eleven-year-old son Warren. The committee had Martin McBirney as chairman, and as well as Bell the members included Rowel Friers, J.G. Devlin and Basil Kelly, QC, MP. The subscriptions sent were usually accompanied by letters expressing appreciation of the man and shock at his sudden death. Among those who dealt directly with Bell were colleagues David Hammond, Ronald Mason and Maurice Leitch and friends such as Brian Friel. One letter from Denis Tuohy, the television presenter, advised Bell that Barbara Mullen (Janet of the earlier *Dr Finlay's Casebook* television series) was anxious to know about the arrangements.

Among those whom Bell rang on the day of Thompson's death was James Young, who with his partner Jack Hudson had taken over the running of the Ulster Group Theatre. Young declined to serve on the committee, saying in his letter, 'in view of our late friend's very stormy association with the Theatre . . . my presence on such a committee

might not only prove embarrassing for all concerned, but would revive unhappy memories'. The reference was, of course, to the controversy stirred up by Thompson's play about sectarianism in the shipyard, *Over the Bridge* (1957). The play had been accepted by the Group Theatre but the board, finding it too controversial, demanded substantial changes in the script. When the author refused to agree to them, the play was withdrawn and James Ellis, then the artistic director, resigned, as did Harold Goldblatt who had been one of the Group Theatre's founders in 1940. In January 1960 Ellis staged the play in the Empire Theatre where it was an outstanding success (it transferred to the Prince's Theatre in Shaftesbury Avenue the following May). Bell's copy of the programme for the Belfast opening night (26 January 1960) bears the autographs of his friends Louis MacNeice and Martin McBirney and a dedication from the author: 'To Sam Hanna Bell, the man who inspired me to write.'

Bell had met Thompson in the Elbow Room in the mid-1950s and, impressed by the awkward fluency of his conversation, urged him to write for radio and theatre. The first feature Thompson wrote for Bell was *Brush in Hand* which was transmitted on 17 February 1956 (it had three repeats and new productions in 1962 and 1965). It told the story of a shipyard painter who recalled the craftsmanship of his apprentice days:

> That's right! Sparingly. Brush it well, up and down, up and down. Man, you're shaping rightly. Now cross brush it. That's right. Another dip now. Och you're too heavy this time. Rub your brush out tight to the side of the pot. Now, once more up and down, lightly this time, as little weight as possible on the brush. That's it! That's what you want – fine brush work.

This 'fine brush work' was contrasted with the new techniques that seemed to the painter to constitute shoddy work: 'The last time we were down here the cabins were getting seven or eight coats. Now they're lucky if they get four ... And we have the spray gun.'

Bell had already written and produced a feature about the shipyard – *The Islandmen* (28 January 1953) – but here was the authentic voice of a true Islandman. Thompson was able to follow that first feature with *Tommy Baxter: Shop Steward* (29 January 1957) and *The General Foreman* (15 May 1958). A script exists of a feature *We Build a Ship* which seems to have been commissioned early in 1958 but had not been received by October 1959. I can find no record of it having been broadcast. The

opening narration gives some idea of Thompson's growing skill and confidence as a writer:

> It is the end of another day's toil in the Belfast shipyards, and all roads out of the harbour estate are thronged with buses crammed with men. Thousands of bell-ringing bicycles weave crazy patterns to avoid motor cars who honk impatiently at the slow dungareed pedestrians who block their way. A crazy disordered spectacle, all leading out of the shipyards. But what do they leave behind them these men who are shipbuilders?

The picture is very much that of the late fifties, with MacNeice's clanging trams a distant memory.

Thompson went on to write two other stage plays. *The Evangelist*, which was produced for the Gate by Hilton Edwards and starred Ray McAnally as Pastor Earls, was one of the hits of 1963 and was presented by the company in the Opera House in June. McAnally's performance as the charismatic Madison Avenue preacher was one of the finest of his career. *Cemented with Love*, about the chicanery of the old-style Unionist Party at election times, was shown on television in May 1965, three month's after the author's death. Bell's radio version of *The Evangelist* (produced by Ronald Mason and with McAnally in his old part) was transmitted on 29 November that year.

Bell produced a radio tribute on 30 May 1972 called *A Profile of Sam Thompson*, using archival material which included James Ellis's account of the eventual staging of *Over the Bridge*. Bell appeared in a television documentary called *Sam Thompson – Voice of Many Men* made in Dublin by Donald Taylor Black in 1986 with Stephen Rea as Thompson. As Bell records in his diary, he felt Thompson had faults as a writer and at times a stormy personality that alienated his friends. One one occasion – in the sedate Chalet d'Or – Thompson threw a bottle at Bell. On another, Bell threw Thompson down the stairs in a club: a wit, in retrospect, described this as *A Bridge Too Far*. Yet there was no doubt about Thompson's artistic passion, his commitment to non-sectarian principles, and his personal experience of working life. Bell played down in conversation any help he may have given the raw talent he discovered. Thompson died too young to realise his potential; a second Sean O'Casey with a Ballymacarret accent did not after all materialise.

12
THE HOLLOW BALL

*T*HE HOLLOW BALL, which was published in 1961 by Cassell, is a literary sport in that it has an urban location and, set only a presumed twenty-five years before the time of its publication, is less of an 'historical' novel than Sam Hanna Bell's other fiction. *December Bride* (1951), *A Man Flourishing* (1973) and *Across the Narrow Sea* (1987) can be regarded as an fictional trilogy covering different epochs in the history of east Ulster. *The Hollow Ball* in a sense bears the scars of recent experience, both Belfast's and Bell's own. The constantly repeated figure of 'thirty-thousand unemployed in the city alone' becomes a kind of mantra, and the state of worklessness is spoken of with raw acquaintance: ('From the unanswered applications, the morose homecomings, she began to apprehend something of the invisible barrier that rose between the employed and the workless.')

Belfast had suffered as much in the depression as other manufacturing cities through the industrial world. As Emmet O'Connor notes in his *A Labour History of Ireland, 1824–1960* (Dublin, 1992): 'The over-capacity and over-supply created during the war continued to affect shipbuilding and agriculture, while changes of clothing and lifestyle were consigning linen to the status of a luxury good.' In 1931 there were 50,000 idle in Belfast, of which 14,000 were eligible for outdoor relief. This dole was available for married men only and administered by miserly boards of guardians who had introduced a hated means test. One result was, as noted in Chapter 2, a hunger march on 11 October 1932 combining 20,000 Catholic and Protestant workers in an unprecedented display of unity. During the disturbances two men were killed by the RUC.

By the time of the not precisely specified action of *The Hollow Ball* (presumably later in the same decade), conditions were somewhat better. Unemployment was still very high but actual hunger was less of a threat than it had been. Nevertheless, the threat of unemployment, when its results were so evident, was still a potent means of ensuring that those lucky enough to be in the workforce were underpaid and quiescent. Boney McFall, the socialist-minded friend of the novel's chief character, David Minnis, tries to interest David in the social conditions of the city from which he is about to escape because of his football skills:

> Bonar indicated the crowded pub . . . 'What are those to you?'
>
> 'Just – ordinary fellas.'
>
> 'To me they're *extra*ordinary fellas. The pile-drivers of the richest civilisation in the world and this is all it has to offer them at the end of the day–'
>
> 'They don't *have* to come here.'
>
> 'Where else would they go? The pictures? The dogs? To see you playing football?'
>
> 'That's the sort of thing they want.'
>
> 'Aye. Oddly enough that's what they get. Even when they're outa work it's fixed so that they still get the pictures, the dogs, the drink –'

(The voice is clearly that of the youngish socialist who sold *Labour Progress* at street corners at the end of the 1930s.)

The asectarian comradeship of the very early thirties yielded to unofficial manipulation of religious differences as the decade advanced. But in *The Hollow Ball* there is no overt sectarian bitterness, partly because the novel is set in the lower Ormeau Road area, a part of the city that then had few if any Catholic residents. To the minds of the protagonists 'papishes' are at best a conundrum and at worst a potential rather than an actual economic threat. The practice of the mainly Protestant employers and the majority of local authorities where a unionist ascendancy was maintained (by fair means if possible) was to employ 'our own'. (The same was true of the far fewer examples where the boot was on the other foot: Catholic firms and the councils of Strabane, Downpatrick and Newry employed Catholics by choice.)

The brief violence of the early 1920s was still a vivid memory. The thirties saw ugly incidents in 1932, 1933 and 1934, most of them associated with the Orange Order. In 1935 the Silver Jubilee of George V was marked by anti-Catholic pogroms and vicious rioting during which eight Protestants and five Catholics died and many were injured, most of them Catholics. Yet the city of *The Hollow Ball* is relatively quiet – the resilience of all Northern Ireland people amazes when it does not chill outside observers – and the economic situation is not as dire as even five years earlier. The austere sense of justice of David Minnis's widowed mother is established by her action in sheltering the children of Mrs Cassidy, a Catholic woman whose family 'had to leave their home hurriedly and fly to a sister's house in the Falls Road' during 'the Troubles'. It was Mrs Cassidy who had arranged for Mrs Minnis, on her husband's death, to do sewing piecework for the local garment factory and when the widow was congratulated by her neighbours for her subsequent kindness to the Cassidys (and courage, though this was not stated), 'her answer, calm and quietly spoken, was always the same, "The woman was kind to me once." '

The index of the relative political awareness of David and Boney is neatly established by their memories of violence:

> In Cromac Street, Bonar paused and looked round as if in search of something. 'Did you see any of the Troubles?' he asked.
> 'Only a papish fruitshop burned out in the Dublin Road when I was a kid.'
> 'I saw a man shot dead – there.' Bonar pointed to the street corner opposite.

(Bell had seen a man shot dead in York Street in the 1920s.) The violence that is to claim Boney's life is nicely foreshadowed by his awareness of the nature of their society and his preoccupation with the bullet that 'the peelers' had dug out of a windowsill at the scene.

There were, of course, Catholics employed in Hamilton's wool warehouse where David 'got his start', their numbers neatly calculated to match the perceived number of customers of the same persuasion:

> ... the new apprentice who had replaced Conniff was not there because he was eager to devote his life to the woollen trade, but because he was a Catholic – a tactical necessity from the management's point of view – and knew it. Already he was behaving to everybody with the wary hostility of his predecessor.

115

The only other reference to 'the situation' is the account of an attack during a match with the Bogsend team. David's 'Siamese twin', Mulhern, is attacked by a section of the crowd as a 'fenian bastard', although 'everybody knows you're a Prod. . . . It was your name that foxed them. They're a simple-minded lota buggers round Bogsend.'

David Minnis is a flawed protagonist, solipsistic and not especially courageous – and the more interesting as a character on that account. The hero in the classical sense is Bonar Law McFall. Boney's father, as earlier established, is a working-class autodidact, 'a boss night-watchman – when he's working' who has 'devoured three libraries, covers and all'. The father's fatal flaw is that the bureaucratic and unofficial social work that he does for his fellow workers is rewarded by drink, earning him the name Cowld Pint. It is Boney who, eventually sacked from Hamilton's for union agitation, becomes the activist his father wants to be. And the logical development is membership of the then radical IRA and death for an imprecise cause. The effect on the family is shocking and summed up by David's young brother Freddie: 'We've got to go on living here, y'know!' David is on a trip home as an international footballer and is anxious to talk to Boney's father but will not risk meeting Boney's sister Maureen (whom he jilted) or his mother (who 'goes about her work. She never complains'). Mr McFall's grief results in a betrayal of all he held dear throughout his life:

'And yourself, Mr McFall? You'll have to keep yourself busy. What about your work, the Almanac?'
He felt a shiver go through the man opposite. 'That cursed thing? It's scattered, burnt destroyed! If it hadn't been for that kinda fooling my son would be alive today!'

It is a meeting of two oddly similar people, the one now conscious of his own lack of logic and of his cowardice ('I talked to him about destroying things that I wouldn't have dared to lift a finger against!'), the other self-centred, ambitious, opportunistic and in a way as hollow as the ball that is the symbol of his freedom.

The book, however, is not all gloom and rancour; Bell manages to re-create the urban pleasures that Belfast offered, however provincial:

They were strolling homeward in silence under the beech trees in University Road, where, for a few hundred yards, their vast market town took on the grace and elegance of a city.

116

There are dances, picnics, occasional excursions in friends' cars. There is also romance for a time, as David courts Maureen. The period is well realised both in its details (trams, the universal wearing of caps or hats both by men and women) and its morality (girlfriends' preservation of their virginity). Here and there, however, a postwar slang phrase such as 'not on your nelly' is true not to its period but to its time of writing.

Above all else in David's case there is football, played by amateurs, semi-professionals and the Olympian full-timers, who are paid fees and given perquisites that are risible by today's standards. (Bell was himself a keen athlete, and his papers indicate the playing of rugby and soccer, and word of a trial for Ulster. A postcard dated 9 November 1931 advises him that he has been selected by the committee of Cooke Rugby Football Club to represent the first xv against Ards on the fourteenth: 'Bus leaves Oxford Street at 1.40 sharp.') The descriptions in the novel of tactics and play have a jargon-free detail and excitement that impress. Some 25 of its 248 pages are given over to actual descriptions of games which even those with no love of spectator sports must find interesting. Some deserve places in any anthology of fictional sports. Of equal or greater interest are the details of scouting, signing, and boardroom politics.

When David leaves Belfast to play for a West Midlands top-of-the-Second-Division-soon-to-be-promoted team the book loses some of its urgency. His sloughing-off of Maureen, though not explained, has an air of authenticity: David, for all his attempts at introspection, is neither a deep thinker nor an effective examiner of his own psyche. The author discussed the matter in correspondence with his editor at Cassell:

> Leaving aside the reasons for it, there seems to me to be X – an unknown quantity – in the love between a man and a woman. (This is neither an original nor a profound conclusion on my part!) Both may well bring a good appearance, sincerity, fidelity, wit, passion and compassion, and yet without this quite unpremeditated gift or ability to fuse their personalities, it's no go. This is what happened to D. A well-meaning well-wisher could have told him that Maureen had everything that is desirable in a girl. He would have agreed. Yet, he can't quite make it. That is why he breaks off their correspondence. So defeated, and indeed frightened, by this inexplicable inability on

his part, he takes refuge in emotional sickness – a revulsion against everything in her that should spell joy and pride.

The details of his life in England and doing holiday work in Scotland are almost perfunctory. The characters in his lodgings are well-observed but seem to belong to a different novel. The gradually developing interest in his fellow lodger Gibby (Miss Gibbon the librarian), leads to expectations that are not fulfilled in the course of the book, though the description of 'the soft fall of her hair, illumined by the flamelight' suggests some future connection.

The central flaw in an otherwise naturalistic novel is David's ability on the football field. In a sense to endow a character with what amounts to a magical gift detracts from the realism of the rest of the book. Though it is central to the novel's theme, the effect of this one talent is to marginalise the character, or perhaps to make the novel a diptych, one portion a marvellous social novel, a rare account of the life of Belfast at a significant time, the other a singular tale of a particular individual with an unusual talent. Without the support of Belfast, the character David Minnis shrinks into the role of chorus, a mere commentator and perhaps this explains the sense of deflation once he leaves his home.

For all this, *The Hollow Ball* is a remarkable achievement, in its way the one of Bell's four novels that set him the greatest difficulty and that reflects most obviously the facts of his own life without the psychological safety net of historical distancing. Mrs Minnis is a character drawn from some characteristics of Bell's own mother who eked out her widow's pension with long hours of sewing and the sufferance of lodgers. More fundamentally, the character of David, an ordinary man who becomes a success but is diminished by it, reflects the tensions and divisions Bell was conscious of in his own life: between the active radical socialist of his youth and the bourgeois comfort of the BBC and marriage into the middle class.

The book contains many interesting characters: the lodger Mr Rankin, who is instrumental in getting David placed in Hamilton's and acts as a kind of surrogate father to him, lending him books and implicitly indicating the nature of gentility; Mr McFall; and the almost silent Jew, Mr Shriberger, who buys garments from the store and who is eventually revealed as an anarchist refugee from the Balkans. *December*

Bride was a brilliant picture of rural County Down at the turn of the century; *The Hollow Ball* presents the city of Belfast more than three decades later and, in the sense of overcoming difficulties, it is the greater technical achievement.

Among the reviews of *The Hollow Ball* was a short note in a Dublin monthly review called *Focus* (February 1962) by Martha Gray-Stack which commends 'the general picture of the social situation of Belfast in the thirties' but is wrongheaded about Boney's membership of the IRA: 'his downfall was doubtless caused by his affection for a papist girl'. The concluding paragraph is a neat summary of a particular contemporary Southern view of 'those people up there':

> Is this whole book designed as a parable to illustrate that in Northern Ireland there is no room for constructive and intelligent opposition and that the really wise people concentrate on the hollow ball?

Other reviews were more in sympathy with the theme and atmosphere of the novel but none were raves. Ten silent years is a long time in a novelist's life. Bell's name was still known, but as that of a radio stalwart, and *Erin's Orange Lily* had only briefly broken the literary silence. Those with an interest in local writing were interested though. The most favourable review was that of Brian Friel on 23 September 1961 in the *Irish Times*: the author is described as 'a mature man who knows his job, a careful worker who has his main characters drawn and his readers involved after five minutes'. It commends the

> . . . vivid and accurate portrayal of working-class Protestant people.
> . . . This is not the Ulster of the slogan-writers and Pope-cursers; nor is it the wholesome Ambridge-like Ulster that the BBC (NI) would have us believe; but Ulster – or, at least, six counties of it – as it is.

Friel added, 'Happily we are given a minimum of description of football matches.' The *Sunday Independent*'s unsigned note printed the previous Sunday found it surprising that a man who had been features producer for fifteen years and was almost as well known 'south of the border . . . should have let loose on the public what reads like an unfinished and sketchy piece of literature'. Further, the reviewer notes 'the uncertainties of the author in handling his characters' and 'an indeterminate background through which Belfast is but mistily recognisable'.

The Belfast papers were more polite; the unsigned review in the *Belfast News-Letter* found it not to be 'the success one would have expected from a writer with his feeling for Ulster and Ulster people'. The atmosphere was not as powerful as in his 'moving' *December Bride*. 'The scenes in the drapery establishment are much more convincing than those on the football field, where too often the author relies on the language of the sports journalist.' Martin Wallace, who reviewed the novel in the *Belfast Telegraph* on 7 September and a month later on John Boyd's regular radio feature *The Arts in Ulster*, was on the whole favourably impressed. He did not find David Minnis a sympathetic character but judged the novel entertaining and observant. All agreed about the graphic account of the hungry thirties in Belfast though the *Belfast News-Letter* reviewer compared it unfavourably with Michael McLaverty's *Lost Fields* (1941).

A few points may be made: David Minnis is not, in Wallace's broadcast words 'a more unlikeable, unsympathetic hero than Sam Hanna Bell intended'; he is all the more interesting because of his flaws and apparently fully realised according to the author's intention. The Belfast of the novel's period, though necessarily imprecise, is portrayed by a man who was in the fray. McLaverty's account is that of the child's experience of lost content, remembered and reconstituted from the author's own youth.

The reader's ambivalence towards David is nicely sketched by John Hewitt in a letter to Bell written from Coventry on 10 November 1961. Hewitt is full of praise for the novel, and as a Belfastman who was translated to the English Midlands himself says he 'can't find you wrong in any detail'.

> But what I find really memorable about the book is that you have achieved that very difficult thing, of making me believe in Minnis and feel that I know him, understand his attitudes, sympathise with many of them, yet at the same time feel critical of his actions and annoyed by his selfishness. This is a kind of Brechtian thing, the V-effekt: like Mother Courage, that old rip, we admire her and deplore her simultaneously; and we see her as we do Minnis, firmly enmeshed in society.

13
THE DIARIST

S AM HANNA BELL KEPT A DIARY INTERMITTENTLY, indeed with large lacunae, from 1956 until the week before his death in 1990. The first sections were written in an 8-inch by 5-inch commercial post book with a black 'all-weather cover' whose front endpapers are decorated by two excellent caricatures, one full-face and in ballpoint signed 'Rowel Friers 1965', the other a profile done in pen and black ink with no attribution but probably by Douglas Carson. Also on the inside cover, written in pencil is the National Insurance number HM/28/ 33/71/C which may be Mildred's since her date of birth, 20 April 1911, and the date of their marriage, 31 October 1946 at Donaghmore Parish Church, Newry, are written below it. At the bottom is a quotation from the Authorised Version of the Bible: 'Better is a handful with quietness, than both the hands full with travail and vexation of spirit' (Eccles. 4: 6). Almost the last entry (the book was only half used) is the wording of the plaque for Mildred's ashes, though the last page has a quotation from A.E. Housman which was one of Bell's own rules: 'Accuracy is a duty, not a virtue.'

The black-covered journal was begun on 24 November 1956 and ended formally on 24 August 1977. It is a record of plays seen, books read, occasional social events and dismayed references to drinking. The list of books read during 1957 includes works by his favourites Dostoevsky (*The Idiot*) and Turgenev (*Virgin Soil* – reread). He enjoyed

Henry James's *The Princess Casamassima* (part one in May, and the rest in July) and studied an essay on the work by Lionel Trilling. He had not much time for *The Quiet American* (1955) by Graham Greene:

> June 9th [1957]: Glad to get back to Princess C. (Vol. 2). Finished Greene's Quiet American. Fed up with his sinful helpless floundering good-natured Aunt & Uncle Sallys put up to be knocked down by R.C. understanding.

There were also books about books: *The Russian Novel in English Fiction*; *Introduction to English Novels* (volumes I and II), *Thomas Hardy's Notebooks*, Bertrand Russell's *Portraits and Essays*, *Leo Tolstoy* by E.J. Simmons.

The 1958–59 list includes such new books as *The Feast of Lupercal*, Brian Moore's bitter story of a teacher in Ardath College, Belfast, a thinly disguised St Malachy's, scene of the author's not very happy schooldays; and two by friends, *The Choice* by Michael McLaverty (about Tom Magee's need to decide whether on the death of his wife to stay with his grown-up family or return, as he had always wished to do, to his birthplace), and *One Small Boy* by Bill Naughton (1910–92). There were also such catchings-up and rereadings as *Room at the Top* (1957) by John Braine, *The Catcher in The Rye* (1951) by J.D. Salinger, *Prisoner of Grace* (1952) by Joyce Cary, *As a Man Grows Older* (1898) by James Joyce's friend Italo Svevo (the English title being Joyce's version of the original Triestean *Senilità*), and Somerset Maugham's pleasantest novel *Cakes and Ale* (1930). Stendhal's *Scarlet and Black* was reread, as was Jane Austen's *Emma*. An interesting voice from the past was *Saturday Night at the Greyhound* by John Hampson, whose later work was too explicitly homosexual to be published, even by the Hogarth Press.

It was characteristic of the list maker (and the relentless autodidact) that he should compile a kind of progress report on his reading. The yearly roster of books read was abandoned, but notes about current reading are to be found scattered through the diary entries:

> August 16th, 1959: Finished *The Irish Writers (Literature under Parnell's Star)* by Herbert Howarth. Most enjoyable although author is hard put at times to yoke his writers (Gregory, Yeats, Moore, Æ, Synge, Joyce) to Parnell. Revealing the disgust of Yeats and Æ at the Ireland that app. after 1916. A quotation from Yeats (originally applicable to Lady G.) might well be applied to the Ulster businessman: 'They

despise the Bohemian above all men till he turns gypsy, tinker, convict or the like, and so finds historical sanction, attains as it were to some inherited code or recognised relation to such code' . . . January 10th [1960]: Read Lawrence's 'The Man Who Died'. [This was a long short story about Christ originally entitled 'The Escaped Cock' (1929).] Lush, snobbish, lush, lush lush. They did it much better in the New Testament, I think.

Balzac's *The Peasants* (20 May 1960) calls forth the comment 'In praising this novel for its "honesty" the Marxist critic George Lukacs rather understates Balzac's detestation of the bourgeois *and* the peasants.'

During the summer holidays of 1960, Bell read *Culture and Society 1780–1950* (1958) by the Marxist novelist and critic Raymond Williams and Saul Bellow's *Henderson and the Rain King* (1959), while in the autumn he finished 'J.M. Thompson's *French Revolution* – a most illuminating piece of research and graphic story-telling. I had known little or nothing about the period, apart from an adolescent skimming through Carlyle's book' (14 September) and Draper's *American Communism and the Soviet Union.* 'Not a pleasant story as Draper tells it' (22 September). He read *Barnaby Rudge* (8 January 1961) without comment; one would have liked his opinion on riots – and anti-Catholic riots – and his estimate of Dickens's portrayal of the crazed Lord George Gordon (1751–93). Twelve years later (28 January 1973) he is appreciative of Martin Chuzzlewit and quotes Old Martin's confession of paranoia with implicit approval:

> There is a kind of selfishness – I have learned it in my own experience
> of my own breast – which is constantly upon the watch for selfishness
> in others, and holding others at a distance by suspicions and distrusts,
> wonders why they don't approach, and don't confide, and calls that
> selfishness in them. Thus I once doubted those about me.

As the years pass, fewer books are mentioned though he continued to read voluminously (a pun he would have appreciated), carefully preserving his paid invoices from William Mullan & Son, Booksellers, for tax purposes. (One dated 1 January 1973 was for poems by 'Heaney [presumably *Wintering Out*] and Donne'.) A book bought on 14 June 1977 – *And the Cock Crew* (1945) by the Scots writer Fionn Mac Colla – continued to interest him to the extent that he offered it to friends who had not read it. He had heard of it first on an edition of *The Critics*, the Home

Service radio programme that was soon to be transferred to the Third. *And the Cock Crew* is set in the time of the Highland Clearances in the first decades of the nineteenth century and depicts the betrayal of his flock by the Calvinist minister Maister Zachary because of what 'the life-denying beliefs of Presbyterianism' impose upon him. The title is, of course, from Mark 15: 68. The entry concludes with the interesting admonition: 'Will repay careful reading against *The Planters*.' [This was the working title of what was to become *Across the Narrow Sea*.] The use of the Lallans preposition 'against' to mean 'in preparation for' is typical.

As well as being a journal, the diary also served as a commonplace book, with observations about life and literature culled from many sources, including his own experience. Bell also marked the deaths of friends with meditative obituaries. The humorist Lynn Doyle died in August 1961. He had been one of the dramatists of the Ulster Literary Theatre, and had been the subject of one of the most popular programmes produced by Bell, *Enter Robbie John*, written by David Kennedy in 1954. Doyle had been born Leslie A. Montgomery on 5 October 1873 in Downpatrick, part of which was the Ballygullion of his extremely funny stories. He joined the Northern Bank in 1889 in Belfast and served there until 1906 when he was transferred to Skerries as manager. His comedy *Love and Land* was presented in the Grand Opera House, Belfast, in 1913 but because of the perceived dignity of the 'banking service' of the period he found it judicious to find a *nom de théâtre*. Seeing a bottle of linseed oil for sale in a shop window he called himself with characteristic geniality Lynn C. Doyle. The *C* was dropped for *The Lilac Ribbon* (1919) and *The Turncoats* (1922). (For some unrecorded reason he called himself Leslie Lynd for his 1918 play *The Summons*.)

Bell was naturally interested in the passing of an Ulster humorist who was as popular and as talented as George A. Birmingham and nearly as good as the much less genial Somerville and Ross. He recorded his death in the entry for Monday, 14 August:

> Lynn Doyle died this past weekend (Sunday I think). I remember our meetings very clearly. He was a good companion at a convivial gathering – Arts Club or elsewhere. He always drank sherry. On one occasion he told me as we left Lavery's that he dearly wished his 'serious'

novels to be given the credit he felt they deserved. When I said I felt any writer would be very pleased to have created Ballygullion or Dear Ducks, he smiled but I doubt if I really convinced him. I am not so sure that I was being only polite. Fiddling Farmer and his other writings are not very important but his comic characters may indeed still be read years hence. As Denis Ireland called him in B. T. [the *Belfast Telegraph*] article he was indeed 'The Man Who Was Ulster'. I shall always remember him with pleasure – even his intense dislike of W.R. Rodgers' image of the rooks 'tumbling about the sky like tealeaves'.

Lynn Doyle was an obvious subject for a memorial feature and *Mr Doyle of Ballygullion* was broadcast on 19 June 1962. Among those taking part was Sam Waddell, who as Rutherford Mayne had been the premier playwright of the Ulster Literary Theatre, and author of *The Drone* and *The Turn of the Road*. He was to figure largely in Bell's survey of Ulster drama. From letters and cards written by Waddell in February and March 1962 from his home in Foxrock, County Dublin, it is clear that he and Bell discussed the first stagings of 'my old play' and that Bell had asked for any responses at the time. Waddell was able to send him copies of excerpts from contemporary reviews including a letter from John Galsworthy urging the young playwright: 'Go on – you will do fine work.' (This information, including the full text of Galsworthy's letter, was later incorporated in Bell's 1972 book *The Theatre in Ulster*.)

The entry for 3 September 1963 begins: 'Many months since I've written in this diary. Today Louis MacNeice died in St Leonard's Hospital, Shoreditch, age 55.' Bell follows this with sections of an obituary he had written for the *Irish Times*, notably the sentences: 'Louis MacNeice was a cat who walked by himself. . . . He was not (like Auden, Spender, and C. Day Lewis) deeply committed politically or philosophically but was from the start a broadly liberal humanist.' He continues:

This evening in the six o'clock news I gave a tribute (Sound and TV): 'I would rather speak of L.McN. the man than of L.McN. the poet. He was a friend and colleague for almost twenty years. Shortly after the war, the BBC sent him here to NI to look for new writers for broadcasting. It was a happy choice, for McN. always acted as a leaven among his fellow writers, encouraging them, guiding them, opening doors when inspiration seemed to have flagged. It was also a happy choice in another way for he always enjoyed returning to his native province. We knew him, of course, with Spender, Auden & C. Day Lewis, as one of the foremost poets of his generation. But in conversation he was disinclined to talk of literary matters and never about his own work. What we talked about were rugby, the Ulster countryside, Ulster politics, Ulster painters and writers, but above all rugby. Louis would have gone almost anywhere to follow the Irish rugby fifteen – most certainly he went to Paris, Edinburgh, Cardiff and Lansdowne Road. The appearance or disapp of an Irish back at the beginning of the season was to him a matter of supreme importance. If radio writing can claim to be a form of art, L.McN. was one of its masters. Here I shall mention only his radio play *The Dark Tower*, which in its wedding of sound and voice has influenced almost every writer since. I had the privilege of being present at the first rehearsals of this production. I remember how he would stop to explain how he got an effect, a transition, a run of voice and music. But that was MacN., a man of brimming talent – he believed in sharing his skill, and did so, with endless patience and generosity. This generosity and kindness he carried out among us who had the rare privilege of knowing him.'

Here one should interpolate that MacNeice taught Bell well, for the same talent, skill and generosity were characteristic of his protégé too. The entry concludes with a private note:

My memories are of respect and affection – around Soho, the evening at Cheyne Walk and the walk next morning through sunlit London when he showed me [Edward James] Moeran the composer in a pub. Those jollities with W.R. Rodgers in the early days, the evening when he read 'Bagpipe Music' to McBirney and me at Cregagh Road. Affection and respect. But he would have killed you with the liquor!

On 10 September, MacNeice's ashes were buried at Carrowdore Parish Church, in the Ards Peninsula. Bell went there with Ronnie Mason and James Boyce, and appreciated the comic aspects that are so often part of an interment:

Archdeacon Quinn made gallant, if not very successful effort to appear at home with Louis as a poet. . . . Hedli [MacNeice's wife] very effective in black veil bore ashes down the aisle and deposited casket in a small hole in grave followed by a bunch of red roses. Observed rector dissuading sexton from filling in hole then and there.

One of Bell's own protégés was recalled in the entry for 15 February 1965:

> This morning Sam Thompson died. He was 48 years of age. ... What does one say? I produced all his radio work – that was his apprenticeship to writing. Many times he said he had much to thank me for. But in time it became a bit of boasting. What in fact has he done? Two plays, badly written, no construction, yet vivid and bursting with life. It would be unfair to [say] S.T. did not work on his plays. He worked very hard, talked about them, boasted about what people said about them – agents, TV prods etc. Then his incredible naïvety – obscene cursing of BBC and all its officials then asking me to help him, advise him. A more considered evaluation later.

Another, much sadder note followed the murder of his friend Martin McBirney by the IRA on 16 September 1974. McBirney had been serving as a Resident Magistrate and was shot on the same day as the Catholic judge Rory Conaghan, like him seen as an oppressive member of the occupying forces. That summer he had been a member of Bell's team on the Radio Ulster/RTÉ literary quiz programme *Quote – Unquote*.

> Monday Sept 16: This morning Fergus phoned me from Newry to say that Martin McBirney had been murdered by the Provisional IRA. He had been preparing breakfast before setting out for court. The gunman appeared at the kitchen door in the gable of the house and shot Martin twice, once in the back and once in the head as he swung round. His wife Pat and son Ross were upstairs at the time. I called this afternoon and found Pat remarkably composed and in control of the situation. She told me she hadn't heard the shots and when she found Martin lying on the kitchen floor she thought immediately of a heart attack. He had been complaining of feeling unwell on the previous day. This, to some extent, blunted the shock.
>
> I first met Martin about 1939. We became very friendly. In the early years of the war he worked in a munitions factory. After the war he was appointed as a civil magistrate in Germany. Then he took up residence in London on his admission to the English Bar. When I crossed to London to attend BBC Training School I stayed with him at his flat. We went to the theatre a lot and had many enjoyable evenings with Bertie Rodgers, MacNeice, Laurence Gilliam and the Features crowd in Rothwell House. After his marriage to Pat Cooke, Martin

returned to NI and took up practice at the NI Bar. (I've just stumbled on a letter giving the address of the flat in which I stayed with Martin – 10 Southside, Dalmeny Avenue, Camden Road North, London.) He had an overriding ambition to be a writer and for a time it took precedence over his work as a lawyer. He wrote a couple of radio scripts for me, and later two or three for the present Features Producer. A man with creative ideas (it was he who suggested the shape of *That Woman from Rathard* from *December Bride*) nevertheless there was a lack of coordination between his head and his fingers. He had an excellent library of the 30s–40s, particularly in the novel. Often I asked him, if he wanted to write, to turn his mind to critical essays, or something of that form. It is sadly lacking here – and, as Seamus Heaney says, a literature requires its critical tensions. I'm not sure if Martin ever gave my suggestion serious thought. Of late he had the fun of working as a member of the NI *Round Britain Quiz* team. He told me a few days before his death that he had offered the BBC the idea of a script of his days in Germany. Some time ago I had turned up a couple of letters he had written to me from Germany and sent them to him. But of course that was blotted out at 8.30 a.m. by a young thug. Martin was a fine man, not only as a magistrate (he was that as is evident from the tributes of his legal contemporaries) but as a friend and good companion.

One of Bell's memorial diary entries was political:

Sunday 19th [August 1973]: The *News Letter* was delayed on morning of Sat. due, presumably, to death of Lord Brookeborough. This man was largely the author of the present strife and bloodshed in Ulster. His bigoted Toryism, indeed blatant sectarianism, drove a chasm in this unfortunate community. He was like something out of the eighteenth century.

Another, the entry for 15 November 1973, was a threnody for a lost resort:

This afternoon stood at the door of the Windsor Castle pub (the Elbow Room) on Dublin Road and saw the devastation after last night's bomb attack. Recall that over the years many writers and artists drank here: Louis MacNeice, Bertie Rodgers, Lennox Robinson, Lynn Doyle, Laurie Lee, Colin Middleton, Dan O'Neill, Joe Tomelty, Sam Thompson, Roy McFadden, Frank O'Connor, Seán O'Faoláin, Brendan Behan, Brian Friel, Tom Carr, James Boyce,

George McCann, Jack McQuoid, Michael Duffy, Harold Goldblatt, Rowel Friers, Colin Blakely, James Ellis, Denis Ireland, J.D. Stewart, Sean O'Boyle, Maurice Leitch. It was the only pub that could really claim to be a convivial centre for artists, writers and actors. This was largely due to the fact that it was the BBC's tavern for 30 years. Artists from other places made their way there by hearsay and instinct. Now it's all a shambles . . .

Bell had a continuing interest in theatre until worsening deafness made it pointless to attend:

24/11/1956
Went to New Theatre, Bangor with R.McB. [Martin McBirney]. Enjoyed Cibber's *The Careless Husband* [1704] although it seems an odd choice for a company drifting towards the rocks. Gave James Ellis the new play *The Sliddry Dove*. New car running well.

4/12/56
Read *Long Day's Journey into Night*. A harrowing play: well written. Cannot resist the irritable feeling that so much drama is made up of highly compressed sequences running for the requisite number of acts and hours, the lot floating in a colourless substance. Surely it's false to show the Tyrone family on the precise day they are falling apart from morphine and alcohol? Why not on any of the days when they were happy?

Though I sympathise – my God, I sympathise!

Feb 14th [1958]: To Arts Theatre with Fred McNeill to see *All My Sons* by Arthur Miller. A very bad production, so bad it was impossible to say how good (or otherwise) the play.

Mar 28th [1958]: Group Theatre with Fred McN. – *Summer of the Seventeenth Doll* [by Ray Lawler (b. 1922)]. A bad production. All far too proper to give the bed-odour of this play. Colin Blakely [1930–87] the exception.

An important opening was that of Sam Thompson's controversial *Over the Bridge* at the Empire Theatre on 26 January 1960:

Uproarious, splendid opening. Joe Tomelty v. poor. I'm afraid poor J. is finished. Boyce unforgivably weak on his cues. But a great theatrical occasion. A firm slap in the teeth for the frightened men who banned the play from the Group Theatre.

Later that year Bell attended a features conference in London and met Ronnie Mason and Moore Wasson who were there for TV training. On 3 July the three of them went to see Bernard Miles in Bertolt Brecht's *Galileo*: 'This is probably a good play but not in Miles' production.' On 12 June 1961 he went with a friend to see Arnold Wesker's *Roots* (1959):

> My first visit to the new Arts [in Botanic Avenue]. Very attractive theatre. Too much to hope perhaps, that Wilmot will give us a sequence of plays as good as *Roots*. The 'message' obtruded a bit, but the young actress, Gail Starforth, did a good job and at least the play said something to the audience. Could be moved to Antrim or Down or Fermanagh without too much dislocation.

On 25 November 1964 Bell records that he has written to Mrs Capper of the Arts Council offering to write a history of the Ulster theatre. The entry for 15 January 1965 is uncharacteristically edgy:

> ... today W.R. Rodgers arrived in Belfast to attend Arts Council Standing Committee. I suspect that he has been elected on to this body so that he could write the History of Ulster Drama. Nothing would please his proposer, A.A. [Alfred Arnold] more. Anyway, Rodgers was angry, rather drunk and apparently reluctant to meet me (according to J.B. [John Boyd]). I am sorry about this but this is twice that Arnold has meddled in something he knows nothing about. The first was Loudan's failure. I now await Mrs Capper's reply to my letter of the 25th Nov. and the decision of the council.

The next day Bell met Arnold at a party. He proved 'very affable, offering me the story behind Loudan and the book on Ulster Theatre'. Bell's proposal was accepted on 9 April and it was Rodgers himself who rang to tell Bell that it had been agreed that he should write the book with a fee of £600: 'Wonderful news and I have been unfair to W.R.' In fact Rodgers was one of the main movers in having Bell commissioned to do the book. The formal offer of an advance of £200 – 'rest on completion' – arrived on 14 April. The completed book was delivered on Tuesday, 21 June 1966. By then 'that play of mine' had been chosen as part of the new season of Mary O'Malley's Lyric Players. 'Old bones stirring.'

Fergus was an occasional companion at plays. Not long after his eighteenth birthday they had seen Turgenev's *A Month in the Country* with a spectacular performance by Bob McLernon as Shpigelsky, the local doctor. On 5 April 1966 they went with Barry Sloan to see a production of *Caligula* (1944) by Albert Camus, and at the end of August 1971 they saw Joan Littlewood's *Oh, What A Lovely War!* (1963) at the Arts Theatre. In September 1971 the pair travelled to Scotland on a short holiday and saw *Rattle of a Simple Man*, the comedy by Charles Dyer (1962), at Ayr Civic Theatre.

It is hard to decide, as with diaries of all good writers, whether the entries were meant for his eyes only or perhaps intended for others to read. Many entries have professional skill and elegance, even in the abbreviated and impressionistic style used. The entry for 10 May 1977 is a drama in microcosm:

> Following a morning's filming at Martin farm I travelled to Porta-ferry to check on butcher's shop for another episode [the programme was called *Beef* and produced by Tony McAuley] – lunched at hotel. Coming out of P'ferry took a secondary road to cross peninsula to Greyabbey. Stopped to enquire my way. When starting off, was clouted in back by BMW driven by a Father P. McCollum PP of Porta-ferry. I could have been in the wrong. Just possible I hadn't flicked my indicator. Road here narrow with switchback rises. My car not much damaged – one rear light cluster and bootlid a bit twisted – or so I thought! When I got back to film unit Tony's secretary Maeve said a priest shouldn't be driving a BMW – and orange-coloured at that!

The estimate for repair of the damage came to £258.

Two aspects of Bell's personal life run like threads through the entries, his deafness and the business of his drinking. In 1960, when Bell was fifty-one, a specific entry labelled 'Dec:' reads, 'Over this past month or so my hearing has been rather worse. Trying unsuccessfully to get off smoking.' In February 1961 he attended Dr Gordon Smith at the Royal Victoria Hospital about his hearing and was given 'a new tablet drug – Perdilatal – which speeds up, I understand, the blood in the inner ear'. On 24 March he was back at the clinic. Dr Smith tested his hearing again and reported a marked improvement. 'I seem to feel much less pressure and noise in my ear. This is v. good news.' The entry for Sunday 2 July strikes a deeply gloomy note: 'I fully realise that I'm going deaf.' Yet thirteen years later, on 14 March 1974, he was cheerfully back with Dr Smyth [sic], now at University Square. 'Relieved to hear him say that an aid could help – although this cost £70–80! To call with a Mr Lomas at Clarke's, Donegall Sq. W. late next week.' A week later he collected a Qualitone hearing aid – 'price £95!'

> Tues 26th: Hearing aid packed in – will phone Lomas tomorrow morning.

> Wed 27th: hearing aid all right – simply clogged up!

On 4 February 1977 he records that he had

> suffered a most embarrassing and depressing period of deafness these past two weeks (my hearing aid made practically no difference). I had an appointment this afternoon with Gordon Smyth, the consultant. He extracted large quantities of hardened wax from my ear, and to my relief discovered that this was the cause. V. glad as I had looked forward to the London visit with much foreboding.

The visit was for the investiture of the MBE (see Chapter 14). In fact the problem remained but though distance hearing was usually impossible and made theatre-going and attendance at lectures pointless, his hearing was perfectly fine in normal conversation and on the telephone.

For Bell, as for most men of his time, drinking was a normal social activity. The bright sparks may have congregated in Campbells in the forenoon, but in the evening the venues were Mooneys or Laverys or, for 'tourist' divilment, hostelries of dubious reputation. He was a witty man with a Ulster-Scot laconicism and in the company of fellow imbibers he could be as unbuttoned as the next man. The producer who at one of the weekly post-mortems at Ormeau Avenue responded to the head of programmes' statement that a particular programme did not in his opinion 'come off' with the terse 'It's a programme; not a pair of knickers,' was not going to be bound by conversational niceties. In *The Middle of My Journey* John Boyd recalls a not untypical story from the BBC years:

> I remember one afternoon when Sam and I escaped from our offices to this relaxing sanctuary [the Elbow Room] and we were joined by Jack Loudan, a sandy-haired ex-journalist who was then in charge of CEMA – the Council for the Encouragement of Music and the Arts, the organisation which preceded the Northern Ireland Arts Council. Jack was a good conversationalist, a playwright and the author of a book on Amanda McKittrick Ros, the novelist from Larne whose euphuistic style had attracted the attention of Aldous Huxley and Denis Johnston. Sam was himself an engaging conversationalist and the hours

passed quickly until Jack, pointing to a travelling bag at his feet, announced that he was bound for London that evening and wanted to be on board the Heysham boat well before sailing time; he asked us to go with him by taxi to the docks, and join him on board the boat for a final drink to round off the evening. I decided not to go, but Sam accepted Jack's invitation. The next morning I got a telephone call from Sam.

'I'm ringing from Manchester . . .'

'From where?'

'Manchester. From the BBC here . . .'

'Oh . . . Anything wrong?'

'No, all's well . . . I want you to do something for me if you're not too busy at the moment . . .'

On Sam's return he told me what had happened. The conversation in the ship's bar had become more and more engrossing and when Sam asked the steward whether the time hadn't come for him to leave, the steward had replied, 'Sir, you cannot disembark now. We are already past the Isle of Man.'

After Bell's retirement from the BBC the stress level dropped and though he did much work, the entries indicate a much more relaxed man. In a letter written on 9 February 1988 to a friend, Tom Adair, with whom he had a regular correspondence in the late 1980s, he wrote:

You are, of course, absolutely right about the family and home life. For years I drank too heavily, an incubus that fell (miraculously) from my shoulders the month I left the BBC. I also, from my twenties, have suffered from Ménière's Disease, and intermittent deafness is not the most useful attribute for a radio producer.

Certainly in my experience of knowing him for the last thirteen years of his life, he never drank or showed the least abrasiveness. He was kind, genial and witty, and as helpful and considerate to young aspirants as ever. It is likely that the stress of originating, writing and producing features was added to by the fact that for most of his brilliant career, like his friend John Boyd, he could not rely upon support from the local BBC establishment. Throughout that career, especially in the earlier days, his position was so anomalous and disapproved of (when not misunderstood by the higher ranks who had to placate Unionist Party HQ at Glengall Street) that he felt that his job was insecure. He felt that both he and Boyd had been kept out of the development of television programming by local management; it rankled that he had been involved only as a contributor, never a producer. Furthermore, the abolition of the Features Department in the 1960s altered Bell's position fundamentally, so that he had to keep his head down from then on.

All these difficulties may help to explain his almost incredible output of programmes. He was a man of great industry, working right up to his death but an output of several series plus close on three hundred individual features, forty of them written himself suggests embattlement, an attitude at times like that of the Red Queen: 'Now *here*, you see, it takes all the running you can do to stay in the same place. If you want to get somewhere else, you must run at least twice as fast as that.' Like his friends MacNeice and Rodgers, he had come to regard drink as the punctuation of life, and places like the Wheatsheaf and the Elbow Room as extensions of office and studio, and rather more congenial than either.

Bell kept several diaries, used *aides-mémoire* as much as anything else, but the post book with its all-weather cover gives the man in his troubled middle years. The original pithy observations on life and literature together with those sedulously copied down make the journal an uncommonplace book. The journal reveals the man's unstudied love of and interest in wife and son, his taste for anecdote, his irritation at slovenliness, his industry, his deeply felt disappointments and exhilarations, and his instinctive and untrumpeted kindnesses. It expresses his love of life, art and literature, his curiosity, his egalitarianism, and a view of economics in which frugality and generosity are curiously mixed. His unabashed awareness of his own worth is expressed in the entry for 26 October 1960, in which he notes that, as instructed by Cassell, the publisher of *The Hollow Ball*, he has removed 'nearer 10% than 20% but this seems to be the maximum – some good writing gone!' The diary contains many examples of his appreciation of Northern Ireland. It also reveals that he returned, without weakening his socialism, to a kind of Christianity: if not the strict practice of his childhood, then one in which spirituality played a considerable part.

One anecdote about not himself but one of his heroes might be taken as the keynote of the journal as a whole. It occurs in the entry for 31 August 1957:

St. J. Ervine tells of how, on a visit to Max Hill [Max Gate, Hardy's house near Dorchester] he saw Hardy send a poem to some journal enclosing a s.a.e. in case of rejection – this was when he was famous. Ervine removed the stamped envelope and gave Hardy a good talking-to on account of his modesty. Characteristic of both, I should say.

14
SAM HANNA BELL MA (*HONORIS CAUSA*), MBE

B ELL RETIRED FROM THE BBC in the autumn of 1969 in spite of
efforts on his part to stay on. A letter from Waldo Maguire,
BBC Controller, Northern Ireland, sent on 13 October 1967
and marked 'personal', regretted:

> that it will not be possible to offer you an extension of service after
> your sixtieth birthday on 16th October 1969, and you will therefore
> expect to be retired on that date. We will, however, review the posi-
> tion before you reach the age of sixty in case circumstances should
> have changed.

The diary entry for 5/6 July 1969 notes:

> Yesterday rehearsed and recorded my last dramatised feature, 'The
> Greatest Storyteller' – a centenary programme on William Carleton
> [who died on 30 January 1869]. A studioful of actors – Goldblatt,
> Cathie Gibson, Louis Rolston, dear Michael J. Murphy, Michael
> Duffy, Bob McLernon – all three Belfast theatres represented.

His retirement dinner was held at the Stormont Hotel on Monday 13
October, three days before his sixtieth birthday. Mildred and Fergus
were present, and many old colleagues – including Gerry McCrudden,
John Boyd and Billy Boucher – 'made very complimentary speeches –
all in all, a memorable last bow', as the diary records. As a souvenir of
the occasion someone had the idea of filling a child's autograph book

with personal comments from the whole BBC staff. Gerry McCrudden's had the nicest touch, the entry written in the form of a broadcast script:

(FADE) You have been listening to Sam Hanna Bell – a life-study in the illustrious career of a distinguished Irishman. Taking part were hundreds and hundreds of grateful associates, artistes, colleagues and friends, among them, one Gerry McCrudden.

At drinks beforehand, during the usual jolly chat expressing envy at his 'being shot of all this', how much they wished they had the freedom, et cetera, Bell mentioned in a purely conversational way that he might write his memoirs with particular reference to his time in Ormeau Avenue. It was noticed that shortly after this remark, Waldo Maguire, left the gathering. Amidst the speculation this caused, Bell opined that Maguire had gone home to change his trousers.

In fact, Bell's twenty retirement years were to be almost as busy and as fruitful as the previous thirty years. At the dinner Ronnie Mason asked him to continue with *Country Window*. (This verbal commitment was formalised at the end of November. Bell noted: 'I'm to carry on . . . monthly. Very acceptable @ £40 p.m.')

The following week, in the canteen of Broadcasting House, the Controller, Northern Ireland, presented Bell with 'a very handsome watch'. It was inscribed: 'To Sam Hanna Bell from his friends in the BBC, 1969'. Offers of work continued to come in, particularly from the Schools Department. Cowan Watson, the editor of the *News Letter*, took Bell to lunch in the Grand Central Hotel and offered him a column. There were further retirement tributes: on Monday 17 November Mildred and Bell were entertained at the Arts Club and presented with a plaque and teak garden seat. The plaque bore the words: 'Presented to Sam Hanna Bell by his friends in the acting and literary professions. October 1969'.

It is possible to gauge from the laconic and intermittent entries in the diary the mood of slight disarray and decompression that followed his retirement. Othello's occupation was gone, at least temporarily. Family worries obtruded: his brother Bobby was taken to the Moyle Hospital with a coronary on 28 October 1969. He was showing some improvement by 21 November but was still kept in hospital. He was eventually allowed home and was stated to be progressing favourably, but he was still at home in February 1970.

On 5 September 1969, J.J. Campbell sent Bell a version of the auto-biography he had requisitioned seven years earlier, asking him to bring it 'up to date, correcting and amending as you think fit'. The document was written in the third person but apart from mentioning the comple-tion of the 'history of the theatre in Ulster from 1902 until the present day', it was substantially as Bell had sent it. The purpose of the update was revealed in a letter from F. Arthur Vick, the Vice-Chancellor of Queen's University Belfast, sent on 28 November. It began:

> I write with great pleasure to inform you that the Senate (the Govern-ing Body) of the University has unanimously and cordially agreed to invite you to accept the honorary degree of Master of Arts at a gradua-tion ceremony on Monday morning, 6 July 1970.

There were the usual warnings about confidentiality and an invitation to the ceremony and dinner on 7 July included Mildred. There was also an invitation to lunch in the Vice-Chancellor's Lodge after the confer-ring. Bell replied on 2 December happily assenting, and on 11 Decem-ber Vick wrote to say that the news had been released to the press. Congratulations streamed in from such colleagues and friends as Harold Goldblatt, G.B. Newe of Prospect House, Cushendall, Norman Harri-son, Waldo McGuire, John Boyd, Ronnie Mason. A card showing the photograph of a genial old party in cap and gown with Bell's name and the message 'Your friends are honoured too' came from his close friend Jim Ryan, who was to be one of Bell's special guests. Afterwards Jim Ryan sent Bell a photo of himself wearing a Moscow University T-shirt, labelled Jimsky Ryansky D.Theo (1690). It read:

> Sam Thank you for the honour to me and mine in having us at your conferring. I am sorry we could not find you afterwards. I hope you will be my honoured guest at my conferring (Doctor of Theology) Affection regards Jim

G.R. Cowie, secretary to the university, wrote on 7 January advising Bell of details of dress and robing, and requiring his hat size. The letter also listed the other honorary graduands and asked for names of parti-cular friends he would like to invite. Bell's reply stated that his hat size was seven and a quarter and that he wished to invite Major Gerald Reside (Mildred's brother) and his wife, Dr James Ryan and his wife, and Beryl Thompson, Mildred's colleague from Richmond Lodge.

After the ceremony, at which the degree was presented by Dr Vick, Bell and Mildred joined the other honorary graduands (and guests) for lunch with him. The dinner in the Great Hall afterwards was a 'very dignified and *enjoyable* affair'. Bell sat between Lady Fraser and Mrs Collinson Black. 'Her ladyship remarkably radical in her opinions; the pretty young Mrs Black equally conservative.'

Six years later, Bell's now busy-as-ever career was again interrupted by public honour. On 29 November 1976, on returning from recording a piece on his first publisher, Richard Rowley, Bell found a letter marked 'Urgent and Personal'. It was from Kenneth Stowe, Parliamentary Private Secretary to the prime minister James Callaghan, advising him 'in strictest confidence' that the PM had submitted his name to the Queen as an appropriate Member of the Order of the British Empire.

> I thought at first it was a jape, for I could think of no reason why this should arrive at my present age, or who would put forward my name for such a distinction. But the idea pleased M. I filled in the form intimating that I would accept the Order and posted it on Wed. Dec 1st (delay due to postmen's strike).

The award was announced as part of the New Year's Honours List on 31 December. The *News Letter* and *Belfast Telegraph* had photographs and the *Irish Times* 'a generous biog. supplied by the BBC, no doubt'. As the diary records:

> M. delighted. At 5.15 I was summoned to Broadcasting House to be interviewed by Sean Rafferty on the MBE award. Much to Gerry McCrudden's derisive disgust, Sean asked me, 'now that I have been given this honour, would I continue with my writing'. Letters and phone calls arriving. One to my surprise from Sir Jack Longland; the last time I saw him, relations cool, owing to a muddle over meals and hotels for *Round Britain Quiz*. Still very nice of him.

Messages of congratulations came from many friends and agencies with which he was associated, including the Northern Ireland Tourist Board, Ulster Television, the BBC, Gilnahirk Horticultural Society, the staff of the *Ulster Tatler* (per Dick Sherry), the Ulster Bank (per Sir Robin Kinahan), and the Senate of Queen's (per G.R. Cowie). There was also one from John N. Knipe MBE, chairman of the Association of Ulster Drama Festivals, who having been through the process was able to assure Bell that he would find 'the presentation a most satisfyingly memorable occasion': 'The ceremonial is impressive and is carried out in the high style, accompanied by unfussy good humour and lack of pomposity. It is an excellent example of the British flair for this sort of thing.' George Thompson wrote on his own behalf and that of the Ulster Folk and Transport Museum, as did Ken Jamieson for the Arts Council of Northern Ireland.

On 8 February 1977 the necessary morning suit was collected from Parsons and Parsons. (A receipt for an amount of £5.70 is among the Bell papers.) The Northern Ireland Office had sent a schedule of travelling and subsistence for investitures, and with Bell's usual precision the air, bus and coach tickets are pinned to the sheet detailing expenditure of £182.15. (This was in the days before the Piccadilly Line ran to Heathrow.) The party consisting of the laureate, Mildred and Fergus flew to London on 9 February and found the Strand Palace Hotel 'not very much changed in the intervening years', though they were shocked to find that the carvery lunch now cost £3.90. Fergus went for a haircut ('an odd time') while 'M. and I mooched about the hotel'. That night the parents went to a performance of Terence Rattigan's *Separate Tables* (1955) at the Apollo, Shaftesbury Avenue, while Fergus kept a dinner appointment. Bell had been attracted to the show by the excellent cast of John Mills, Jill Bennet, Margaret Courtenay, Raymond Huntley and other West End stars but though the seats were expensive, Bell heard very little. Mildred enjoyed the evening very much though it was marred by their having to trudge home taxiless from the theatre.

There is a characteristic hint of irony – and discomfort – in the erstwhile socialist's account of the next day's events. In the morning, in 'ceremonial togs' they queued in their taxi in the Mall while their French driver at first complained and then in Gallic fashion acquiesced. Once inside the palace gates, recipients were separated from their guests and each went their separate ways. In the company of about forty other men and women, Bell was shown up an imposing staircase which was guarded at intervals by figures in imposing uniform bearing glittering breastplates and drawn sabres. Their stolid indifference to 'the crocodile of soberly garbed civilians in morning coats and gowns' struck him as hardly surprising. The company was eventually shown into a long salon decorated with splendid canvases including some recognised by Bell as Van Dycks. His nearest companions were a Scot called Begley, who was being honoured for his work in organising factories for the disabled in Scotland, and 'a most amiable Yorkshireman active in the natural gas industry'. Also in the company was 'a solidly built fellow in kilts' called Anderson, a champion caber thrower who was being rewarded for his work in organising Highland games.

There were some moments of advice from two officials in long tight military coats, and trousers with a crimson stripe, as to how they were to comport themselves when presented to the Queen Mother. They were ushered in in alphabetical order, Bell relieved that there were a handful of *A*s and even a couple of *B*s in front of him. He noticed a man in a wheelchair being pushed by a palace flunkey; this was Harold Hobson, then seventy-three, who had been knighted that morning (paralysed in the right leg from the age of seven, Hobson had managed for many years to write brilliant drama notices for the *Sunday Times* and the *Christian Science Monitor*, his praise of *Waiting for Godot* in 1955 had established Beckett's English-language reputation).

The presentation was 'admirably stage-managed' – praise from an expert. The recipients were lined up at a side entrance to the scene of the investiture, the Grand Ballroom, and 'released one by one'. As one recipient was presented the next stood ready three paces back, accompanied by a court official.

> I was duly presented to the Queen Mother who hung the Order on the hook for that purpose. She asked where I came from.
>
> 'Belfast, Your Majesty.'
>
> 'Things are very disturbed and difficult there.'
>
> 'Yes, Ma'am,' said I.
>
> 'I hope that you may soon see peace return.'
>
> 'Thank you, Ma'am,' said I, 'for your good wishes.'
>
> I retreated my three steps, looked up to see her eye still upon me, which called for a further bow answered by the much-publicised smile. Sharp turn to the right and out of a side entrance. Here, upon a long table, lay rows of black jeweller's cases. An official removed my Order, dishooked me, slapped my medal into one of the cases and I was out. (No time wasted.) A circuitous route by the corridors and I was back again in the Ballroom, ushered to a seat to watch the rest of the recipients decorated. When the Queen Mum had left the chamber, escorted by her retinue, I joined M. and Fergus, who had had a good view of the proceedings in a sort of raised rostrum behind.

The official photographers charged them £12 for a group photograph but 'it was not an opportunity to be missed'. And afterwards there was a splendid lunch provided by Fergus in the Café Royal. 'Years since I'd been there, in the company of MacNeice and Bertie Rodgers, where we met V.S. Pritchett. Waiters most attentive – delicious rib of beef etc.' Back at the hotel they got out of their finery and headed for home. On 22 August a letter from the Central Secretariat at Stormont announced that a large envelope had arrived from the Central Chancery Office 'in connection with the honour you have received'.

15
THE THEATRE IN ULSTER

IN THE YEARS OF HIS RETIREMENT Sam Hanna Bell had five books published: two further novels, a retrospective anthology of northern Irish life called *Within Our Province* ('an old horse running again!'), a collection of 'tales' from the *Ulster Tatler*, and the survey of Ulster drama which had been commissioned by the Arts Council in February 1965 and completed the following year.

Bell was an entirely appropriate choice to write *The Theatre in Ulster*, which was the study's title when it was eventually published seven years later by Gill and Macmillan on 10 March 1972. (The cover which arrived by post on 3 January had been designed by Cor Klaasen. It was 'very colourful with a Celtic dog design – but in orange and blue!') The commission gave Bell an opportunity to give the story of the Ulster Literary Theatre a fifty-page survey – apart from an academic study, *The Ulster Theatre in Ireland* (1931) by Dr Margaret McHenry, it had largely been ignored. Its premier playwright, Rutherford Mayne (1878–1967), brother of the medieval scholar and translator Helen Waddell, had bequeathed to the Irish theatre the comedy *The Drone* (1908), and to the amateur drama movement its soundest prospect. As Bell recounts:

> The play has been published and republished. In the length and breadth of Ireland there must be few drama societies which have not

staged *The Drone*, and many times at that. John McBride, the Ulster actor, recalls that when he first appeared in it he expressed an uneasiness about his lines to the producer, Fred Morrow. 'Don't worry,' Morrow reassured him, 'if you need a prompt the audience will prompt you.'

Bell, of course, had always been intensely interested in theatre. He was approximately the same age as *The Drone* and was friendly with the personalities of the Ulster Group Theatre (the Ulster Literary Theatre's successor), especially its chief playwright, Joe Tomelty, whom he had suggested as the only possible scriptwriter for BBC Northern Ireland's most successful comedy soap, *The McCooeys*. Many of the features Bell had written and commissioned in his days at the BBC were in dramatised form, even though based on fact. He had collaborated unofficially with Martin McBirney in the writing of *That Woman At Rathard* and with Gerry McCrudden on *The Sliddry Dove*, and inevitably the Ulster theatre had featured in his radio features.

Enter Robbie John, Bell's radio feature on the Ulster Literary Theatre, was first broadcast on 25 November 1954 and was repeated on 11 May 1955. The script was by Bell's friend David Kennedy who was a colleague of J.J. Campbell on the staff of St Malachy's College. A battered copy of the original script among the papers has a pencilled note: 'Mr Bell, I found fascinating, HMcM': praise indeed coming from the then BBC Controller Northern Ireland, Henry McMullan. The story was told with narration, dramatised scenes featuring the words of Rutherford Mayne, Bulmer Hobson, Gerard Macnamara (Harry Morrow, who wrote the Ulster Literary Theatre's other hit, *Thompson in Tír na nÓg*), Padraig Gregory, James Winder Good, Cathal O'Shannon, Forrest Reid, Whitford Kane and Larry Morrow, and excerpts from *The Drone* and *The Turn of the Road* by Mayne, *The Little Cowherd of Slaigne* by Joseph Campbell, *The Enthusiast* by Lewis Purcell (David Parkhill), and *Thompson in Tír na nÓg*.

The Drone has all the ingredients of the kitchen comedy. There is the decent, hardworking John Murray, a widowed farmer whose daughter is a poor housekeeper, his slothful brother Daniel, who 'has a great head on him', a neighbouring spinster with an eye to a breach-of-promise suit, and a 'Scotch engineer'. All this and the genial air of happy endings were to have an influence on George Shiels and on such Abbey dramatists as Lennox Robinson, Brinsley MacNamara and Louis D'Alton. They also influenced Harry Morrow's one-acter about the Orangeman Andy Thompson, whose 'ould gun blew up' at the Scarva Sham Battle, sending him to Tír na nÓg, the Valhalla of the Celts. There he has to try to explain Ulster politics to Cúchulainn, Fionn Mac Cumhail, Maev of Connacht and other Irish heroes. *Thompson in Tír na nÓg* was even more popular than *The Drone*, since its length and simple set made it suitable for Young Farmers' clubs and community groups. It was first staged in 1912, when the agitation against Home Rule was gaining momentum, and was all the more effective for its timing.

The title *Enter Robbie John* refers to Mayne's serious play *The Turn of the Road* (1906), which may be read as the clash between spiritual and materialistic values or the conflict that faces the artist in a Puritan society such as turn-of-the-century Ulster. Robbie John is the second son of a County Down farmer and a gifted violinist. His family regard such a talent as unmanly and unsettling, but Robbie John resists all pressures ('To the fire with it') and leaves home to pursue his proper career.

On 9 December 1965 Bell presented a radio feature written by himself on the Ulster Group Theatre called *A Gathering of Players*. In making the feature, which was repeated on the Third Programme on 24 January 1967, he had the advantage of having most of the Ulster Group Theatre actors available to tell their stories. The programme followed the pattern devised by Kennedy for *Enter Robbie John* with excerpts from such representative Ulster Group Theatre plays as *All Souls Night* (1948) by Joseph Tomelty and *Friends and Relations* (revised 1951) by St John Ervine.

Bell's radio programmes were points of departure for his book, which was begun on 18 April (Easter Sunday) 1965. By 26 January the first two chapters, those on the Ulster Literary Theatre, were typed and Bell noted in his diary that he would send them to David Kennedy for his comments. On 15 February he spoke to the Belfast Drama Circle on 'Ulster Theatre' and had a 'good audience and a good reception'. He noted slightly sourly that 'amateurs are, largely, indifferent to the professional theatre'. The completed manuscript, then entitled 'The Dramatic Movement in Ulster', was delivered to the Arts Council on 21 June. Four years later – most of Bell's books took a long time to be published – he sent the typescript to Michael Gill of Gill and Macmillan, Dublin, and on 2 November 1970, Michael Longley of the Arts

Council of Northern Ireland informed him that Gill and Macmillan were to publish his work as *The Theatre in Ulster*. Contracts were signed and witnessed on 12 March 1971 and his editor Mary Dowey, who came from Belfast, complimented him upon it: 'It certainly looks interesting and is extremely well presented.' Michael Gill was very pleased with the finished book and the reviews were 'pretty good'. One in *Fortnight* by Kathleen Boehringer struck Bell as 'rather silly'. 'She thinks I should have written quite another sort of book – all about the plays, analysing them. Unfortunately, the bulk of the plays aren't worth it – even if I wanted to do it.'

The book is very readable, a good job of journeywork. It lacks an index, but the author in three appendixes lists all the first productions of the Ulster Literary Theatre, the Ulster Group Theatre and the Lyric Players Theatre (1951–71). With characteristic serendipity he found an appropriate couplet in Swift to launch the project:

Gallants, this Thursday night will be our last
Then without fail we pack up for Belfast.

Like other Irish cities, Belfast had its theatres, music halls and concert rooms. The glory was Frank Matcham's Opera House and Cirque built in 1895 but there were others, including the Theatre Royal and later the Empire. The Divine Sarah (Bernhardt) and Mrs Patrick Campbell were regular visitors, and the young Robert Lynd (1879–1949), the essayist and nationalist friend of Bulmer Hobson, would often absent himself from afternoon class to see Marie Lloyd, Little Tich and Vesta Tilley, and lose his heart to Marie Studholme, the most beautiful and popular actress of the day. Yet it was the unIrishness of this commercial fare that drove Hobson and his friend David Parkhill to establish in Belfast an equivalent of the Irish Literary Theatre of Yeats, Gregory and Hyde.

Bell tells their story well and since it is a very satisfactory story the first section of the book is the most interesting. The other sections, dealing with the recent past and the active present, were harder to do. Nevertheless the accounts of the Ulster Group Theatre, the Belfast Arts Theatre of Hubert Wilmot, and the Lyric are extremely valuable and full of fascinating nuggets of off-beat information. The word *Ulster* in the study's title was interpreted liberally. Exhaustive accounts of the plays done in Ulster theatres, of whatever origin, are given, as are accounts of plays by Ulster-born dramatists whose work may not have

146

originally appeared in the North. It is ironical that the work of that quintessentially Ulster playwright George Shiels had its first productions in the Abbey – and, moreover, that his plays of the twenties, thirties and forties such as *Paul Twyning, Professor Tim, The New Gossoon, The Passing Day*, and *The Rugged Path* were often the Abbey's bread and butter, put on when funds were low. Other writers born in Ulster who for obvious reasons found their natural outlet in Dublin and on Broadway rather than Belfast were Brian Friel and Eugene McCabe. Bell's study includes a succinct account of the career of Sam Thompson and of how his play *Over the Bridge* changed the face of Ulster drama (see Chapter 11); characteristically, Bell makes no reference to the part that he played in Thompson's beginnings as a writer.

A concluding chapter, entitled 'The Scene Today' notes the continuing popularity of the amateur movement, the existence of several active local 'little theatres'. It also bemoans the fact that 'The Empire Theatre has been demolished, the Grand Opera House and the Hippodrome are now ornate picture-houses.' Bell was conscious that the Arts Council of Northern Ireland, working with the Department of Education and local authorities, had plans in time to provide local theatres, and indeed he lived to see the Opera House restored to its former opulence and modern theatres built in Coleraine and Enniskillen. The persistence of theatre's popularity (in spite of the Troubles, the resurrection of the cinema and the coming of satellite television) and the creation of many local semi-professional companies seem to bear out his conclusion:

> ... more often than is recognised, we have had good, sometimes outstanding playwrights. I am confident that there are young men and women among us today who will write fitting drama for the new theatres, for the skilled actors, and for our delight.

16
A MAN FLOURISHING

ONE FEATURE OF THE PROCESS by which Sam Hanna Bell's novels came to publication, apart from the slow and meticulous care with the writing and its often evolutionary nature, was the welter of correspondence with his agent David Higham Associates during the gestation periods and the sometimes longer process of getting them placed. Initially work on *The Hollow Ball* was handled by Paul Scott (1920–78), the future author of *The Raj Quartet* (1966–75) and Booker prizewinner for *Staying On* (1977). He had written to Bell on 13 October 1959 announcing that he would retire the following year and on 22 March, nine days before his retirement, he handed him over to the care of a colleague, David Bolt. It was not until 16 January 1961, almost a year later, that a contract to publish *The Hollow Ball* was signed with Cassell. An early mention of the germ of Bell's third novel occurs in a letter written to Kenneth Parker, the head of Cassell's editorial department, on 14 June 1961. This was connected with the usual option clause: 'of publishing the Author's next novel on the same terms' and with a decision 'within six weeks':

> I have already started work on a novel running from about the 1798 Irish Rebellion up to about 1912. This story of three or four generations will be spun round the linen trade and the working title is *Damask*. Do you think there is still a market for the history of a textile family? I need

hardly add that the history of Ulster since 1798 has been a pretty tumultuous one – almost certainly full of more exciting incident than any other region of the British Isles. I should appreciate your comments.

The answer came from Annette Carter, another member of the editorial department, on 22 June. She commented as publishers often do: 'If it is a good novel then there is always a market for it, whatever the subject and background.' She warned Bell, however, that since 'family sagas tend by their nature to be lengthy and publishers are apt to look askance at large-scale novels unless they are very, very good . . . anything larger than 90–100,000 words . . . would not be an economic proposition'. Bell noted her advice and promised to do his best 'to make this new undertaking both well-behaved and good'.

Actually the book had been started on 20 April 1960, five months before David Higham Associates had succeeded in placing *The Hollow Ball* with Cassell. As a flourish in the diary puts it: 'Started, at long last, my novel "Damask"!' On 20 April 1961 he brought out the 50,000 words he had written and found they looked all right: 'Now for the hard work in reading up Belfast 19th century. I intend to keep a list of the books I read.' (In fact except for a glance at the future of Aggie McDowell, the maid, the action of *A Man Flourishing* (as the novel was finally called) takes place in the years 1798–1805.) One of few diary entries for 1966 is that for 28 August which has its own – and unexplained – drama: '12 noon. Have resolved to finish "Dwellers at the Ford" – this is a crisis in my life, writing and otherwise.' (That title had been in existence for nine years: the diary entry for 1 April 1957 reads: 'Consider a possible collection of stories about Belfast – working title "Dwellers at the Ford".')

The crisis must have passed for there is no mention of the novel until 30 December 1968 when he records: 'This evening I started to type my novel "Dwellers at the Ford".' Something over a year later, on 9 February 1970, he was able to record:

Wrote 'The End' to 'Dwellers at the Ford'. I'm passably satisfied with the work. To type the last few pages and then off with the m.s. to the binders – and my agent, who says he's looking forward to it (D. Bolt).

The typescript was left to be bound on 19 February and was dispatched to David Higham Associates on 27 February. David Bolt replied on 19 March:

I must say this comes as quite a surprise and very different from the last novel of yours I read. You must have done a tremendous amount of work in research! I found the beginning a bit complicated, but once into the book settled down and thoroughly enjoyed a very solid and entertaining read. I very much hope Cassell will like it as well as I did.

Bell made a waspish entry in his diary for 23 March:

Letter from David Bolt acknowledging 'Dwellers at the Ford'. Still registering astonishment that it is a period novel and seems to me not v. taken with it. But I must remember that agents rarely commit themselves and that it took 10 months to sell *The Hollow Ball* and over a year (I think) to place *December Bride*.

The note of disenchantment continued in spite of a placatory letter from Bolt assuring Bell that he did enjoy the book and that he had forgotten that Bell had earlier mentioned that 'the new one would be a period novel'. On the evening of 9 May Bell decided not to write a fourth novel but to consider the possibility of writing a play. Cassell rejected the novel with praise but said it was not consonant with their new fiction policy of 'concentrating very much on novels for which there will be a large market in the Commonwealth countries', as Cassell's Edwin Harper wrote to Bolt at David Higham Associates. Bell suggested that Bolt try Charles Monteith at Faber and Faber. Monteith had been educated at Inst, he had met Bell several times, and had expressed an interest in writing from Ulster. Meanwhile Bolt tried Collins. The unease of waiting was mitigated a little by the excitement of the honorary MA, but on 20 July Bolt had to tell Bell that Collins did not want it because it did not 'develop with sufficient power' though Monteith looked forward to reading it: Bolt tried Heinemann and Hutchinson and on 25 November had to tell Bell that Monteith did not think the novel suitable for the Faber list. The novel was also rejected by Hodder and by Eyre and Spottiswood, whose reader mentioned 'James's adultery', an adventure that was removed from the final novel.

The winter and spring of 1971 were taken up with work on extending *The Theatre in Ulster* for Gill and Macmillan and with schools broadcasts work. February brought a small drama in a personal letter from David Higham announcing that David Bolt was leaving with Sheila Watson, another member of the staff, to set up an independent agency.

In the confusion the manuscript of 'The Dwellers at the Ford' was misplaced. Bell elected to stay with David Higham Associates in spite of the new partners' wishes to retain him on Bolt and Watson's books. The manuscript (which Bolt had taken with him) was traced to the new offices and a letter written on 10 August to Bell advised him that it would be returned to David Higham Associates 'with all speed'. It was clear from Bolt's letters that he was very disappointed that Bell had not come with them: 'I mentally had you down as one of the ones with us.'

Some time between 13 and 27 September, after prompting from David Higham, the novel's title was changed to 'A Man Flourishing'; a letter from Higham noted that it seemed better in every way – 'And I remember the relevance of it also.' The laborious work of trying to place it continued: on 1 November Bell sent a copy to Jim Gracey who with his wife Diane had founded the Blackstaff Press. Macmillan's answer to David Higham on 22 November was 'a reluctant no' because it seemed to their reader to be 'nearly a very good novel'. The following August he was heartened by a very favourable report from Peter Sinclair, a reader for Hart-Davis, Macgibbon, who rejected it because 'fiction set in Irish history hasn't been doing at all well for us'. Finally on 5 October 1972 Higham wrote saying that Kevin Crossley-Holland of Gollancz would publish the book and send a £400 advance subject to Bell agreeing to cut between 10,000 and 12,000 words from 'its present 98,000 words' (their estimate). This was a matter for jubilation since Gollancz was the sixteenth publisher to whom the book had been offered, and the work of redrafting was started on 15 October. Bell followed the advice of Crossley-Holland as to the parts to be deleted and the emended text arrived at Gollancz's offices on 21 November. The contract was signed and witnessed on 29 November.

There was one last disagreement, about the title. Crossley-Holland wrote that although 'A Man Flourishing is by no means a bad title, there might be a case for settling on something that places the novel more precisely. . . . Our sales manager has suggested: AN IRISH MERCHANT, which though rather flat, is probably moving in the right direction.' Bell's response was swift:

I'm happy that Mr Kenneth Kemp [the sales manager] thinks that the novel should do well, and sorry that he doesn't like the title. But I'm afraid that the suggested alternative, An Irish Merchant, opens no window on the story for me. The novel, as I see it, is not about James Gault selling groceries, but selling his earlier principles, bit by bit, until he has achieved that sure mark of heavenly approbation recognised by the Ulster Scot – material prosperity. (MacNeice couldn't have written the verse I quote about a southern Irishman). The present title echoes the psalm quoted by Gault, and seems to me to describe, I trust with a touch of irony, the progress of the central character.

Crossley-Holland's response was wittily acquiescent: 'A Man Flourishing it is. Those you have not won over, you have knocked over.'

The MacNeice verse, chosen by Bell as the book's epigraph, was from the early poem 'Belfast' (written in 1931):

> The hard cold fire of the northerner
> Frozen into his blood from the fire in his basalt
> Glares from behind the mica of his eyes
> And the salt carrion water that brings him wealth.

The psalm quoted by Gault is the First Psalm, recited 'in your dissenter's doggerel':

> He shall be like a tree that grows
> near planted by a river
> Which in his season yields his fruit,
> and his leaf fadeth never –

The idea of 'material prosperity' as a mark of justification before the Lord, Bell's 'heavenly approbation', was not a tenet of Presbyterianism. Indeed the Presbyterians among the United Irishmen would have disdained such a mercenary view, but once the separatist United Irishmen rebellion of 1798 was over and the Act of Union with England was an inevitability, many dissenters settled for an honourable Nonconformist respectability. Many indeed flourished, a 'touch of irony' that Bell refers to in his letter, whose overriding concern with Gault's moral progress is apparent, despite its light tone. The progress to respectability of Gault, of course, has parallels with Bell's own life, and it seems that this novel originated from the same tensions that produced *The Hollow Ball*.

The novel begins in the summer of 1798 when, influenced by the radical cries of *liberté* and *egalité* from revolutionary France, many young Presbyterians in counties Antrim and Down rose in arms. Led by Wolfe Tone and Henry Joy McCracken, the United Irishmen were ardent republicans, advocates of separation from England, and also counted Catholic Emancipation among their aims. But already loyalists had flocked to join the county yeomanries, the Orange Order had been founded, in 1795, with the blessing of the Church of Ireland, and by 1797 General Lake had effectively 'disarmed' Ulster by arming the Orangemen. (One notorious example of Lake's misdeeds was the hanging of farmer William Orr in Antrim, despite a jury's recommendation of mercy, for 'administering unlawful oaths'.) In the summer of 1798, with more spirit than wisdom the northern radicals rose in rebellion in solidarity with their brothers in Carlow and Wexford. McCracken's men engaged the army and their yeomen allies under Colonel Durham in Antrim on 7 June and two days later the County Down chapter of the United Irishmen led by the Lisburn linen draper Henry Munro held the field of battle at Montalto, near Ballynahinch, for three days against the army of General Nugent who had previously razed the towns of Saintfield and Killinchy by fire. Munro was hanged opposite his own door and in sight of his wife and children on 15 June. Two days later McCracken was hanged in the Cornmarket in Belfast, close to the tavern in Crown Entry where the Society of United Irishmen had been founded in 1791.

It was against this background that the beginnings of the career of James Gault, student of divinity at Glasgow and a radical Presbyterian, are traced in Bell's novel. The scene is the Ravara of *December Bride*, and familiar names occur like landmarks. Hugh Purdie notices the preparations for insurrection:

> In the past few days the armed men had begun to trail by in the dawns and dusks. . . . There were faces and figures he recognised; his cousin Stewart Purdie, Rab McIlveen, Hans and David Echlin of Rathard. And he knew of others who had taken the rebel oath. Men like Kate's sweetheart, James Gault.

In fact James Gault never makes it to Ballynahinch; the 'randyvoo' at Killyleagh does not materialise because the leader of their band, Willie McKeever, stays home to please his mother. (He is hanged just the same, as are the six of his group who do not make the safe crossing of Strangford Lough.) James heads for Belfast, hoping for a passage to America, and finds shelter with the master of a thieves' kitchen, Dr Luke Bannon, whose habitation close to the docks is safe from interference by the authorities because of the doctor's special position in the town. One significant early incident describes how the Purdies, though innocent of involvement in the rising, are arrested by 'yeos' and made to strip to prove that they have not just ridden hard from Ballynahinch. The English major is decently impatient of his captain's insistence that Kate Purdie strip too. This captain, Nugent Mullan, is well known locally as a lout – 'Mullan o'Comber', who plies the trade of leather chandler – and his later career entwines with that of Gault and his wife in an episode of blackmail and murder.

The theme of the novel is the corruption of power and the strength of the manacles of respectability. The mode, however, is one of irony and indeed understanding. The plot is cleverly contrived from start to finish. Gault's austere rectitude is proof against all the temptations to gluttony, fornication and dishonesty that Bannon puts in his way. It is only when he is able to break with Bannon and take his place as a town merchant, when in fact he is a man flourishing, that his integrity falters. The novel is not a tract and there is nothing of what Sir Walter Scott called the 'big bow-wow' strain. There is instead a nice mixture of history, character studies, action and even, if a little straitly expressed, romance. One issue in relation to such a well-wrought work is whether the cuts suggested by Crossley-Holland damaged the structure. Some of them are probably cosmetic enough:

> We feel that most of the cuts could come from the sections that deal with the home life of the Gaults and the Purdies. Much of this has only slight relevance to the main theme. Sam Gault [James's uncle] is indeed a redundant character. . . . James's pursuit of Daniel Echlin in the final chapters is out of character and a digression, as is his encounter with Sophia. True, that he should let himself be seduced by Sophia is in revealing contrast to his high-principled rejection of the whores provided by the Doctor when he was in hiding, but I'd be inclined to cut that passage too. The Cornwallis visit could be cut too and less made of Mrs Masterton.

The trouble arises not out of the shedding of 'redundant' characters but of the damage done to the architecture of the novel. The published novel's only (minor) fault is that, once established, James Gault is just another city merchant and his life and dreams are those of a grocer. All contradiction in his character has been erased. Excitement and drama pass him by (apart from one commercial setback). It is Kate Purdie, now his wife, who is left to deal with finality with the blackmailing Nugent Mullan who, heavily indebted to the unrecognised city merchant and sorely pressed by him, has suddenly realised that the respectable Kate is the 'plump morsel' whom he forced to strip on the day after Ballynahinch. The traumatic effect of Mullan's murder on Kate, and her agonised and impotent remorse at her incrimination of the doctor's amanuensis, Aeneas Gordon, leave her increasingly smug husband unmoved.

The episode of the seduction of Gault by Sophia that was part of the original novel, and the intended highlighting both of Gault's hypocrisy and his residual passion, would have given a balance to the somewhat headlong third section. Sophia had been his pupil, the niece of his benefactor Pringle Hazlett, and in a moment of rare tenderness she announces her love for him. In the final novel, Gault's rejection of her in mutually embarrassed confusion is the last we see of her. One cannot help feeling that the original episode might have wrung from the reader, as was clearly intended, a last piece of sympathy for an increasingly unpleasant character. In an interesting way the action level matches the character at different points in his evolution. At the novel's beginning, when a young rebel in his early twenties, Gault is vigorous and resourceful, brave and physically competent. He is more than a match for a fellow fugitive, William Kean, and is none the worse for a mud bath in the Lagan. His 'unco guid' response to the amoral Bannon and all his works is genuine and exemplary. But the love of money, as his New Testament might have warned him, proves to be the root of many evils, the chiefest a decline in self-awareness. The final seal on his moral dissolution is his shipping off to Canada of Hugh Purdie, who once idolised him, to prevent the embarrassment of having a radical brother-in-law. Gault dismisses Hugh to the care of Captain Ferguson, the master of the *John and Phoebe* bound for New Brunswick: 'There's twenty guineas there ...' As he looked at the small heap of gold he thought fifteen would have sufficed. This *aperçu* on the penultimate page is an even more effective comment on the title of the book than the last chill sentences:

'We've paid a big price, husband.'
James lowered his book. 'It'll be worth it, if he flourishes.'

He heard her sob as she rushed past him to the door.

A strange family, he sighed, leafing over a page.

Kate, the other main character, though a true daughter of the manipulative and corrupt Sim, is more consistent and has less distance to fall. She is a more effective cashier than her husband and just as ruthless in her self-centred manipulation of those who serve her. She brings Aggie, a schoolfriend, to be her housekeeper, and on the way to Belfast they talk of old times. But once in the town Aggie is relegated to the position of servant. Kate becomes so dependent upon her as resource and minion that she aborts a likely match between her and Hugh: 'So little Aggie McDowell stayed with the Gault family, her name changed to Agnes, her loyalty committed unquestioningly, her meat and raiment assured, her virginity sealed.' The other betrayal is much more deadly: that of allowing Aeneas Gordon to hang for her crime; it was Gordon who gave her as a wedding present the engraved pistol with which she killed Mullan and whose love for her was proved by his refusal to defend himself lest he might incriminate her.

There is not a preachy word in the book; Bell 'is fair to all his characters, even the most despicable, and lets them reveal themselves with a soft irony that is far more telling than any blood and thunder treatment', as Peter Sinclair put it in his favourable report for Hart-Davis, Macgibbon. The book depends on irony to make its point and it is the most relentless thing that Bell wrote; compared with it *The Hollow Ball* and *December Bride* seem wildly romantic. The moments of lyrical description that kept breaking into the earlier books are hard to find here. What does compensate for the harrowing of all the main characters is the sense of historical authenticity. The research was prodigious, though less than would be required for his next and last novel. The original 214-year span intended for the novel was reduced to four or five years. Instead of a linear chronology of how Belfast was 'dragged up from the swamp in the last hundred years', we are shown the seeds of time and can tell how they will grow.

At a significant moment of the book, perhaps the turning-point in Gault's character, he and his mentor Pringle Hazlett take a turn about the garden after dinner at Hazlett's country mansion at Stranmillis and look down at the town.

Below them the lights shone in broken rows and clusters. A single light, the most distant, crept at a steady pace across the darkness. The two men recognised it as the mast lantern of a vessel heading into the mouth of the river. In the town, lamps and candles set in windows pricked the gloom. Under a constellation of flaming torches, the fiery glow thrown back by tall gables, James could see men, like ants, working around a new house.

'*Belfast*,' said Mr Hazlett, slowly. 'They tell me that in the old tongue it means the place where men crossed the river on their journeys. Now we've come to halt on its banks. We are the dwellers at the ford. And prospering, James, draining, raising, prospering.'

The alternative, 'black' economy is personified by the grotesquely picturesque Bannon with his irregular army of thieves, bullies and whores. His liberal education (and quixotic kindness) do not disguise his ruthlessness and malevolence. This dwarfish polylingual ambivalent figure remains to haunt the reader, making a much greater impression than the main characters. It is no surprise that Bannon joins forces with the rascally Sim Purdie in his exploitation of the Catholic sharecroppers who work his steadily growing acreage – nor is it a surprise that the enigmatic, cultured Aeneas Gordon should become their go-between. In the end the tenants-at-will are driven murderously off their patches by a compliant militia: as an unidentified yeoman puts it: 'Papish rebels. Gie us the word, sir,' he said in an eager whisper, 'and we'll whitewash the walls wi' their blood.'

The ending of Bannon's empire can be seen as symbolic of change. His death, attended by Gault in a rare mood of charity, provides a moving setpiece. A quotation from *Julius Caesar* about the deaths of beggars, whispered ironically by Bannon, is the prelude to a near-revelation of the truth about Mullan's death.

The novel was generally well-received, except for a 'hatchet job' (as the diary entry for 23 August 1973 describes it) in the *Irish Times* by Barbara Bourke:

> it is quite well written, interesting in parts, but unless Mr Bell has a family connection with a possible James Gault, I cannot really understand why he expended the energy to write 250 pages on such a priggish, narrow-minded bore and his avaricious wife. . . . The North has often been neglected in Irish historical novels and it is a point in Mr Bell's favour that he has tried to rectify the situation. Unfortunately he has chosen a badly-lit and ill furnished shop window from which to

display his wares – James Gault, merchant supreme, would have known better than to do that.

The attacks are perhaps less offensive than the patronising pats on the head for readability and writing about the North. The review rankled for years, and shook Bell's confidence severely to the extent that four years later when we became friends he asked me to read the book and give my response. On 1 September Bell is happy to note a 'favourable, indeed enthusiastic review of AMF in today's *Irish Press* by a Beatrice Coogan. Very warming but wonder if this is not some private vendetta between Dublin female scribes.' In fact Beatrice Coogan (the mother of the paper's editor, Tim Pat Coogan, and widow of the first deputy commissioner of the Garda Síochána) knew her history and was sent the book for review by David Marcus because she had already written a historical novel, *The Big Wind* (1969). The anonymous reviewer in the *Times Literary Supplement* (24 August 1973) found that the novel 'helps to explain how the present "Troubles" are rooted in past battles, military and economic, which still haunt the Irish imagination'. When *A Man Flourishing* was reissued in 1986 by Blackstaff Press, Mary Leland, reviewing for the *Irish Times*, found it 'a substantial and satisfying read'.

17

'RETIRED' BROADCASTER

SINCE SAM HANNA BELL had not been anxious to relinquish the position of member of the 'established' staff of BBC Northern Ireland, it is fortunate that his official retirement turned out to be simply a kind of punctuation, a *reculer pour mieux sauter*. The finishing of *The Theatre in Ulster* and *A Man Flourishing* and the idea for an Ulster anthology did not blunt his interest in broadcasting, both in sound and vision. The features writer in Bell could not be stemmed, and the years of retirement produced not only several books but many excellent features for schools which, in the assessment of producer Douglas Carson, recalled the golden age of BBC radio features. The BBC archive held in the Ulster Folk Museum, Cultra, contains tapes of thirty-nine radio programmes made with Bell's involvement as writer or performer between 1970 and 1985. The offer made by Ronnie Mason that Bell should continue to do the series *Countrywide* had been happily accepted (see Chapter 14), and his papers suggest that the first programme went out on 26 October 1971: 'Modestly successful – sort of pilot programme,' he recorded in his diary. On 23 November, however, after another edition (praised by Mason as 'very enjoyable'), Bell decided that he did not want the series back even though it meant the loss of £40 a month: 'My idea of what a country broadcast should be is wholly at variance with the young set.'

Another fact that inhibited him at the very start of his retirement was the cap on the amount of extra income a BBC pensioner could earn, which meant that some offers of work from BBC Northern Ireland had to be refused. This regulation was not amended until 1975. He used an accountant in these retirement years, and on his instruction kept documentary evidence of legitimate expenditure for his 'vocation' of part-time writer and broadcaster.

Bell continued to live the life of the professional writer, still working in his upper room where so many words had already been written. The talks about literature, history and life (often memories of his own boyhood) that he wrote with such swift and elegant professionalism could be printed as articles in the *Belfast Telegraph* after having been broadcast on such magazine programmes as RTÉ's *Three-O-One*, earning '£7.50 per piece which is v. nice', as the diary entry for 13 September 1972 records. Some of this material appeared in extended form in articles for the *Ulster Tatler* and eventually was published in his collection *Tatler Tales*. Bell could delve into a vast store of accumulated knowledge on most aspects of Irish life and culture, particularly his 'native' province, and bring out appropriate material to be reworked and embellished for the particular purpose. This was especially true of the programmes he made for schools with producers Douglas Carson, David Hammond and Tony McAuley, who were all happy to have the services of the old master. As Carson recalled, Bell 'saw a chance of translating to Schools the energies that drove him in the fifties'.

Typical of Bell's imaginative work for schools broadcasting was the invention of the character Flames McKeown, a herring cadger whose father was such an unearthly performer on the uilleann pipes that the fairies stole him each night, much to the annoyance of his wife:

> If only, son, your da was playing at decent Christian hoolies, where he could earn an honest penny! He's so dead bate when he gets back in the morning that he's fit for nothing but putting away the pies and tumbling into bed.

Flames, who gets his herring fresh at Kilkeel, roves about County Down to sell them at three ha'pence for six. Eventually he seeks out the chief of the fairies, Sean MacAnanty, who lives under Scrabo Hill, and works out a deal according to which Dan the piper will be required only for 'May Eve and Hallowe'en, and such-like important occasions'. As a token of friendship, Flames is given a magical brass collar stud which secures him the services of a leprechaun – who proves as tricksy and bad-tempered as most of that breed. Bell's file, included in his paper, contains the script as broadcast on 14 January 1977, certain correspondence, and copies of three brilliant illustrations by Rowel Friers to be used in the schools brochure.

With a slightly different surname, Flames had sprung into life six and a half years before the broadcast, as a diary entry indicates: '4 October 1970: Opened page on "The Adventures of Flames McKenna".' In all Bell wrote four adventures for Flames. Though they were fanciful and played like stories, they subtly lived up to the implicit schools brief of the series *Today and Yesterday* (later *Today and Yesterday in Northern Ireland*). The first was broadcast as *The Travelling Man* on 30 October 1970 and was designated 'a semi-dramatised script' and produced by Douglas Carson. Two other Flames stories exist literally in manuscript form: 'The Four Reapers' and 'Flames Goes on an Errand'. (In 1971, Bell intended to write a book of Flames McKeown stories, intended specifically for children.)

Hammond, Carson and McAuley have each commented upon the rare ability Bell showed in his capacity as an educator. It is clear he would have made a splendid teacher, as his three producers, themselves ex-teachers, avouch. This was demonstrated in termly broadcasts called *Postbag*, which Bell compiled and introduced and which used original writing by young people. Tony McAuley believes that *Postbag*, together with the semi-dramatised programmes based upon his own boyhood in Raffrey, and the Flames McKenna/McKeown cycle prove that Bell would have been as remarkable a writer for children as he was a kindly and matter-of-fact interviewer. (Interestingly the music for the edition of *Postbag* broadcast on 13 June 1975 was supplied by the Phil Coulter Orchestra.) Such scripts as *The Tinker and His Three Wishes* (2 May 1975), *The King of Green Island* (3 October 1975), and three programmes about Fionn Mac Cumhaill (broadcast in October and November 1976), all produced by McAuley, certainly bear this out.

The topics chosen had to suit the audience for *Today and Yesterday* (broadly, the older children in primary schools). Certain themes and attitudes are predictable. *Bundle and Go*, transmitted on 14 May 1976, was summarised: 'This story follows the journey of the McIlveen family from their farm in Ayrshire, Scotland to a farm in Ireland in 1607'; it had recorded inserts from Edinburgh. It was followed a week later by

Across the Water, which Bell also wrote and in which he took part. This describes the McIlveens' settling in a farm near Newtownards and fending off an attack by displaced Irish whom the Planters called 'woodkerns'. These tales were from 'store', part of Bell's large body of work in progress, not all of which came to fruition; these particular themes were to gain their fullest expression in Bell's last novel, *Across the Narrow Sea*.

Bell's fertile imagination and remarkable knowledge of Ulster's history allowed some unlikely people to figure in his *Today and Yesterday* brief. One very successful programme dealt with the adventurer Edward Bruce, brother of the more famous, arachnophile Robert. Edward invaded Ireland in the early fourteenth century. The first *ard rí* since Rory O' Connor (d. 1198), he was the kind of anti-establishment figure who seemed to appeal to Bell. Edward Bruce was killed at Faughart, County Louth in 1318. Another subject was Lambert Simnel (*c*.1477–*c*.1534) the impostor who tried to oust Henry VII, the founder of the Tudor dynasty, claiming that he was the son of Edward IV and thus the rightful Plantagenet heir to the English throne. The dramatised account of his career was transmitted on 10 March 1982. Writers, too, were close to Bell's heart, and schools programmes on such old favourites as Allingham, Carleton, Goldsmith and Swift must have lightened the load of many an English teacher.

Among the significant figures of Ulster history who received the Bell treatment were the Huguenot exile from Picardy Samuel Louis Crommelin (1652–1727), 'Father of the Linen Industry'; Alexander Chesney, the eighteenth-century excise officer of Kilkeel and Annalong; Jemmy Hope (1764–*c*.1846), the Templepatrick weaver who rose with McCracken in 1798 and survived; Edward Bunting, the preserver of Irish music (1773–1843); Francis Crozier (1796–1848), the Banbridge explorer who perished on the Franklin expedition to find a northwest passage to Asia; and Vere Foster, the Belfast philanthropist (1819–1900). (Some of these programmes were adapted from earlier scripts, not all originally written by Bell.) Social life was not neglected: *The Ulster Railway*, a programme about the second Irish line – built in 1842 from Belfast to Lisburn and extended to Portadown – was transmitted on 21 September 1979; the programme *Turning Wheels* (4 September 1977, and apparently a new production of an earlier script) dramatised an early coach journey from Cornmarket in Belfast to Derry via Coleraine, and included among its actors a young man from Ballymena called Liam Neeson.

The schools brief included geography and folklore, and there were few in the Ulster of the time who knew the province better or were more cognisant of the nature of its changing folklife. One obvious linking of today and yesterday was supplied by the programmes *A Country Childhood* (16 January 1970) – in which Bell recalled in semi-dramatised form his own boyhood – and *Strangford Lough*, transmitted on 25 February 1975. The second of these dramatised a boy's youth, largely Bell's own, growing up near the lough shore, helping with the work of the farm, and going on cockle-raking excursions and boat trips; it also touched on the history of the place in the twelfth and fifteenth centuries.

What used to be called 'nature study' was catered for by programmes like *My Singing Bird* (15 June 1973) in which the characteristics of many types of birds, from wren to eagle, are distinguished, with poems and songs such as 'The Songs of the Birds' and 'The Little Red Lark' to illustrate their individual features. The programme concluded with a typical Bell flourish: a court session in which the birds decide who should be their king. His flair for unusual anthology programmes was seen in *Winter Customs* (21 November 1984) which featured poems by Joseph Campbell, Allingham, and his friend 'John O' The North' (Harry T. Brown), and prose by other old friends such as Michael J. Murphy, Joe Tomelty and Denis Ireland. A programme called *Oak, Ash and Thorn* transmitted in June 1973 was a lively reminder of the variety of, and need for conservation of, Ulster's trees. It was intended to encourage creative work by the listeners.

The producers involved still speak with a mixture of appreciation and awe about Bell's breadth of vision, the professionalism of his broadcasting, and the quality of both his scripts and performances. He was, of course, no newcomer to schools broadcasting: long before BBC Northern Ireland was given its own service he had supplied programmes to the network.

In all his work he was conscious of the need for appropriate music. His knowledge of the classical repertoire was extensive, and just as he had realised the need to preserve the dying folk music soon after his appointment to the BBC, so too in later decades he was aware of the recovery of traditional music and the growing popularity of such groups as the Chieftains, Planxty and the Bothy Band. Tony McAuley, who first met Bell when he was used as a singer for some of his features, is convinced that Bell was significant in making Ormeau Avenue aware of traditional music. Bell decried the relaying to Northern Ireland of such programmes as *The White Heather Club* and *The Kilt Is My Delight*: not because of any intrinsic faults, but because Ireland had its own songs, dances and folk traditions and did not need to rely upon Scottish imports. It was due to him in no small measure that such series as *Listen Here A While To Me* and *Sing North, Sing South*, which involved McAuley and Maurice Leitch (and which Bell occasionally introduced) enabled BBC Northern Ireland to be in the forefront of the 1960s folk revival. Up until then, the main gesture towards local music had been the popular but somewhat ersatz *Irish Rhythms*, which featured David Curry and his orchestra.

The indexing and publication of the Sam Henry Collection for which Bell was responsible were impressive enough achievements for any archivist. He was later to present a programme to celebrate Henry's work, which was broadcast five days after the centenary of the man's birth on 9 May 1878. It included David Hammond's well-known recording of 'The Wee Falorie Man', as well as 'Finvola, the Gem of the Roe', sung by Francie Brolly (which was to be the subject of one of Bell's last radio features). Certainly he chose the music for his programmes with care, often using it for atmosphere when it was not the actual theme of the programme. For *The Big Wind*, about the hurricane that struck Ireland on the night of 6 January 1839, he used dance music played by a band of young uilleann pipers. (Memory of the Big Wind was used in Ireland as proof of age when the old-age pension was introduced in 1909.) In *The Singing Town,* made at the height of the Troubles in May 1974, children were reminded of the rich store of street songs associated with Belfast in a more peaceful past. In March 1976 he delivered six *County Mixture* scripts to Ken Savidge, an Englishman who became a television producer in Belfast; Bell's diary records: 'work went smoothly enough except that I feel he has made some v. odd musical choices to illustrate counties'.

An Echo of Voices, written and presented by Bell and first broadcast in September 1974, was repeated as a tribute on 4 March 1990, a month after his death. It begins thus:

When I arrived in Broadcasting House in Belfast in the Autumn of

1945 it was an empty cavern of a building. In the months that followed, the echoes I heard were not so much those of voices as of the demolition of the air-raid shelters in Linenhall Street. Since then Broadcasting House, like my memory, has become a hive of voices.

The greater part of his career as a broadcaster was spent in radio, and like MacNeice and Gilliam, he played his part in defining the sound feature. But he was also interested in and anxious to come to terms with the new medium of television. As we have seen, his first appearance before the cameras was in December 1959 when he told a story from *Erin's Orange Lily* ('after laborious memorising'). Television was messier, full of *longueurs* and less lyrical; yet, as he recorded in his diary on 16 March 1960, it had its positive aspects:

> Introduced my first TV show 'The Lilt of Music' – a sort of St Patrick's Eve half-hour of Irish song, dance, etc. A tremendous success. Forty phone calls, letters, etc. This augurs ill for the future! For all that I seem to have some small flair for the picture box that the people like.

One can sense the scant respect for the 'picture box', but also the realisation that the golden days of radio were coming to an end. He also introduced the series *Make Music*, which ran from 23 October 1963 until the March of the following year, and he was occasionally in demand for programmes that were essentially radio anthologies adapted for television – sometimes including dancers. Typical were *Christmas Eve* (24 December 1962) and *For Heaven's Sake* (23 January 1963).

In 1964 he wrote and presented a television feature, *Water from the Rock*, about the building of the Mourne reservoir at Silent Valley. It was one of several programmes devised by him about the Mournes, beginning on radio with *Kingdom of Mourne* (22 May 1946). Others included *The Mountains of Mourne* (16 March 1969), done as part of a series for Radio Four called *Holidays in Britain*; 'Fishing at Kilkeel', a piece written as teaching notes for a David Hammond programme on 3 March 1970; and *Look Stranger: Mountains of Mourne* (27 October 1971). *Water from the Rock* was shown on 30 September 1964. It began with a shot of Bell speaking to camera at the Ben Crum Reservoir. A few minutes later he mentions that

> the two dams are fed by springs and mountain streams, clean clear water rising through granite sand – a very different matter from the source used by the early inhabitants of Belfast – the busy malodorous Farset that runs down High Street.

There was, of course, a singer to beguile those suffering from too much straight narration. One song serendipitously trawled described the rail-track specially built from Annalong Harbour to draw anthracite, cement and other materials to the dam:

> I am a bold engine-driver;
> From Annalong Harbour I go
> Along the switchback to the Valley
> With my big load of granite and coal.

The programme ends with the observation that Belfast continues to grow and that the water commissioners are looking for other sources of water:

> But the Silent Valley will be the main source for many years to come. From its mountain-shadowed reservoirs and running streams thousands of millions of gallons of pure water will pour out to satisfy the thirst of a city.

Other television programmes that he made while still on the staff of BBC Northern Ireland include *The Trident Port* (25 March 1966) and profiles of his friends the artist William Conor (11 February 1968), Joe Tomelty (17 March 1971) and Michael J. Murphy (8 June 1971). The series *I Remember* (1969), produced by Gerry McCrudden, showed Bell to be as good in front of the cameras as behind the microphone. As Douglas Carson notes in an *Irish Review* article:

> When television came to Northern Ireland, the cameras were at first reserved for others: Sam felt excluded from production and direction. He contributed, however, as writer and interviewer, as critic and presenter, and as a source of ideas. In black and white there were archival conversations with painters like William Conor and actors like R.H. McCandless. He also worked in colour, and on film: in 1975, for instance, he conducted viewers round the Ulster Folk Museum; and in 1976 ... he explored the river Lagan from its source to the sea.

Bell's appearance could cause the first-time viewer a little perplexity. Rowel Friers, who provides a superb pen drawing of him in his autobiography *Drawn from Life* (1994), describes this nicely:

> I first met Sam Hanna Bell at the Hewitts' flat. There were many characters there, but only one stuck out that night in my eyes. Perhaps it was because it was my first sighting of Sam, but I still think it was

because of the fact that he was seated lower than everybody else. He was on a stool and I thought, That's a big man, he must be about six foot six, at least. He had a towering brow, with fair, bushy eyebrows pulled down, throwing his piercing blue eyes into shadow. A large romanesque nose hung over and dominated a straw-coloured moustache, an exact match of his eyebrows. All this was set off by a large and very determined-looking chin. Every now and then he would twitch his nose, close his eyes and thrust his chin forward – a nervous habit that served only to emphasise or draw attention to the strength of his face. Huge hands rested on his knees and these, too, added to the impression of a really big man. When he stood up he shrank to being an averaged-sized person with above average head and hands. The head was an essential for the brain he had, and the hands he certainly put to good use.

In 1974 Moore Wasson prepared a television portrait of the north Antrim coast. The result was *Proud Dunluce* (subtitled *A North Antrim Idyll*), recorded in June 1974. It told the story of the McDonnell castle on the north Antrim coast and gave the lore of the surrounding countryside. There were stories about Dunluce, the Giant's Causeway and the wreck of the Armada galleon the *Girona*. The music included a translation of 'Airde Cuain' and a song by David Hammond about 'The Causeway Tram'. As Bell's diary records the filming:

> 20 June 1974: For this I chose a number of pieces of prose and verse which, although they had no direct connection with the place, seemed to me to lend themselves to the history and legends of the castle. All went passably well – some nice speaking from Bill Hunter, Aine McCartney and Barry Cowan – two good young singers. My contribution rather marred towards the end (late Tuesday evening) by rain which blurred everything – including my cue card!

Bell continued to work in both radio and television until the end of the 1980s. His work included reviews for various arts programmes on radio and television, thumbnail sketches of characters from Ulster's past – his particular forte – and versions of books for dramatisation or reading. Among these were his own *December Bride* (prepared for *A Book at Bedtime* and read by Margaret D'Arcy in 1974); *The Gates* by Jennifer Johnston (abridged in five parts for reading by Kate Binchy in May 1975); *The Hard Road to Klondike* (February 1976) from Val Iremonger's translation of Mici Mac Gabhann's autobiography *Rotha Mór an tSaoil*

(The wheel of destiny); and ten fifteen-minute episodes of Synge's *The Aran Islands* (under the title *An Island of Love*). He wrote about Amanda McKittrick Ros, but was disappointed that a feature on John Steinbeck's maternal grandparents (who came from Eglinton) could not be broadcast because Steinbeck's publishers would not give permission for the use of quotations from the novel *East of Eden*. Bell was often asked to contribute to features about writers he had known: F.L. Green, Louis MacNeice, George Shiels, John O'Connor. He also took part in programmes on institutions dear to his heart – a radio feature on the Linen Hall Library and a film about the Ulster Folk Museum, for example.

The last programme I can trace was *Finvola, Gem of the Roe*, about the heroine of the ballad which describes the love match of the princess of the O'Cahans and Angus MacDonnell, the lord of Islay. A letter written on 18 October 1988 to the producer Kathryn Porter to accompany the script contains the remark 'nothing improves a script like cuts'. It was a wryly characteristic conclusion to a long script-cutting career.

18

WITHIN OUR PROVINCE AND TATLER TALES

S AM HANNA BELL WAS ESSENTIALLY A WRITER. In the twenty years of his retirement he was rarely idle and never without a project. Between 1960 and 1987, in addition to his broadcasting work, he was engaged in the slow process of writing two novels. He also found time for two 'little' books that reflect his local knowledge – and local patriotism. These were *Within Our Province* and *Tatler Tales*.

The idea of a miscellany of Ulster writing had been in his head for some time, since at least the time of the writing of *Erin's Orange Lily*, but it had its origin in the many journeys and features of BBC days. The first recorded reference is the diary entry for 20 January 1972:

> Discussed with Jim Gracey my idea for an Ulster Miscellany – a sort of chapbook of refs. to Ulster. He is interested in the idea as a publishing project for the Blackstaff Press and asked me to go ahead.

On 13 February 1972 Bell visited Jim and Diane Gracey at their home in Wandsworth Road, Knock, to discuss 'my idea of an Ulster Miscellany to be published by Blackstaff Press'. As the diary entry records: 'Favourable response and I'm to go ahead and compile.' Three weeks later the letter of confirmation arrived from Blackstaff. 'Odd clause: – "Clearance of copyright would be in your hands, and any fees would be at your expense." I've never come across such a stipulation before.' The reaction of David Higham, Bell's agent, was equally unenthusiastic:

'My agents don't think much of it. Have suggested that Blackstaff could cover first £50.00.' The matter must have been resolved by 16 October, the date of the drawing-up of the contract, since there is no mention there of the author's responsibility for clearance and payment of copyright.

Two thirds of the text was delivered to the Graceys on 29 June 1973, and the balance was ready by 3 August. One of the diary entries describes Bell's returning the letters of Mrs Delany (1700–88), the great Georgian Irish correspondent, friend of Swift and wife of the Dean of Down, to the Ulster Folk Museum: 'Have made some extracts for W.O.P.' The book was due to be published 'late in October', presumably to catch the Christmas market. By 6 December Bell had delivered the first half of the corrected proofs. He noted that there had been an obvious delay and that the book should be ready by 18 December. In fact it was not ready until 22 December, as the diary entry for that day makes clear:

> Today (and a few yesterday) *Within Our Province* made its appearance. Jim Gracey has had a most awful time getting it into the bookshops before Xmas. . . . My book – a meagre 500 – looks well with the illustrations excellently chosen and placed by Diane Gracey. . . . J.G. is upset and v. angry at the treatment he has had from printers. Lost out just before the Christmas rush.

One of several inadequacies of the book is the lack of a list of credits for the illustrations. Of thirty-two of these, thirteen are by Seaghan Mac Cathmhaoil, and eight by 'C-M'; with the exception of an engraving of the White Linen Hall in Belfast done by Clayton and Nelson, they are all unlabelled. The Gaelic name partially hides the identity of John Patrick Campbell (1883–1962), who was the brother of the poet Joseph Campbell, the subject of one of Bell's features for schools, *The Mountainy Singer* (5 February 1971). 'C-M' was *Ceann-Maor* (literally, 'head keeper') which was the name Joseph Campbell used for his own line drawings and which decorated his book of verse *The Rushlight* (1906). The younger brother's illustrations are a mixture of Beardsley and early Yeats and were originally used as illustrations in *Ulad* and as such were entirely appropriate for inclusion in *Within Our Province*. 'C-M' was also an apt choice and his meticulously executed drawings and woodcuts of turf fires, curraghs, bellows, churns, psalters and creels increase the pleasure of the book.

The book also lacks a table of contents and a biographical index, and any reissue should include these. It begins with John Hewitt's fine fricative poem 'Ulster Names' – 'each clean hard name like a weathered stone' – and finishes with an envoi by William Allingham. In between those two sober poets are accounts of Ulster life and character. Mrs Delany appears three times, disapproving of horse racing, the rural diet, and fashion:

> I am very sorry . . . that wine and tea should enter where they have no pretence to be, and usurp the rural flood of syllabub, etc. But the dairy-maids wear large hoops and velvet hoods instead of the round tight petticoat and straw hat, and there is as much foppery introduced in the food as in the dress – the pure simplicity of the country is quite lost.

There is Lord Dufferin on a dinner in Government House in Reykjavik in which he matched his host glass for glass, for the honour of the Irish peerage. There are excerpts from the journal of John Tennent, apprenticed to Samuel Givin, grocer, Coleraine, July 1786–July 1790 recording '– a continued round of insipidity and vexation being obliged to keep company to a man I hate'. And there are inclusions from old friends, both actual and literary, such as William Carleton, Shan F. Bullock, Forrest Reid, Michael J. Murphy, Robert Lynd, E. Estyn Evans, Mary Ann McCracken (1770–1866), Æ (1867–1935), St John Ervine (1883–1971), Richard Rowley, Robert Lloyd Praeger (1865–1953), Lynn Doyle, Denis Ireland, Bertie Rodgers, David Kennedy, Jack Loudan, and Ralph Bossence of the *Belfast News-Letter*. The earliest piece is a translation by J.J. Campbell of a piece from *Aislinge meic Conglinne*, the medieval vision of a world composed entirely of food and drink, as seen by a clerical student at Armagh. Chronologically there is a leap of five hundred years to the next entry, also gluttonous, describing a Christmas entertainment in Lecale in 1603 ('There were pies of venison and various kinds of game; pasties also, some of marrow, with innumerable plums; others which they call Tarts, of divers shapes, material and colours, made of beef, mutton and veal.')

As well as literary inclusions there were many short page-fillers:

> So dense were the woods in the time of our forefathers that a man might make his way from MacArt's fort [Cave Hill] at Belfast to Lisnagarvagh [Lisburn] without his foot touching aught than the tops of the trees.

When a weaver had woven 40 yards or a 'cut' he was paid for his work. Too often he went to the pub and got cut with the money. Sometimes the linen merchant paid out a 'sub' when a 'half-cut' was woven. Hence the expression 'he's half-cut' meaning that someone is half drunk.

Kilrea for drinking tay,
Garvagh for asses,
Limavady for Irish lace
And Coleraine for lasses.

The book also contains the authentic text of the often-corrupted 'Ballad of William Bloat' by Raymond Calvert (1906–59). Another extract concerns a horse whisperer, a man from Mayobridge, who could cure farcy (glanders) by speaking 'in a very low voice into the horse's ear'. Finally Bell included anonymously two *aperçus* of his own, taken from the radio feature *In Praise of Ulster*. 'Ulster: where every hill has its hero and every bog its bones'; and 'Armagh: where two cathedrals sit upon opposing hills like the horns of a dilemma'.

In a letter to Tom Adair written in September 1987, which accompanied a copy of *Within Our Province*, Bell mentions that most of the copies were destroyed in a bomb attack on Blackstaff's store in Wellington Place.

Tatler Tales was published in 1981. It was a selection from a series of stories that Bell had retold for the *Ulster Tatler* with the general title 'It Takes All Kinds'. The first story, 'Sweet Dolly Monroe', about an eighteenth-century beauty from County Down who almost became the wife of Viceroy Townshend, appeared in February 1969. The stories continued regularly, with at least ten each year until August 1977. (Two months later Bell's main energies were to be devoted to the *Ulster Tatler*'s Literary Miscellany.) Altogether, there is a store of more than ninety published pieces. The book simply repackaged eighteen of the tales, retaining the original print from the magazine, and was published by Ulster Journals, the holding firm for the *Ulster Tatler*. The result was startling in its typographical variety, but the stories, as the cover describes them, 'in various moods, dramatic, humorous or eerie', were well-written and engrossing. There was no attempt at editing or annotation and, apart from a flyleaf note explaining that they had appeared in the *Ulster Tatler*, no introduction.

The idea for the book had surfaced some time before 22 October 1973. As a diary entry indicates, on that date Bell had coffee with the Graceys to plan a Christmas sales campaign for the paperback edition of *Within Our Province*:

> At the same time discussed a new book for Blackstaff Press, *The Clue of the Four Soldiers and Other Strange Tales* which I'll draw from UT [the *Ulster Tatler*]. Jim and Diane Gracey v. interested in the idea and I've to go ahead and collect material.

The matter is not mentioned again until 29 August 1975 when Bell called at Blackstaff Press and 'Diane Gracey expressed interest in my idea for a book of "strange tales" and suggested it might range outside Northern Ireland. I promised to look into the idea further.' On 5 February 1976 he delivered nine 'strange' tales to Blackstaff and there the story ends as far as the diary can show.

The nine stories submitted to Blackstaff were 'Sweet Dolly Monroe'; 'The Hounds of Auld', a ghost story, also from Down; 'The Golden Boat of Broighter' about the treasure discovered near Limavady in 1896; 'The Clue of the Four Soldiers' (this had been broadcast as a dramatised feature on 15 May 1962), about the capture and execution in 1823 of a murderer called Bernard McCann from Newtownhamilton; 'The Flower of Sweet Prehen', the story of the famous 'Half-hanged MacNaughton' and his killing of Mary Anne Knox; 'The Ordeal of Mary Dunbar', about a witchcraft case in Islandmagee in 1711; 'The Doctor from Nowhere', the story of a nineteenth-century confidence trickster calling himself Dr Pinkston Blackwood and his activities in Bangor; 'He Lies in Armagh Jail', about a Clones murder case; and 'The Ghost that Crossed Water', the story of a Fermanagh family haunted by mysterious tappings and other phenomena associated with a poltergeist.

Of these, three (the second, the fifth and the eighth described above) were not printed in the book but there were plenty more to choose from. The final selection must have been based upon quality and perhaps popularity. The dozen chosen to complete the text included four about murder ('The Poisonous Cherry', 'The Terrible Affair at Croft Lodge', 'The Treacherous Nephew', and 'An Eye to Murder'). Six others also concerned the law: Charles Macklin (?1697–1797), the great Irish actor, arraigns the claque who nearly drove him out of business;

Daniel O'Connell, the greatest of Irish pleaders, 'catches a shark with a fly' in a marvellous revelation that a pun could constitute perjury; the successful counsel in a breach of promise case is horsewhipped by his female client; a woman appeals to the House of Lords in 1864; a court-martial takes place in Newry after a duel; and a supernatural witness helps to settle a Carrickfergus court case.

Though admittedly journeywork, Bell's 'It Takes All Sorts' series for the *Ulster Tatler* nevertheless deserves a more substantial and accessible publication than *Tatler Tales*. The picture the stories present of Irish – and particularly Ulster – life in the eighteenth and nineteenth centuries is fascinating. It is to be hoped that this archive will find a suitable editor.

19
LITERARY MISCELLANY

T HE FIRST MENTION OF THE LITERARY MISCELLANY occurs in the diary entry for 2 August 1977:

> Invited to lunch at Balmoral by Dick and Noreen Sherry of UT [the *Ulster Tatler*]. They want a literary section in the magazine. We discussed this at length and I got the feeling that they were really serious about it this time. [There had been several abortive attempts before.] Noreen admitted that they should have appointed an editor to look after the intake and selection of material. This Dick and Noreen proceeded to do: they asked me to take the idea away and consider it. Remuneration – £70 per month. The idea appeals: I like editing and it would be an excellent opportunity for local writers.

Bell was by then an old *Ulster Tatler* hand. As well as the 'It Takes All Sorts' stories, he had written a column with the general title 'Talking about Books', which appeared intermittently between April 1968 and February 1970.

At about this time he also became a kind of informal literary editor. Dick and Noreen Sherry felt they could not decide themselves about the merit of an increasing number of unsolicited articles, mostly of literary, historical, or local interest. They also relied upon Bell to provide reviews of the occasional books that were sent for consideration.

Among Bell's papers are short reports, recommendations to print, and as many rejections. 'An article on the Brontës is a good idea but [this] is not well enough written for the *Tatler*.' 'Hanging over the Half-door *and* May Day in South Armagh. Both very nice articles. The May Day one would be particularly appropriate for the May issue. It is the better of the two.' 'I would say *no* to this article. It is not well-enough informed and consists of too much long quotation from Moira O'Neill's verse, all of which is still subject to copyright payment.' The response was as ever professional, astringent but enthusiastic about worth. To become the editor of a proper and permanent literary section was manifest destiny.

By the June 1978 Elgy Gillespie was drawing the attention of the readers of the *Irish Times* to the section's existence:

> The *Ulster Tatler Literary Miscellany* is a fairly new section edited by Sam Hanna Bell, and augurs well to be as much of a fairy godmother as New Irish Writing is in the South. To date, it has shown itself of a very high standard and though you can't buy it down here, southern poets like John F. Deane and Padraig Daly have been welcomed. It also pays well (£5 for a poem).

Elgy Gillespie had published a profile of Bell in the *Irish Times* on 30 December 1977 in which he had approved the work done by David Marcus in the New Irish Writing page of the *Irish Press*. Then well into its tenth year, the page had not only published new work of established Irish writers but had also been tremendously influential in its discovery and encouragement of new ones. In reply to a letter from Marcus (already mentioned in Chapter 8) Bell gives his own account of the experiment:

> You may be interested in the beginnings of the *Ulster Tatler* Literary Miscellany. It was the idea of Richard and Noreen Sherry, editors and directors of the UT. We didn't know how the readers of a firmly established glossy/commercial journal would take it. Approvingly, it would seem. Anyway, they tell me sales have increased. My friends rallied round willingly; Michael and Edna Longley, Ray and Judith Rosenfield, Maurice Leitch, Paul Muldoon and John Hewitt, and the two new luminaries, Sam McAughtry and John (Confessions of Proinsias O'Toole) Morrow, have all sent me material. Short stories seem hard to come by. There has been so little opportunity in the

North. In my day we broadcast about two stories a week from NI BBC. Now it seems one a month. In a word I hope that the story-writers will come to realise that the Miscellany is in existence, and for them.

The dearth of short stories was remedied by an *Ulster Tatler* competition run in collaboration with the BBC; entries had to be between 2,250 and 2,500 words 'to suit Paul Muldoon' for the broadcast, and the closing date was 28 February 1979. The first prize of £100 was won by Ian Wilson of Bangor, who wrote to Bell on 24 June thanking him for his 'telegram and subsequent letter'. He was also pleased with the way his story was read on *Bazaar* (a Radio Ulster literary programme of the time): 'Several short passages which I wasn't consciously aware of as being significant to the whole gained importance through the sympathetic reading.'

Once in its stride, the Literary Miscellany was usually about six pages long with stories, poems, four to five review articles and (as often as possible) an appraisal of a literary figure or work. These appraisals were usually commissioned. My own reappraisals included *My Lady of the Chimney Corner* (1913) by Alexander Irvine (1863–1941); the novels of Peadar O'Donnell; *Come Day, Go Day* (1948) by John O'Connor; the non-comic work of Joseph Tomelty; the folk writings of Michael J. Murphy; *Father Ralph* by Gerald O'Donovan (1871–1942); and the fiction of Julia O'Faolain. Other writers who contributed literary articles included: Robert Greacen on Forrest Reid, Patrick MacGill, Kathleen Coyle, Rudyard Kipling, Patrick Kavanagh, Joyce Cary, Robert Lynd and Robert Graves; Sophia Hillan King (who also contributed stories and was a runner-up in the competition) on Charles Lever and Maria Edgeworth; Derek Stanford on Dylan Thomas, William Allingham, and Sheridan Le Fanu; and J.J. Campbell on Samuel Ferguson.

Some contributors to the Literary Miscellany were established writers. Roy McFadden, for example, wrote reviews and poems and 'some nine or ten short stories'. Others were new. As ever, the rejection slip was the editor's friend, but often refusal was mitigated by comment. Bell's *Ulster Tatler* file contains many letters that accompanied submitted manuscripts: these letters are invariably annotated with short indications of response. Mostly the annotations are as brief as 'rtd' followed by the date. Sometimes one finds 'returned with note of encouragement on rejection slip'. On occasion the response is mildly cynical: 'returned with "helpful" note'. At the foot of a letter offering a sonnet, Bell wrote: 'His "sonnet" was a piece of doggerel, 56 lines long.' When the material had worth, he usually wrote a letter pointing out flaws, for example: 'It seems to me that [this] lacks the fluency and ease of the earlier story.' Elsewhere a writer is advised to choose a better title and devise a more satisfactory conclusion. One such letter which had advised that the writer should not 'burden nouns with such a load of adjectives' concludes with a heartfelt maxim: 'A warning: be careful of people who want to rewrite your story.' One typical note reads: 'Editor Regrets with "sorry – I felt that I should have been more moved by this."' Only rarely does one come upon such an extreme response as: 'Awful!' The writer of one rejected Christmas story received the following reminder: 'I should add that material intended for Christmas ... should be submitted no later than September.'

In October 1980 the Literary Miscellany was three years old and as part of the birthday celebrations a partial list of the contributors was given:

> This month Literary Miscellany enters its fourth year. It was initiated in September 1977 to offer the readers of *Ulster Tatler* a selection of interesting reading and to give writers, established and new, an opportunity to have their work published. Contributors in the three years have included: Maurice Leitch, Sean Breslin, Paul Muldoon, Ruth Baker, Sean McMahon, Derek Stanford, Paul Wilkins, Michael J. Murphy, Edna Longley, John Cronin, Robert Greacen, Sam McAughtry, Leland Bardwell, Robin Glendinning, Patric Stevenson, Meta Mayne Reid, Frances McEnaney, Ann Ruthven, John Morrow, Shirley Toulson, Roy McFadden, Jack McQuoid, Ewart Milne, Norman Harrison, Ray Rosenfield, Medbh McGuckian, Michael Longley, Anne Hartigan, Padraig J. Daly.

In 1981, a little weary of 'poetry' and in the hope of encouraging lighter prose material, Bell asked regular contributors including Robert Greacen, myself and others to write the sort of articles that were the staple of the magazines and periodicals of the first half of the twentieth century and that were then unashamedly called 'essays'. The names of such expert practitioners as E.V. Lucas (1868–1938), or Alpha of the Plough – the pseudonym of A.G. Gardiner (1865–1946) – or Belfast's own Robert Lynd meant little or nothing to the readers of the 1970s, but their work was the ideal Bell aimed at. So Robert Greacen wrote as

Jack Pembridge, I as John Benedict. The pieces were personal, ephemeral, generally unpretentious, and rarely rejected.

The *Ulster Tatler* for September 1982 was mildly and justifiably self-congratulatory:

> The Literary Miscellany completes its fifth year this month. When it was introduced in October 1977, its main purpose was to extend the interest and entertainment of *Ulster Tatler* readers. But it was realised that new writers would welcome the chance to have their work published in a region where opportunities are limited.
>
> In the five-year period there have appeared in the Literary Miscellany over one hundred original short stories, one hundred and fifty poems and numerous articles on writers and their work. A feature, Tailpiece, was introduced a year ago to facilitate the publication of articles of a general nature.
>
> On its introduction the Miscellany was welcomed by established writers and the Literary Editor would like to express his thanks particularly for their practical contributions to the reviews section.

One contributor to the Literary Miscellany came out of a completely different sphere in Bell's life. He was an assiduous philatelist: one large box file among his papers is crowded with correspondence with dealers. His main interest was in Republic of Ireland stamps. A fellow enthusiast combined stamps and literature in an ingenious way that interested Bell. This was Robert A. Dunbar who, before his move to the staff of the Church of Ireland College of Education in Rathmines in 1980, had taught in Rainey Endowed School, Magherafelt. The point of contact between Bell and Dunbar was *Lit-Phil* (1977), a typescript journal produced by Dunbar with articles about famous literary figures featured on stamps worldwide. The first number was published in January 1975 and included Bell among the list of founder members. It included news of stamp issues with a literary element. It noted that Greece had marked the 150th anniversary of the death of Lord Byron in 1824, and that the United States had commemorated the centenary of the birth of the New England poet Robert Frost. It also looked forward to the 1975 British issues that would celebrate the bicentenary of the birth of Jane Austen with stamps showing characters from *Emma*, *Northanger Abbey*, *Pride and Prejudice* and *Mansfield Park*.

The next issue, that of April 1975, contained a short piece by Bell about how the theme of 'Literature on Stamps' should be interpreted.

He felt that a literary stamp should bear a portrait of the writer it commemorated, and he was looking forward, 'through *Lit-Phil*, to learning from more experienced collectors the most fitting manner in which to write up my thematic collection'. It was clear that Dunbar put a great deal of work into his magazine, and that his efforts were appreciated by a host of thematic collectors. Preserved in the same file as the Dunbar correspondence and the copies of *Lit-Phil* is a list from a Liverpool firm offering examples of 'Literature on Stamps' and 'Music on Stamps'. Some issues are to be expected: Dante and Ariosto in Italy, Stephen Leacock in Canada, Robert Louis Stevenson in Samoa. But they also include Dickens in the Cayman Islands and Shakespeare in Panama.

In a letter to Dunbar on 3 February 1976, Bell said he had hoped to write for *Lit-Phil* on either James Clarence Mangan or Tomás Ó Criomhthain, author of the Blasket Island autobiography *An tOileánach* (1929), both of whom had figured on Irish stamps. 'But I've been so busy on my own work (a pensioner can't afford to pass up on an assignment these days) that I didn't get a chance to do the background reading.' In April 1978 he wrote again to Dunbar saying that he had begun to edit the Literary Miscellany and asking him to submit an article:

I'm thinking of something on 'Literature and Stamps' or some title of that nature. Length about 1,000 words at current *Tatler* rate of £12.50. If the idea appeals to you, you could base it on Irish–British issues or roam wider. The only guidance I would suggest is that the emphasis should be on the literary aspect, as the readers of the *UT* are likely to be a non-philatelic audience.

Dunbar was still living in Magherafelt at the time and promised a piece within a fortnight. A letter written two years later from the college in Rathmines indicates that Dunbar was happy to be in Dublin and anxious to start writing mainly critical articles. He wanted to make a start 'by enquiring of yourself and the "Ulster Tatler" '. Bell's answer gives an incidental account of the system under which the *Ulster Tatler* operated:

Articles should be about 1,500 words or so, dealing with literary or historical works – single books, and/or authors and their output. These pieces are particularly welcome; but if the idea appeals to you, please let me know what you had in mind, as we've covered quite a range of writers in the Miscellany.

Because of economies a radical change has taken place in the review situation. Publishers no longer send out books on 'spec'. Nowadays I write to publishers requesting titles from their lists. In the Republic, Poolbeg Press send us a pretty comprehensive selection for review; O'Brien Press and Gill and Macmillan occasionally, and Mercier of Cork infrequently.

In fact the reviews were remarkably wide-ranging, though naturally with a tendency for the books to be of Irish, and if possible, Ulster interest. History and literature predominated, but not in a highbrow way. Accessibility without writing down was Bell's policy. Such works as *The Irish Renaissance* by Richard Fallis, *The Meaning of Irish Placenames*, by James O'Connell, *A Belfast Woman* by Mary Beckett, *The Anglo-Irish Novel I* by John Cronin, and *Silver's City* by Maurice Leitch were reviewed alongside *The Agatha Christie Who's Who*, the Hong Kong thriller *Sci-Fi* by William Marshall, *Will* by G. Gordon Liddy (of Watergate burglary fame), *The Official Sloane Ranger Handbook*, Barry Norman's *The Movie Greats*, and *Three Women* by Nancy Thayer, a quintessential 'woman's book'. The editor used his right of anonymity to review books that interested him, using either the pseudonym Finlay McIlveen or the more obscure R.F.K.

The Literary Miscellany was successful but it meant a great deal of work for Bell, including commissioning articles, dealing with review copies, reading unsolicited manuscripts (including often dire verse), chasing fees and trying to improve proofreading. By the beginning of 1983, he was ready to relinquish the editorship. He wrote to Dick Sherry on 24 February.

After considerable thought I have decided to retire from the editorship of the Literary Miscellany.

Needless to say I have come to this decision with regret. If the opinion of readers can be relied upon the Miscellany has been a success. I very much appreciated the confidence of Noreen and yourself in entrusting the work to me and I certainly enjoyed the challenge of compiling the feature month by month. The *Ulster Tatler* is due a considerable amount of praise in encouraging new writing.

Now at the end of five years I feel that the Miscellany is falling into a set formula. My BBC experience warns me that this is the time for fresh thinking on the project. Apart from that I am beginning to find the work a bit of a strain – I'm in my seventy-fourth year!

Needless to say I'll carry on for the next month or two or until such time as you appoint a successor.

As it turned out, the last Literary Miscellany that Bell was responsible for was that of May 1983. After that, Sean Breslin took over for a few years. With typical efficiency Bell made a list of unpublished but accepted material so that the handover could be achieved without disruption. The Literary Miscellany for June carried a boxed item which read:

Six years ago it was decided to add a literary section to the *Ulster Tatler*. Sam Hanna Bell was appointed editor; no better choice could have been made. He was a distinguished novelist, critic and literary historian while his long and fruitful service in the BBC had earned for him the respect and indeed the affection of the Irish literary world. He was therefore uniquely fitted for the task of bringing into being and nurturing the magazine's Literary Miscellany, his own chosen precise title.

His aims were threefold. The Miscellany would be an outlet for Irish writers in a society where they are not as plentiful as they should be. The Miscellany would encourage Irish publishers. Finally – and of equal importance – it would give pleasure to the readers of the *Ulster Tatler*.

His success is manifest. The list of contributors reads like a *Who's Who* of Irish writing. Established writers have been generous in their support and new writers have been given their opportunity.

There is nothing quite like Sam Hanna Bell's Miscellany in the British or Irish magazine world.

We pay here our tribute to the man who created it and whose efforts have been so successful. We hope to maintain his standards.

In fact the Literary Miscellany was Bell's own invention: he had given it its shape and, with the old broadcaster's sense of audience, he knew both how to present a pleasingly balanced edition and when to close. The material was remarkable in its variety and though it could not command the same standards of writing as Marcus's New Irish Writing it was an important part of the literary life of the North in a dark period of the Troubles. It was 'a little magazine' as significant as *Rann*, *Threshold* – and even *Lagan*.

20
ACROSS THE NARROW SEA

THE USEFUL STUDY OF SAM HANNA BELL that Deborah Keys made for her 1982 MA dissertation concludes with an excerpt from his last novel, *Across the Narrow Sea*, which was subsequently published by Blackstaff Press, in 1987. It was characteristically kind of Bell to allow this exposure of work in progress. The excerpt is in fact in its final form (it appears early in the finished novel, as pages 38–43 of the 299-page published book). The text features some passages of Ulster Irish put in the mouths of members of the Mac Cartan family – indigenous Gaels who have lost their best lands in the Ulster plantation which, at the time of the novel's action, 1608, has just begun – as well as passages of Scottish Gaelic spoken by the hero, Neil Gilchrist. These texts were obtained from a friend who was an honours student in the Celtic studies department of Queen's University Belfast in 1979 (and who afterwards received an inscribed copy of the book). It is evidence of the deliberate and meticulous nature of Bell's approach to his novels that the book took at least eleven years from the original idea to its successful realisation. At the book launch held in the Linen Hall Library on 27 June 1987, Bell joked that if anyone in the audience had a burning interest in researching the period he had a trunkful of papers that he would gladly relinquish.

He was not exaggerating the amount of research he had carried out: filled notebooks, typescripts and a drift of papers (usually the backs of old broadcast scripts, plus used envelopes carefully rendered into their original rectangles), the contents written mainly in pencil, show just how precisely he investigated matters of dress, farm implements, weapons, roads and other aspects of terrain, shipping, the nature of the kirk and school house, the anomalous position of the original Gaelic aristocracy, and the language. Among many interesting files in the Bell papers was a *Glossary of Words and Phrases used in Down and Antrim*. These dialect words were the residue of the lexis of the Galloway settlers who created the new order in northeast Ulster.

The use of Lallans by the people who crossed 'the narrow sea' – from Portpatrick in Galloway to Donaghadee in County Down, a distance of something less than twenty-two miles as the coble, with a following wind, flew – fascinated Bell. All through his life he kept something of a Scots cadence in his own speech, and he retained the dialect words of his childhood. Since these were preserved in the aspic of rural isolation they were as appropriate for the Echlins of *December Bride* as for their grander forebears in *Across the Narrow Sea*. Though highly salted with dialect words, the vocabulary of the MacIlveens and the Purdies presents the Irish reader with no difficulties. As with, say, the plays of Synge, the exotic vocabulary is soon acquired and the flavour is relished.

For this book, for the first time as a novelist, Bell had an editor. As he put it with wry resignation in a letter to Tom Adair dated 11 May 1987:

> The Ms has undergone the strictures of Jeanne Marie Finlay, an editor, the first time this has happened to me (which shows how long it is since I wrote anything substantial). Her concern for the 'lazy reader' – what would he/she do with a dozen or so archaic words scattered through the narrative – irked me somewhat. In the end I conceded a few. On the other hand her suggested deletions made good sense. They do, undoubtedly, tighten up the narrative and add pace to the story. Hilary Parker of Blackstaff, with whom I worked through the proposed shifts and changes, tells me that everything, even compilations of factual material, is now fine-combed like this before publication.

Among many ripe words that survive are 'bodie', 'coof', 'gommeril', 'grummly', 'callan', 'fissling', 'smiddy', 'caddy', 'chiel', 'spiering', 'chaffer' and 'pease-bogles' – all readily construable by onomatopoeia or context.

In an interview with Terry McGeehan for the *Sunday Press* (10 June 1984), Bell observed; 'I have a quaint conception that [*Across the Narrow Sea*] taken with an earlier novel, *A Man Flourishing* about the 1798 rebellion and *December Bride*, the three will make up a kind of trilogy.

He gives no indication of when the idea of the trilogy occurred to him but as already noted, certain surnames are to be found in each of the novels, including McIlveen, Purdie and, of course, Echlin. A strong stimulus, as any working writer will know, is the publisher's option clause. A diary entry for the week of 12–16 July 1976 mentions correspondence with Kevin Crossley-Holland of Gollancz 'enquiring about a new historical novel from me':

> I wrote offering my two ideas: the Plantation family from Scotland, and the 1907 Belfast family in the period of the Larkin strike. K. C.-H. in a very pleasant letter tells me that having discussed my ideas with his colleagues, 'and given the relative success of A MAN FLOURISHING, and the crying need for good historical novels, we all feel that your novel about the McIlveens (the Planters) is the one that would be most likely to appeal to us'. So I pick up the threads and the research – again.

In the letter mentioned above, sent on 30 June, Bell notes that since *A Man Flourishing* he has been working on two novels:

> . . . a bad thing. It means that I've been in a state of suspended animation between them for too long.
>
> (a) is concerned with a Belfast working-class family caught in the James Larkin dock strike of 1907. The father, a carter of peasant origin, doesn't understand strikes, or why he should stop work, or nascent trade unionism. The son, a shipyard tradesman, understands too well and gets himself killed. There are two daughters. The story largely circles around the elder, who loses her brother and her lover, who emigrates. Briefly it could be described as a 'sad' love story.
>
> (b) is set about 300 years earlier – James the First's Plantation of Ulster, from which we can plausibly trace our present strife. A Scottish peasant family, the McIlveens, are driven off their own farm by a rack-renting laird and cross the Irish Sea to Co. Down, there to try their luck in the 'new' lands of the dispossessed Irish. Strangely there has never been a novel set in this period. The research here is intimidating, but the idea haunts me, probably because it was the beginnings of my own family and stock. The story would remain completely or largely in Ulster. (I don't want to write a pastiche Fortunes of Nigel.)

The Belfast story sounds very interesting. A pencilled page headed 'Strike' in a jotter labelled *Ideas* contains an obviously unrevised opening paragraph of this unwritten novel:

> Around five o'clock in the evening of February 9, 1907 Robert Miskelly finished the last furrow in the one-acre patch he had been ploughing for his father. Robert unyoked the mare and told her to stand there. He scraped the clay off his boots on the frame of the plough. He led the mare across the cobbled farmyard and stabled her. His mother had fried American bacon and oatmeal and potato farl for his supper. She sat at the other end of the table watching him eat. He had been hungry in the field but finishing the ploughing had so exhausted him that he was too tired to eat although he was hungry. His father who had gone to look at the work came in looking well pleased. Robert told him he was out of practice, he had lost the touch for ploughing. No, said his father, that's a good job. He was well pleased that the field had been opened before it was too late for sowing.

The rest of the short excerpt reveals that Robert has left the country and lives in Belfast where his wife does piece work and his daughter works in Gallaher's tobacco factory.

The amount of research required for the second option was indeed daunting. The diary entry for 21 August 1976 reads:

> Today started, in earnest, the writing of *The Planters*. My plan is to cut out, if possible, one draft, and watch length with care. Both *The Hollow Ball* and *A Man Flourishing* were set out at too great a length (around 100,000 words) and both had to be cut. This great waste of labour and time.

Progress with 'The Planters', as the work was originally called, was characteristically slow. Between 22 June 1976 and 9 February 1978 nine letters were sent by David Higham asking about the work. No doubt there would have been more but for Higham's sudden death on 30 March 1978.

The story is labelled a romance, largely because of the contrivance of the plot which ends with the romantic escape of Anne Echlin, dressed as a serving-wench in a mop-cap, from her father and his factors. The last sentence is the stuff of romantic fiction:

> 'Gentlemen,' said Neil, 'our bark swings at anchor. Fo'rrard!' He took

Anne up in his arms and, without a backward glance, kneed his way into the surf.

The character of Neil Gilchrist, though much more realistically drawn than the usual run of romantic heroes, could have stepped from the pages of Sir Walter Scott. A younger son, with two thirds of a law degree from St Andrew's, who has been diverted from seeking his fortune at the court of James I and possesses remarkable skill, courage, charm, wisdom beyond his years and, most significant, luck, he falls for the equally gifted Anne Echlin, the daughter of the undertaker, Kenneth, Lord Deputy Chichester's trusted agent in north Down. Their way, of course, is beset with difficulties. But their problems are solved, perhaps a little mechanically, by the death of Neil's elder brother and the discovery that the family house of Balwhanny back in Scotland is not as 'derelict' as Neil had reckoned. The news is brought by Hunter Murray, his old tutor, and it is with high hopes and confidence that Neil and Anne, Murray and Archie Gill (the carter who will be steward of Balwhanny) cross back in the same coble that had brought Gilchrist to Donaghadee in the first place.

Tom Adair, in his review of the book for the *Linen Hall Review*, felt that the coming of Murray was not handled with Bell's usual confidence:

> ... in the end, the tale turns crucially upon Neil's meeting with Anne Echlin, the laird's daughter, and traces their subsequent illicit courtship to its moving and irrevocable conclusion. Only then does Sam Hanna Bell's assurance fail him, for the return of Neil to Balwhanny in the final act depends upon making plausible the appearance of a messenger from Scotland, a *deus ex machina*, at the hour of Neil's greatest need. A risky ploy.

Bell's response, in a note written on 14 September 1987, reveals the origin of the word 'romance' in the subtitle:

> I think the review much more than fair – it is as clear-sighted as it is generous. I'm mildly surprised that the arrival of the old tutor, Hunter Murray, should put a strain on credence. Old Balwhanny's heir was dead; he needed his other son. Perhaps I should have suggested that it was the aged tutor who set out in search of Neil. Anyway . . . anyway . . .
>
> What really worried me was the unlikely acceptance of Anne

Echlin's escape from Ravara. Indeed that's why, at the last moment, I dubbed the tale – A Romance. A nice word to hide behind.

The tale is 'romantic' enough in all conscience, and it is interesting that Adair uses the theatrical term 'final act'. The book is full of dramatic set-pieces: the relinquishing of his eventual inheritance by Neil Gilchrist; the successful repulse of the sea attack by the Kintyre reivers; the attack on the McIlveen homestead by the locally dispossessed; Neil's effective defence of the crone Rushin Coatie in the witchcraft hearing; the 'bonny fecht' in which Neil dispatches the giant reiver Lachie Dubh in Belfast; the rescue of young Mac Cartan from Chichester's troopers on the night of the great feast; the romantic moments with Anne beside the lake; the nail-biting suspense of Anne's escape from her family.

The love story is beautifully handled, and is very different from relationships in Bell's earlier novels. The Echlins of *December Bride* were eloquent only in their manual skills; David Minnis relinquished Maureen McFall almost as soon as the Irish Sea separated them; and however courageous, idealistic – and romantic – James Gault may have been at the start of *A Man Flourishing*, these virtues disappeared when the hand of respectability clutched him. How much pleasanter to write in happy wryness about the romancing of Neil Gilchrist:

> A glade led to a mere, on its dark waters a solitary swan. The sun was still high and a beam illuminated the bird so that it shone at the end of the narrow clearing. When the rays were broken by the overhanging bows they fell on the forest floor in splintered silver. Neil's gaze followed her pointing finger and he wondered what should stir him in response. He could think of scores of such glades in Ravara woods. Useless. Too overhung for planting, too cramped to even store cut timber. Anne was looking at him, beseeching him to share her delight. Well, yes, he thought. Yes, if ye looked at it that way . . .

The book is a romance in its organisation of its dramatic scenes, some to urge the action forward, some to paint the picture of the times; but it is much more.

The Gilchrists' future, and that of the two who returned to Ayrshire with them, is left to the imagination of the reader. More than thirty years later, Scotland was to feel the shocks of the English civil war, and Ulster was to undergo the native rebellion of 1641. Bell refers to the latter in one telling sentence: 'Until the house fell in flame and smoke thirty-odd years later, Francis Echlin and his family in refuge, it was the greatest assemblage ever brought together under the roof of Rathard.' Bell is conscious all the time that our present discontents in Ulster spring from the settlements of the seventeenth century. But it is part of his humane genius to show that the planters were as varied as the folk they replaced. The McIlveens, in their flight from rack-renting in Ayr, are like the passengers on board the *Mayflower* a dozen years later.

The formal plan for the Ulster plantations had been drawn up by Sir George Carew (1555–1629) before Elizabeth I died, but they did not concern Antrim and Down. There the 'pacification' was informal and personal. Much of the land had already been ceded to Chichester, Montgomery and Hamilton, and undertakers like Kenneth Echlin were imported as much for the landowners' profit as for the handling of the 'wild Irish'.

Like many of his time, Echlin was a career soldier who emigrated to make his fortune. He could as easily have gone to Virginia. Echlin's marriage above his station to the daughter of the Earl of Finnart induces him to seek a knighthood – which Chichester denies. This disappointment, coming after the revelation that his heir, Hamilton, is homosexual, and the obvious interest that Anne shows in Neil Gilchrist, makes the austere man even less open to compromise. His dismissal, on his wife's instructions, of Gilchrist leads to the grudging thought that 'this fellow was what he would have wished his elder son to be'.

By a piece of literary continuity the elder and younger Echlin brothers have the same names as characters in *December Bride*, but it is clear that over the centuries the family took a long time to recover from the destruction of the 1640's so tersely indicated in this book. Warm as the twentieth-century Echlin farm is, it is a long way from the Rathard House in which the great feast to entertain the lord deputy was held. As it is, the account of the settlers' piety and industry, the lovingly delineated characters of Dan Drummond the factor, Mungo Turnooth the Presbyterian minister, Calum Wishart the all-purpose physician, Angus Ross the dominie, and the McIlveens (Bell's own putative ancestors), as well as the sense of the period, all combine to make *Across the Narrow Sea* a significant and successful novel.

21

THE ARTIFICER

IN A LETTER TO TOM ADAIR written by Sam Hanna Bell on 10 July 1987, there is an unusually revealing paragraph, from a man who utterly ignored his friends' regular admonitions to 'write the autobiography':

> You are kind enough to enquire how I assemble my stories. First the inevitable exercise books, scribbled in pell-mell. Next a fuller shaping on the back of old BBC scripts (I've a stack of them). Then, still in pencil, the complete tale set out on foolscap. Finally a two-fingered typing in which, with luck, there are only minor tinklings and polishings. All very laborious. I could never have made a living at it. Larry (*Odd Man Out*) Green told me he could write 2–3,000 first draft words in a morning and finish a novel in two months. I keep a note book fat with scraps of dialogue, dates, incidents, half of which I never manage to squeeze in. My sight not being what it was I paid a young woman to type *Across the Narrow Sea* for the publishers.

This glimpse of Bell's method of working is borne out by the scraps to be found in his papers. One notebook has eighteen 8-inch by 5-inch pages transcribed from such expert books on soccer as *Feet First Again* by Stanley Matthews, *Allison Calling* by George F. Allison, and *Concerning Soccer* by John Arlott, the latter containing diagrams of play. This was part of his research for *The Hollow Ball*. A few pages further on there is a list of gnomic phrases headed 'Aphorisms for Mr McFall', followed by phrases, notes about soccer tactics, and memos to himself about the actuality of professional football and the details he needed to check.

The same book was used for useful expresssions, *aperçus*, sample paragraphs (some marked in red as 'used') for the novel that became *A Man Flourishing*. This novel was intended to tell the whole nineteenth-century story of industrial Belfast and there are pages of 'key dates' from 1798 until the Ballot Act of 1872. As Dr Johnson observed in Boswell's company on 6 April 1775, 'The greatest part of a writer's time is spent in reading, in order to write: a man will turn over half a library to make one book.' Bell turned over many a library in his time. As one turns page after page of neatly written notes one begins to understand why all his books had such long gestation periods.

The notes are fascinating in themselves; a section labelled 'Clothes' contains such entries as: '1780: the surtout, greatcoat or caped coat: this o/coat was large and loose, and followed the cut of the frock, retaining, however, the front skirt which was not sloped away from the middle line ... Cloaks reserved for army, the learned professions & funerals.' The social detail is minute: calico was one shilling and threepence, and linen three shillings and fourpence a yard in Belfast in 1797; there was a coffee-house there in 1803, and the town's best hostelries were the Donegall Arms and the White Cross Inn. One is left with the impression that Lady Morgan (1776–1859), whose novels were all the rage at the time, did not have as much contemporary information as the assiduous Bell.

As noted in Chapter 20, extensive research was required for *Across the Narrow Sea*, with the added problem of language. But the same meticulous treatment was given to the writings produced much more quickly: the stories, semi-dramatised features, articles for *Radio Times*, introductions, talks for the Carleton Society, early pieces for the *Ulster Tatler*, even the response to his voluminous mail. Today's writers, of whatever talent, whose early sins are wiped from the slate by their computer software will not leave behind so fascinating an archive. The Housman aphorism, at the end of his 'black' diary, that accuracy is a duty not a virtue, was one that Bell lived by. Integrity breathed from the man.

The 'rough notes' supplied to J.J. Campbell in 1962 may be taken as the self-appraisal of a man being as honest as possible. It is therefore interesting to note the achievements he takes most pride in: *Lagan*; 'the series It's a Brave Step and Country Bard' that 'drew on the voices and verses of the country'; the compiling of the archives of folklore and folk music 'that was . . . in danger of vanishing'; the collation of the Sam Henry collection; the programme *This Is Northern Ireland* (1949), written to celebrate the silver jubilee of BBC Northern Ireland; his holding firm to the belief 'that whatever is part of the story of any section or class of our community is material for radio, that no prejudice should be allowed to interfere with this, and that the BBC is under an unavoidable obligation to treat with courtesy and integrity the opinion of minorities'; the features by such writers as Rodgers, Kiely, Campbell, David Bleakley, Norman Harrison, Jack McQuoid, David Kennedy, John O'Connor and Sam Thompson; the planning and writing of *Pattern of Ulster* (1953), 'the first TV film made in Northern Ireland' and of *Rathlin Island* (1957), networked from Lime Grove and 'bought by a number of networks for showing in Europe and America'; membership of the original Committee of Ulster Folklife and Traditions and his contributions to the *Journal of Ulster Folklife*. He could have added years of service with the Arts Council (and its predecessor the CEMA), especially on the Drama Advisory Committee; and many reticent contributions to charities.

One of his most admirable practices was his enthusiastic and swift response to a large correspondence. This included fan mail, reactions from schoolchildren to his programmes, and frequent letters and cards from relatives abroad, especially from McIlveen cousins in Canada. Occasionally he sent testy missives to car dealers and other business people if he felt that he had not been treated properly. He was a mixture of high-mindedness and frugality, kindness and occasional brusquerie, socialism and conventional appearance and lifestyle, asceticism and occasional self-indulgence (sometimes in the Chalet d'Or he would eat a sticky bun with his coffee to the expressed dismay of his friend Norman Harrison), generosity and usually concealed impatience with the foolish or pretentious.

His sterling service to BBC Northern Ireland was appreciated both by the colleagues who best knew his worth and by the listening public. Establishment figures were less generous and decidedly more wary. He was accorded neither the prestige nor the advancement that would have been a public mark of his worth. His disappointment at not being short-listed for Assistant Head of Programmes two years before his retirement was great, but with hindsight it seems never to have been a likely possibility. He was not a safe pair of hands, and fortunately that left him free to continue making programmes. Once, as Gerry McCrudden recalls it, on the occasion of the broadcast of the ceremonial retirement of a Governor of Northern Ireland, things went badly wrong. The initial words of the announcer were broadcast simultaneously with the (recorded) opening speech at the ceremony. All those involved in the disaster were summoned to the Controller's office and admonished: 'We are dealing here with the very Fabric of the State; it must never happen again.' The guilty-by-association were advised that they were lucky to keep their jobs. Soon after, a new Governor was sworn in. The broadcast was live – and during the solemn speeches of inauguration there was crosstalk on the line. 'We heard,' says Gerry, 'two wee Belfast Post Office engineers talking to each other at the same time: "Try yon wee red and black wire, Harry, and see if that works," et cetera, et cetera. Sam saw me the following day and said succinctly, "I believe the Fabric of the State got another sore kick up the arse yesterday!" '

22

YOUNG SAM

FROM 1972 ONWARDS, Mildred's health was a matter of continual concern. Bell's diary records many spells of hospitalisation:

26 January 1972: M. not well; F. and I took her to the Ulster Hospital.
1 February 1972: Today M. back from Ulster Hospital. Better but must take it easy for a time. Great relief.
3 August 1972: M. to Ulster Hospital. She is suffering from a spasm which has brought about a severe diabetic reaction.
7 June 1973: M. Pretty poorly today.
17 February 1974: M. ill with shingles. Aggravated diabetic condition. This afternoon took her to Ulster Hosp., Dundonald.
23 December 1974: Because of M.'s indisposition we weren't able to buy the usual Christmas necessities. No turkey available but, in the end, got a very nice chicken.
3 August 1975: This afternoon M., who has had recurring fits of dizziness, slipped and fell on the bathroom floor. As I tried to get her upright she told me that something had given in her left ankle. Certainly she could not put her foot to the ground. I got her on the carpet and toboggan-fashion we reached her bedroom.

It took from 7.30 p.m. until 1.30 a.m. to get her examined and eventually settled in Ward 12 of the City Hospital. 'All this time the pain of the fractured ankle was increasing but M. bore with it very courageously.' The break was described as 'a bloody awful fracture' and required a pin. On 8 August she was 'rather feverish', and on 25 August she was transferred 'from City to Ulster because of diabetic condition'.

Though she rarely required physical nursing, Mildred's complicated pathology required constant monitoring. From 1982 on she had private treatment from a consultant physician. Sam was infinitely attentive and arranged his life so that he was rarely away from home for any length of time. The patient bore her condition with quiet fortitude and summoned up the necessary energy to attend the conferring of Sam's honorary MA in July 1970 and the much more exhausting investiture on 10 February 1977 of the MBE. She was present in the Linen Hall Library on 27 June 1987 at the launch of her husband's last novel *Across the Narrow Sea*, and her last foray away from home was in June 1986 when she and Sam stayed in Ramelton for Fergus's wedding. The same spirit enabled her to rally after a severe attack of septicaemia in 1988 which was almost fatal. By January 1989 the combined destructiveness of diabetes and its complications at last began to affect her short-term memory and seriously weakened her heart. Her grandson, young Sam, was born on 9 January and though she was happily aware of the event, it wasn't thought advisable to bring the baby to the hospital. She died on 13 January 1989.

In a letter to Tom Adair dated 27 February 1989 Bell wrote:

> There are moments when I cannot really believe she has gone. It is not the big issues that are important. It's the trivialities that a couple have shared that you discover are priceless and irreplaceable.
>
> She had had an operation to her foot and because of her diabetic condition the surgical wound wouldn't heal. She was as you know confused and her eyesight was failing. The doctors assure me she was spared much pain and distress. That and the kindness I've received have done much to console me.

He paid a simple but moving tribute to her in the wording of the plaque that marked the burial place of her ashes in Roselawn:

Mildred Ferguson Bell
1910–1989
Loved Wife and Mother
A Gardener and Teacher

The sadness of Mildred's death was mitigated by the existence of young

Sam. Fergus had married Angélique Day, who was working on the Ordnance Survey Memoirs in the Institute of Irish Studies at Queen's. They met in 1983 at Clotworthy House where Angélique was giving a lecture. Fergus, who like his father has a keen interest in local history, was in the audience. Bell was pleased but cautious in his references to their developing relationship; all he would offer conversationally was: 'Things seem to be going all right. I ask no questions.' Things went very well indeed and Fergus and Angélique were married in St Eunan's Cathedral, Letterkenny, on 21 June 1986, one of the few good days of a miserable summer. Mildred was well enough to attend and Bell, though clearly anxious about her, looked very fine in his Parsons & Parsons frock coat. Most of his time at home was taken up with nursing her, though there were finishing touches to be put to *Across the Narrow Sea*, and arrangements to be made about the launch in the Linen Hall Library, a guest list to be sent to Blackstaff, and complimentary copies to organise.

The day of the launch, 27 June 1987, which was adorned by a breezily witty speech from the author, was also the last day of life of John Hewitt, an old and admired friend. At times Bell had found his austerity a bit trying. Once he was asked if Hewitt was still in the Ulster Museum; 'As an employee, you mean?' Old friends, Michael J. Murphy, Michael McLaverty, Joe Tomelty, all still survived, but though contact of a sort was maintained by letter, they rarely met. By now Bell didn't smoke; he had given up cigarettes in the early seventies but had had the odd meditative pipe. The main spur was the discovery in 1980 that he had angina. He stopped driving in the last few years of his life because he was afraid that his eyesight might not be good enough. Apart from stabilised angina, arthritis (a legacy of sport and car accidents), and deafness, his health was remarkably good and his brain and muscular coordination were as sharp as ever. A very successful and faithful radio dramatisation of *A Man Flourishing* by Trevor Royle (with John Hewitt as Gault and Andrew Dallmeyer as Bannon) was transmitted on 8 October 1988 and removed any trace of residual rankle at Barbara Bourke's review.

The big excitement of these concluding years was the filming of *December Bride*. The story of how this came about reads like the storyline of a soap. Ted Childs, the boss of Central Television, got to hear of the novel when his secretary found the 1982 Blackstaff edition with the

Orpen cover in Hatchards in Piccadilly. She wanted something to read on a train journey and on the Monday, back at work, she urged Childs to take an option on the novel. In time the option was taken over by Jonathan Cavendish of Little Bird Productions. David Rudkin prepared a script (which went to at least seven drafts), and Thaddeus O'Sullivan was appointed director.

Mainly for aesthetic reasons the Rathard of the film was moved closer to the lough shore. A suitable location was found at Island Taggart, near Killyleagh. As O'Sullivan told Ciaran Carty in an interview for the *Sunday Tribune* (11 February 1990), 'The only landscape I could find that was right was an island on Strangford Lough. Our whole schedule was geared to the tides.' (Sadly the clipping was sent to Bell by his friend Robert Greacen, unaware that he had died the previous Friday.) In the film the topography so gloriously photographed is an extra actor. For authentication of the site the film company needed the help of Dr Jonathan Bell, from one of the author's favourite institutions, the Ulster Folk Museum. The museum staff made sure too that the Echlin house and yard (though constructed on the spot) were accurate replicas of the Edwardian original. The meeting house at Ravara was created out of a disused Catholic chapel near Kircubbin with the permission of the local parish priest.

Bell came into the offices of Blackstaff to meet the producer and director, and after a short conversation he was offered the part of Andrew, whose death turns his household into a *ménage à trois*. He was strongly urged to play the part: he looked right, sounded right, *was* right! The filmmakers promised that a double would be used for the more physically demanding scenes, and said that though there would be shots of him tempest-tossed and soaked to the skin, they would see to it that he would suffer only the slightest discomfort. The offer was flattering and very tempting but Bell rejected it without real reluctance. He did, however, pay a visit to the location at 'Ravara', driven there by his publisher, Anne Tannahill, and might, if they had had a costume to fit him, have been an extra for Sorleyson's sermon. He enjoyed meeting the actors and crew and talked for a long time with an old friend, Brenda Bruce, who played Martha Gomartin.

In October 1989 he commissioned a portrait of Mildred, done from photographs by Phyllis Arnold, which took pride of place above the living-room fireplace. That month too he went on his first visit to Italy as part of an eightieth birthday celebration, in the company of Fergus, Angélique and the baby. Their base was Cortona in Tuscany, just across the northern border of Umbria, which allowed him to exult in the glory of the High Renaissance with visits to Perugia, Assisi, Siena and, of course, Florence. He climbed many church steps, and risked neck dislocation as he viewed treasures he had hitherto only read about. Unfortunately he kept no journal, and back home he was reticent about the experience, as if he needed time to encompass all the riches he had seen.

There was no indication of any lessening of powers or even failing health. In a tribute, Robert Greacen noted: 'Only a week before he died I had a short letter from him. His handwriting showed no sign whatever of illness or ageing.' A 1990 diary kept mainly for quotidian purposes reminds him on 5 January to get a card for young Sam's first birthday. On the 15th he sent a cheque for £10 to Helen, the newborn daughter of his Manx niece Fiona, and on the 21st he gave Angélique a gift of pearls which presumably had been Mildred's. The entry for 8 February is a memo to buy a birthday card for Fergus; on the 9th (the day he died) there is a reminder to post it in time for the 12th. The last entry reads: '5 p.m. *December Bride* film, Grand Cinema, Downpatrick.'

Bell took ill with chest pains on Wednesday 7 February and was able to phone his doctor, who arranged for admission to the Ulster Hospital, Dundonald. He recovered quickly and it was assumed by him and the hospital staff that he would soon be home again. He was impatient with hospital protocol and the cardiac monitor, and anxious to be back in King's Road. At 2 p.m. on the Friday he had another heart attack and died. Everyone who knew him was taken by surprise.

The family death notices asked for donations in lieu of flowers to be sent to the Simon Community offices in University Street, Bell's favourite charity. The funeral service was held in Knock Presbyterian Church on the following Tuesday and later at Roselawn Crematorium. There were tributes in the *Guardian* by Anne Tannahill and in the *Belfast Telegraph* by Neil Johnston, and on Sunday 4 March the BBC paid him an hour-long tribute, transmitting *An Echo of Voices* and *A Country Childhood* (which had first been broadcast in January 1970). A press release from Blackstaff quotes Michael Longley's tribute: 'For me Sam Hanna Bell ranks alongside Lloyd Praeger, Estyn Evans and John Hewitt as one of our prophets.' *December Bride* had its première at the fifth Dublin Film Festival on 22 February in the Savoy Cinema. It was a superb realisation of the book and must be included in any list of significant Irish films.

Mercifully swift, Bell's death solved, as death often tends to, a number of problems. After Mildred's death he had examined a number of sheltered accommodation complexes, without having found one to his absolute satisfaction. He was conscious that the house was too big for one person, and that the garden would need full-time care. In a letter to a friend who attended the launch of *Across the Narrow Sea* he described how he managed to keep his lawn in shape: 'I keep mine subdued by doing a little patch now and again. Everything at 160 is overgrown but the roses are splendid.' Meals (on wheels) were delivered daily and the house and his person were kept spotless. Yet his arthritis was getting worse, as was his deafness.

He managed to keep up a brave front. As Anne Tannahill put it in the *Guardian* obituary, 'his lively interest in everything that was going on and his quirky sense of fun made every encounter with him an intensely experienced one'. His sense of the spiritual, which never deserted him even in his socialist days, increased in age. He went regularly to church and would have totally approved his obsequies in Knock. No one knew Presbyterianism, its faults and its sterling virtues, better than he. Let his friend Robert Greacen have the last word:

> Sam was a loyal friend, a wise counsellor, a man totally without bigotry, a man whose socialism was idealistic and rooted in concern for the underdog – had he himself not been an underdog? He had the instincts of a gentleman in the truest sense of an abused word. I believe that his novel *December Bride*, now made into a memorable film, will ensure a place for him in the Irish fiction tradition for generations to come.

BIBLIOGRAPHY

Books

Summer Loanen and Other Stories. Mourne Press. Belfast, 1943.
December Bride. Dobson. London, 1951.
Erin's Orange Lily. Dobson. London, 1956.
The Theatre in Ulster. Gill & Macmillan. Dublin, 1972.
The Hollow Ball. Cassell. London, 1973.
A Man Flourishing. Gollancz. London, 1973.
Tatler Tales. Ulster Journals Ltd. Belfast, 1981.
Across the Narrow Sea. Blackstaff Press. Belfast, 1987.

Editorial

Lagan, with John Boyd and Bob Davidson. 4 volumes, 1943–6.
The Arts in Ulster. Harrap. London, 1951.
'Theatre' izn *Causeway: The Arts in Ulster*, ed. Michael Longley, Arts Council of Northern Ireland. Belfast, 1971.
Within Our Province. Blackstaff Press. Belfast, 1972.

Articles

Labour Progress

'World War'	January 1942.
'Soviet Transport'	March 1942.
'Brighter Belfast'	April 1943.

Belfast Telegraph

'Men who Work Down at the Island'	23 September 1954.
'The Cockle-rakers Excursion'	16 October 1954.
'Fair Day Brought Many a Long Journey'	13 November 1954.
'Swansong of a Boxing-Day Custom'	27 December 1954.
'Let Us Not Be So Unfair to Giants'	22 October 1955.

'Would You Mind Repeating That?'	29 October 1955.
'As Marie Corelli Said to Me . . .'	5 November 1955.
'What Did You Say, Grandson?'	12 November 1955.
'Come All Ye Gallant Ulstermen'	19 November 1955.
'Alas, Poor Hodge'	26 November 1955.
'Take a Pinch of Saffron'	5 December 1955.
'A Host of Solitary Travellers'	10 December 1955.
'The Saints and the Storytellers'	25 May 1963.
'Fiddler's Night'	28 June 1963.
'Salt Water in Their Blood'	(1963).

Honest Ulsterman

'Love and Three Ulster Writers'	October 1968.
'The War Years in Ulster' (contributor)	January 1980.

Ulster Tatler

'Talking about Books'	1968–70.

'It Takes All Kinds'

'Sweet Dolly Monroe'	February 1969.
'The Pliant Soul' (on George Farquhar)	March 1969.
'The Man Who Made the Headlines'	April 1969.
'The Wicked Friar'	May 1969.
'Keeper of Cockleshells' (on Hans Sloane)	June 1969.
'The Co-operative Man' (on Horace Plunkett)	July 1969.
'The Belfast Slave-shipper'	August 1969.
'The Well-intentioned Landlord'	October, 1969.
'The Poisonous Cherry'	November 1969.
'She Hath Done What She Could'	December 1969.
'Star from County Derry'	January 1970.
'The Doctor from Nowhere'	February 1970.
'The Disputed Election'	March 1970.
'The Duchess from Cole's Alley'	April 1970.
'Letter from the Postboy'	May, June 1970.
'The Member for Downpatrick'	July 1970.
'The Clue of the Four Soldiers'	August 1970.
'The Mining Curate'	September 1970.
'The Flower of Sweet Prehen'	October 1970.
'The Wandering Heir'	November 1970.
'The Terrible Affair at Wild Goose Lodge'	December 1970.
'Hanged for a Poem'	January 1971.
'He Lies in Armagh Jail'	March 1971.
'An Easter Playground'	May 1971.
'A Head for a Harp' (Edward Bunting)	July 1971.
'The Golden Boat of Broighter'	September 1971.

'The Hounds of Auld'	November 1971.
'The Sporting Rector'	December 1971.
'A Man of Many Parts'	January 1972.
'The Making of a Shellback' (from Arthur Mason's *Wild Seas and Many Lands*)	February 1972.
'To the Lid of the World'	March 1972.
'The Compulsive Will-Maker'	April 1972.
'The Making of a Shellback' (cont.)	May 1972.
'The Lieutenant and the Widow'	June 1972.
'An Eye to Murder'	August 1972.
'Wife or Mistress'	September 1972.
'Wife or Mistress' (cont.)	October 1972.
'The Man with a Good Story'	November 1972.
'The Ghost with an Errand'	December 1972.
'The Birth of a City'	January 1973.
'The Ordeal of Mary Dunbar'	February 1973.
'A Most Extra-ordinary Case'	March 1973.
'An Affair of Honour'	April 1973.
'Tea and Arsenic'	May 1973.
'The Secret of St Robert's Cave'	June 1973.
'A Man of the Theatre' (on Joseph Tomelty)	July 1973.
'Cats for Peru'	July 1973.
'The Terrible Affair at Croft Lodge'	August 1973.
'He Stage-managed His Own Case'	September 1973.
'The Sinister Doctor'	October 1973.
'The Sinister Doctor' (cont.)	November 1973.
'Paper and Quill of History'	December 1973.
'A Long Backward Glance'	January 1974.
'The Price of Being a Critic'	February 1974.
'Across the Narrow Sea'	March 1974.
'Disturbances in the Playhouse'	April 1974.
'He Wrote His Own Epitaph'	May 1974.
'The Inspired Idiot' (on Oliver Goldsmith)	June 1974.
'The Inspired Idiot' (cont.)	July 1974.
'Oh! for the Open Road!'	August 1974.
'The Kist o' Whistles'	September 1974.
'The Terrible Retribution'	October 1974.
'They Went Bump in the Night'	November 1974.
'Dancer Who Toppled a Throne'	December 1974.
'Too Elementary, My Dear Watson'	January 1975.
'The Amorous Barber'	March 1975.
'A World of Ghosts' (on Sheridan Le Fanu)	April 1975.
'The Witch of Kilkenny'	May 1975.
'. . . But Coffee for One'	June 1975.
'The Milliner's Daughter'	July 1975.
'Tried by His Peers'	September 1975.

'The Pimlico Mystery'		October 1975.
'The Man Who Struck More than Gold'		November 1975.
'The Man Who Invented Christmas' (on Washington Irving)		December 1975.
'The Man Who Invented Christmas' (cont.)		January 1976.
'The Ghost That Crossed Water'		February 1976.
'The End of Soapy Smith'		March 1976.
'The Treacherous Nephew'		April 1976.
'The Gallant Gauger'		May 1976.
'The City That Vanished'		August 1976.
'Hell or a Haircut'		September 1976.
'Flower That Rocked Europe'		October 1976.
'The Aspiring Miss Smith'		November 1976.
'Here Comes I, the Turkey Champion'		December 1976.
'The Magic Slippers'		January 1977.
'Fugitive in the Fog'		March 1977.
'The Floating Palaces'		April 1977.
'The Ill-Starred Twins'		May 1977.
'The Doomed Lovers'		June 1977.
'Man on a Soapbox'		July 1977.
'The Facile Pen'		August 1977.

Radio Broadcasting, 1949–69

SERIES

Country Magazine — 15 May 1949–29 June 1954.

It's a Brave Step — 8 June – 14 September 1949. 18 June 1957–21 July 1958.

Within Our Province

'The Armagh Apple Industry'	John O'Connor	7 September 1949.
'The Housing Problem'	John D. Stewart	21 September 1949.
'The Rope-Making Industry'	Ruddick Millar	18 January 1950.
'The Fight against Tuberculosis I'	Graeme Roberts	3 February 1950.
'The Cattle Industry'	Jack McQuoid	23 February 1950.
'Afforestation'	John D. Stewart	7 November 1950.
'The Fight against Tuberculosis II'	Graeme Roberts	8 December 1950.
'In the Service of Youth'	Norman Harrison	9 February 1950.
'Exports'	Norman Harrison	16 February 1950.
'The Student Nurse'	Janet McNeill	9 November 1950.
'The Ulster Weather'	Alex Walker	29 November 1950.

'Going to School in Hospital'	Janet McNeill	30 October 1952.
'To Be a Farmer's Girl'	Anne B. Latimer	7 April 1953.
'The Herring Fisherman'	Bill Everingham	23 October 1953.

Country Profile

'The Country Editor'	Anne B. Latimer	7 October 1949.
'The Country Dressmaker'	John D. Stewart	19 October 1949.
'The District Nurse'	Anne B. Latimer	2 November 1949.
'The Postman'	John O'Connor	23 December 1949.
'The Solicitor'	Roy McFadden	20 April 1950.
'The Country Breadman'	John O'Connor and Gerald Rafferty	6 April 1951.
'The Blacksmith'	Pat Coyle and J.J. Nihill	11 December 1951.
'The Cobbler'	Michael J. Murphy	18 November 1952.
'The Mountain Sheep Farmers'	James Dalzell	24 June 1953.

I Remember . . .

John O'Connor	23 November 1949.
Roy McFadden	14 December 1949.
John Boyd	5 January 1949 (repeated 12 November 1953).
Anne B. Latimer	27 January 1950.
Michael J. Murphy	22 March 1950.
John D. Stewart	12 June 1950.
C.L. Gilbert	24 October 1950.
Jack McBride	6 March 1951.
Olga Fielden	13 September 1951.
Norman Henry	12 May 1952 (repeated 18 March 1953).
J.J. Jeffs	27 November 1953.

Country Bard	24 January 1951–1 June 1962.
Fairy Faith	11 March 1952–8 April 1952.
Loughs Remembered	20 January 1953–27 May 1954.
Music on the Hearth	30 October 1953–14 September 1956.
Folk Song Forum	5 May 1955–13 March 1956.
Country Town	12 June 1955–1 December 1955.
Law in Action	30 October 1956–13 November 1956.
The Arts in Ulster	30 October 1959–24 February 1960.

Talking Round the Hearth	5 April 1967–15 May 1968.
Other People	9 October 1963–22 August 1967.
Twosome	5 April 1966–17 April 1966.
Country Window	18 April 1967–15 May 1968.

INDIVIDUAL PROGRAMMES PRODUCED BY SAM HANNA BELL (SHB)

Their Country's Pride (17 August 1949): written by SHB.

Ulster Ballads (*passim*): edited by SHB.

This is Northern Ireland (26 October 1949; networked and repeated five times): written by SHB.

Call James Haddock! (28 December 1949; repeated 27 December 1951): written by Norman Harrison.

Between the Clay Walls (6 April 1950): written by Thomas Skelton.

The Night Journalist (27 April 1950): written by Ruddick Millar.

Return to Northern Ireland (27 October 1950; networked and repeated three times): written by W.R. Rodgers.

Rathlin Island (6 October 1950; repeated on network 31 January 1951): written by SHB.

The Mountainy Singer – Joseph Campbell (24 November 1950): written by Martin Morrison.

Fingers Pointing to Heaven (12 January 1951): written by James Fitzmaurice.

The Playful Pedagogue (7 February 1951): written by J.J. Campbell.

The Three-leafed River (16 March 1951; repeated on network 17 March 1951): written by SHB.

Mill Row (16 May 1951): written by John O'Connor.

Canadian Journey (6 June 1951): written by Charles Louis Gilbert.

Dear Mr Allingham (22 June 1951): written by Roy McFadden.

The Pliant Soul – George Farquhar (28 August 1951): written by SHB.

The Poor Scholar – William Carleton (2 October 1951): written by Benedict Kiely.

The Shadow of a Playboy (27 November 1951): written by John D. Stewart.

In Retrospect (30 December 1951): written by SHB.

Songs of the Streets (9 January 1952): written by Hugh Quinn.

Coal among the Bushes (22 February 1952): written by W.R. Hutchinson.

Keeper of the Canon (22 June 1952): written by Diana Hyde.

Come Climb with Me (4 July 1952; repeated 19 June 1963): written by P.S. Laughlin and John Kevin.

The Feis in the Glens (30 July 1952): written by SHB.

The Big Drum (8 August 1952): written by SHB.

Richard Rowley (9 December 1952): written by Graeme Roberts, Jack Loudan and G. MacCann.

In Retrospect (1 January 1953): written by SHB.

The Islandmen (28 January 1953): written by SHB.

The Saint and the Storytellers (17 March 1953; repeated on network twice): written by SHB.

An Ulster Journey (19 May 1953 on network): written by Graeme Roberts.

Nachlat Belfast (29 June 1953; repeated 16 October 1953): written by Ray Rosenfield.

Prisoner of State (27 January 1953): written by Nesca Robb.

As I Roved Out (14 February 1954 on Third Programme): written by Sean O'Boyle.

Hired and Bound (3 March 1954; repeated 25 August 1954 on Third Programme and 16 September 1954).

Irish Voices (17 March 1954): written by SHB.

Dove over the Water (24 March 1954; new productions: 20 January 1955 and 13 June 1963): written by J.J. Campbell.

Ribbon Round the Coast (4 June 1954; repeated 25 May 1960 and networked 16 September 1960): written by Norman Harrison.

A Kist o' Whistles (17 November 1954; repeated 11 November 1955): written by SHB.

Enter Robbie John . . . (25 November 1954; repeated 11 May 1955): written by David Kennedy.

God Rest Ye Merry (25 December 1954 on network): written by SHB.

Passport to Life (28 January 1955): written by Charles Witherspoon.

Irish Voices (17 March 1955): written by SHB.

Song of the Glens (12 April 1955): written by J.J. Campbell.

New World to Conquer (20 April 1955): written by SHB.

(For schools) *A Small Farm in Ulster* (9 May 1955 on network): written by Jack McQuoid.

(For schools) *The Siege of Derry* (16 May 1955 on network; repeated on 12 February 1959).

Who's for Our Man? (20 July 1955): written by Martin Morrison.

No More Returning (21 September 1955): written by David Edmiston.

He Lies in Armagh Jail (25 November 1955; repeated on network 26 July 1956, new production February 1965): written by P.S. Laughlin.

The Return Room (23 December 1955; repeated more than six times): written by W.R. Rodgers.

Men after Jobs (20 January 1956; repeated 13 April 1956): written by Robert Coulter.

Brush in Hand (17 February 1956; repeated three times and with two new productions in 1962 and 1965): written by Sam Thompson.

Irish Voices (17 March 1956): written by SHB.

Broth of a Bishop (13 April 1956; repeated 3 July 1956): written by Norman Henry.

The Lady of the Manse (9 May 1956; networked on 20 July 1956): written by SHB.

Boy in Search of a Future I (9 May 1956; repeated 1 January 1957): written by SHB.

Boy in Search of a Future II (1 June 1956; repeated 3 January 1957): written by SHB.

Twenty-five Years Back (2 October 1956; repeated 28 October 1960): written by Duncan Hearle.

It Happened like This . . . (26 November 1956): written by Isobel McColl.

Dan's New Door (3 December 1956): written by Isobel McColl.

The Corncrake (10 December 1956): written by Isobel McColl.

See the Gay Windows (18 December 1956): written by Norman Harrison.

City Set on a Hill (9 January 1957): written by W.R. Rodgers.

Tommy Baxter: Shop Steward (29 January 1957; repeated 12 June 1957): written by Sam Thompson.

Leeds Gave Me a Job (12 February 1957): written by Louis Gilbert.

Clue of the Four Soldiers (19 February 1957; new production 15 May 1962): written by SHB.

The Warm Side of the Stone (19 March 1957): written by SHB.

Operation Ether (25 June 1957): written by Hugh Montgomery.

Pass or Fail (17 September 1957): discussion chaired by Desmond Neill.

A Home in a City (12 November 1957): written by Louis Gilbert.

The Ulster Soldier (27 November 1957): written by Patrick Riddell.

A Round of Tales (2 December 1957): various Ulster storytellers.

The Submerged Village (December 1957): written by Duncan Hearle.

Music in Belfast (9 January 1957): written by Jack Loudan.

The Filth We Breathe (20 January 1958): written by Duncan Hearle.

Six Days Shalt Thou Labour (10 March 1958): written by SHB.

The Case of the Damaged Chocolates (April 1958): written by Paul Martin.

The General Foreman (15 May 1958): written by Sam Thompson.

The Alibi (19 May 1958): written by Paul Martin.

My Bundle on My Shoulder (30 July 1958; repeated 1 January 1963): written by Jack McQuoid.

Coast and Country (31 August 1958 on network): written by Michael Baguley.

The Down Line (9 October 1958): written by Duncan Hearle.

If Winter Comes . . . (3 November 1958): written by Charles Witherspoon.

The Man from Killyleagh (20 November 1958): written by P.S. Laughlin and John Kevin.

Man Who Made the Headlines – Vere Foster (16 December 1958): written by H.L. Morrow.

From Rail to Road (5 January 1958): written by Duncan Hearle.

To the Lid of the World – Lord Dufferin (January 1959): written by H.L. Morrow.

Neither Wheel nor Hand – James Larkin (2 February 1959): written by David Bleakley.

The Quiet Stream (20 March 1959): written by John Irvine.

Town on the Bann (24 March 1959): written by David Edmiston.

Come to the Pedlar (14 April 1959; networked 23 August 1960, repeated 9 July 1960): written by Norman Harrison.

Year of Victory (13 May 1959): written by Duncan Hearle.

The Ulster Sailor (21 July 1959): written by John Body.

(For schools) *Brian Boru* (21 October 1959): written by J.J. Campbell.

The Battle for Youth (17 November 1959): written by Duncan Hearle.

'Wee Joe' – Joseph Devlin (24 November 1959): written by J.J. Campbell.

'No Music in Himself' (27 November 1959): written by D. Frazer-Hurst.

The Gift (22 December 1959): written by Joseph Tomelty.

Christmas Garland (23 December 1959): written by SHB.

Look Behind You (6 January 1960): written by Norman Harrison.

The Stranger with the Knapsack (9 February 1960): written by P.S. Laughlin and John Kevin.

North Irish Horse (15 March 1960): written by John Body.

Strangers in Our Midst (12 May 1960; repeated three times): written by Duncan Hearle.

Johnston of Ballykilbeg (8 November 1960): written by SHB.

Man on the Beat (20 November 1960): written by Martin Tuohy.

Fly Away, Peter (9 December 1960): written by Maurice Leitch.

Angel of the Workhouse (20 December 1960): written by Louis Gilbert.

From Merseyside to Dromintee (24 January 1961): written by Michael J. Murphy.

Cape with Red Lining (1 March 1961): written by Norman Harrison.

Training Today for Tomorrow (2 June 1961; new production 4 September 1961): written by SHB and Maurice Leitch.

The Flower of Sweet Prehen (24 October 1961): written by Hugh Montgomery.

Table in the Window (9 November 1961): with SHB and Jack Loudan, produced by Maurice Leitch.

The Rise of the City (24 November 1961): written by John Boyd.

The Cooneen Ghost (8 December 1961; repeated 31 October 1967): written by N.C. Hunter.

Journey through Lecale (30 January 1962): written by Ronald Buchanan.

From Peace to War (20 February 1962): written by Duncan Hearle.

Mr Doyle of Ballygullion (19 June 1962): written by SHB.

Main Street Today: Killyleagh (17 August 1962): written by SHB.

Long Summer Day (19 September 1962): written by David Edmiston.

The Signing of the Covenant (27 September 1962): written by Hugh Shearman.

The Brairden Stone (25 October 1962; repeated 15 September 1964): written by P.J. Lennon.

Main Street Today: Larne (6 December 1962): written by Duncan Hearle.

New Life in Kilfad (20 December 1962): written by Norman Harrison.

Young Man in Leathers (31 January 1963; repeated 7 August 1963): written by Fred Stock.

What Price Tantrum? (28 March 1963): written by P.J. Lennon.

The Poor Gleaner – Padraic Gregory (25 April 1963): written by J.J. Campbell.

In Praise of Columcille (6 June 1963): written by James Boyce.

Maybe There'll Be Sunshine Too (31 July 1963): written by Norman Harrison.

Autumn Anthology (4 October 1963): written by SHB.

Death at Seven Paces (24 October 1963): written by John Kevin.

Charms and Cures (15 November 1963): written by Michael J. Murphy.

Portrait of a County: Tyrone (9 January 1964): written by SHB.

The Big Freeze (6 February 1964; repeated 6 February 1965): written by Duncan Hearle.

Year on an Ulster Farm (9 April 1964): written by Jack McQuoid.

Bobby Gray (20 May 1964): written by David McGibbon.

Silver Spoons and Chelsea Moons (31 July 1964): written by Jeanne Cooper Foster.

Listen Here Awhile to Me: Dungannon (11 August 1964): written by SHB and Maurice Leitch.

Listen Here Awhile to Me: Lisnaskea (9 September 1964): written by SHB and Maurice Leitch.

Blow in situ (17 October 1964): written by Jack McGeagh and P.J. Lennon.

Forty Years A-Growing (20 October 1964): written by SHB and Sam Denton.

Houses I Have Lived In (31 October 1964): written by Michael J. Murphy.

Bed for the Night (5 December 1964): written by Sam Thompson.

'. . . and Good Wishes for the New Year' (19 December 1964): written by SHB.

House for Sale (9 January 1965): written by Jack McNamee.

Bob in My Fist (22 January 1965): written by P.J. Lennon.

An Edwardian Remembers – Denis Ireland (5 February 1965; repeated 24 December 1965).

What I Would Like to See? – discussion (20 February 1965).

The Arts in Ulster, produced by John Boyd (4 March 1965), includes SHB on the art of writing.

Buying a Used Car (13 March 1965): written by Larry McCoubrey.

Mindful of Ancient Valour (16 March 1965): written by John Body.

'St Patrick Was a Gentleman' – talk for *Woman's Hour* – (17 March 1965).

The Earl Bishop (9 April 1965): written by Eric Ewens.

Belfast 24635 (27 April 1965): written by Anne Ruthven.

Count Redmond O'Hanlon: The Rapparee (27 May 1965): written by Kevin McMahon.

The Green Wound (25 June 1965): written by P.J. Lennon.

Exit John McCullough (23 September 1965): written by Hugh Montgomery.

Portrait of a County: Down (15 October 1965): written by SHB.

A Gathering of Players (9 December 1965; repeated 28 March 1967): written by SHB.

Behind The Wire (7 January 1966): written by P.J. Lennon.

Tailormade (21 January 1966): written by John D. Stewart.

Return to Rush Hill (31 January 1966): written by Louis Gilbert.

Foster Mothers (18 February 1966): written by Anne Ruthven.

This Torrent of Traffic (3 March 1966): written by Norman Harrison.

Home This Afternoon (17 March 1966): contribution by SHB.

City in Flames (14 April 1966): written by Lawrence Pitkethly.

Una Introduces (6 June 1966): contribution by SHB.

Flowers of the Forest (4 July 1966): written by John Body.

New Schools for Old (29 July 1966): written by B. Smyth.

Night-class People (23 September 1966): written by D. Carleton.

The Countryside Today – insert by SHB (9 October 1966).

Piper in the Corn (14 October 1966): written by P.J. Lennon.

The Ship (28 October 1966): written by Jack McNamee.

Barton's Bay (7 November 1966): written by Ann Johnston McCurrey and Larry McCoubrey.

Rock and Reef (14 November 1966): written by John D. Stewart.

The Face of Down – insert by SHB (25 November 1966).

Fermanagh Lakeland (networked 1 January 1967; repeated 2 March 1967): written by John D. Stewart.

Lough Neagh Bounty (10 January 1967): written by John D. Stewart.

Instant Money (7 February 1967): written by B. Smyth.

Heart Disease (21 February 1967): written by Larry McCoubrey.

Home This Afternoon (17 March 1967): contribution by SHB.

Odd Child Out (27 March 1967): written by Judith Rosenfield.

The Ulster Sunday (2 May 1967): written by Larry McCoubrey.

Forget Not Kindness (23 May 1967): written by Michael J. Murphy.

The Orangemen (11 July 1967): written by SHB.

Strolling in the Park (19 July 1967): written by Lawrence Pitkethly.

The Ulster Grand Prix (16 August 1967): written by Larry McCoubrey.

Go East, Young Man (13 September 1967): written by B. Smyth.

Down the River (6 October 1967): written by John D. Stewart.

The Poet of the Blackbird – Francis Ledwidge (22 December 1967).

The Ring-givers (29 December 1967): written by Kate Pratt.

Holidays In Britain: The Glens of Antrim (31 December 1967): written by John D. Stewart.

Wild Goose Lodge (2 February 1967): written by Jack McQuoid and Michael Duffy.

A Little Bit of Everything (29 March 1967): written by B. Smyth.

The Poetic Highwayman (24 April 1968): written by Michael J. Murphy.

(For the Schools) *Here in Ulster* (23 May 1968): written by SHB.

Radio Broadcasting after Retirement

SERIES

Here in Ulster

   A Country Childhood (16 January 1970): written by SHB and produced by Douglas Carson.

Today and Yesterday in Northern Ireland

   The Roe Valley (15 March 1971): written by SHB; produced by Tony McAuley.

Edward Bunting (14 May 1971): account of the collector of traditional Irish music (1793–1873): written by SHB; produced by Tony McAuley.

William Carleton (12 November 1971): written by SHB; produced by Tony McAuley.

My Singing Bird (15 June 1973): characteristics of and stories about various types of common Ulster birds, including a court session at which the birds decide who should be king; written by SHB; produced by Douglas Carson.

Oak, Ash and Thorn (22 June 1973): nature anthology written by SHB; produced by Douglas Carson.

The Singing Town (24 May 1974): street songs of Belfast; written by Tom Adair; produced by Tony McAuley, SHB taking part.

Oliver Goldsmith (8 November 1974): written by SHB; produced by Tony McAuley.

William Allingham (15 November 1974): written by SHB; produced by Tony McAuley.

Strangford Lough (28 February 1975): a young boy describes growing up around Strangford Lough; written by SHB; produced by Tony McAuley.

The Tinker and His Three Wishes (2 May 1975): written by SHB; produced by Tony McAuley.

Vere Foster (6 June 1975): profile of the Ulster philanthropist; written by SHB; produced by Tony McAuley.

Postbag (13 June 1975): children's writing; introduced by SHB; produced by Tony McAuley.

Postbag (25 June 1975): children's writing; introduced by SHB; produced by Douglas Carson.

The King of Green Island (3 October 1975): fairy story of Manus, son of the King and Queen of Erin, who wins the hand of the daughter of Leona, daughter of the King of Green Island; written by SHB; produced by Tony McAuley.

The Great Invasion—Edward Bruce (7 May 1976): Bruce's fourteenth-century Irish adventure; written by SHB; produced by Tony McAuley.

Bundle and Go (14 May 1976): the journey of the McIlveen family from Ayrshire to Ireland in 1607; written by SHB; produced by Tony McAuley.

Across the Water (21 May 1976): further adventures of the McIlveen family in seventeenth-century Down; written by SHB; produced by Tony McAuley.

The Travelling Spalpeen (28 May 1976): written by SHB; produced by Douglas Carson.

Singers and Storytellers (11 June 1976): links between Scots and Ulster folklore and music: written by Tom Adair; produced by Tony McAuley, SHB taking part.

The Narrow Seas (19 June 1976): the life of the people of the Antrim shoreline and that of their Scottish neighbours across 'the narrow sea';

narrated by SHB; produced by Tony McAuley.

The Coming of Fionn (22 October 1976): early adventures of Fionn Mac Cumhaill; written by SHB; produced by Tony McAuley.

Fionn the Hero (5 November 1976): how Fionn Mac Cumhaill became head of the Fianna; written by SHB; produced by Tony McAuley.

Fionn and His Bard (12 November 1976): further stories of Fionn; written by SHB; produced by Tony McAuley.

Flames McKeown and the Fairy Collar Stud (14 January 1977): fairy story about the fish peddler and the magic ring given him by Sean McAnaty, King of the Irish Fairies, who lives under Scrabo Hill; written by SHB; produced by Tony McAuley.

Turning Wheels (4 March 1977): journey by coach from the Cornmarket to Derry via Coleraine of the Lemon sisters; written by SHB; produced by Tony McAuley.

Travelling Man (11 March 1977): written by SHB; produced by Tony McAuley.

Country Bard (21 October 1977): written by SHB; produced by Henry Laverty.

Gulliver's Travels (18 November 1977): adaptation of Swift's satire; written by SHB; produced by David Hammond and Henry Laverty.

Alexander Chesney (21 April 1978): adventures of an eighteenth-century customs officer from Kilkeel; written by SHB; produced by Tony McAuley.

Jamie Hope (recorded 16 May 1978): written by SHB; produced by Tony McAuley.

The Gift of Ink (5 October 1979): programme about Swift; written by SHB; produced by Tony McAuley.

Coastguard (16 November 1979): written by SHB; produced by Tony McAuley.

The Ulster Railway (21 November 1979): semi-dramatised account of the building of Ulster's first railway (between Belfast and Lisburn): written by SHB; produced by Tony McAuley.

The Big Wind (5 November 1980): account of the storm of 6 January 1839; written by SHB; produced by Bernagh Brims.

Hans Sloane (23 January 1981): about the Killyleagh man who helped found the British Museum; written by Stewart Love; narrated by SHB; produced by Tony McAuley.

Louis Crommelin (30 January 1981): the story of the 'Father of the Linen Industry'; written and narrated by SHB; produced by Tony McAuley.

The Story of Patrick (3 March 1981): account of St Patrick's career; written by SHB; produced by Tony McAuley.

The Story of Brian Boru (17 February 1982): written by SHB; produced by Tony McAuley.

Death at Cooper's Creek (5 October 1983): Robert O'Hara Burke's expedition into northern Australia; written by SHB; produced by

Tony McAuley.

Winter Customs (21 November 1984): written by SHB; produced by
Moore Sinnerton.

Lost Leafony (recorded 27 June 1985): legend of the drowned village in
Lough Neagh; written by SHB; produced by Bernagh Brims.

Relationships – Neighbours (25 January 1989): produced by Bernagh Brims,
including 'Cockle Gathering' (from *Erin's Orange Lily*) by SHB.

Modern Irish History

Wood's Ha'pence (17 February 1969): account of the attack on debased
coinage by Dean Swift as 'The Drapier' (1723); written by SHB;
produced by Douglas Carson.

Explorations II

Other Days Around Me (2 February 1978): Florence Mary McDowell
introduced and described by SHB, with readings by Margaret
D'Arcy; produced by David Hammond.

Medieval Irish History

Lambert Simnel (10 March 1982): account of Yorkist attempt to dethrone
Henry VII in 1487; written by SHB; produced by Douglas Carson.

Individual Features

Country Window (10 September 1970): produced by SHB.

A Profile of Sam Thompson (17 April 1972): written by SHB; produced by
James Boyce.

An Echo of Voices (16 September 1974): SHB recalling his broadcasting
career 1945–69; written by SHB; produced by Brian Barfield.

Belfast Calling – BBC Northern Ireland 1924–74 (18 September 1974):
written by Rex Cathcart; produced by Brian Barfield; SHB taking
part.

The Gates (recorded May 1975): Jennifer Johnston's novel, adapted in five
parts by SHB, read by Kate Binchy; produced by Bill Morrison.

Ireland, My Ireland (27 June 1975): selection from the writings of Louis
MacNeice; produced by Brian Barfield; SHB taking part.

Montgomery and the Black Man (23 November 1975): account of the Arian
controversy in the Presbyterian Church in the 1820s; written and
narrated by SHB; produced by Brian Barfield.

Hard Road to Klondike (15 February 1976): adapted from Val Iremonger's
translation of Micí MacGabhann's *Rotha Mór an tSaoil* by SHB;
produced by Paul Muldoon.

Bazaar (19 September 1976): arts programme; produced by Paul
Muldoon; contribution by SHB.

Book Ends (2 January 1977): books programme, introduced by John
Fairleigh; produced by Brian Barfield; contribution by SHB.

The Belfast Strike (1907) (11 September 1977): written by SHB; produced by Paul Muldoon.

Sam Henry (14 May 1978): written and presented by SHB; produced by Judith Elliot.

Harold Goldblatt (15 March 1981): SHB in conversation with the actor; produced by Anthony Knox.

William Conor (17 May 1981): programme to mark the centenary of the birth of the artist; produced by Judith Elliott; SHB taking part.

The Linen Hall Library (2 August 1981): written and narrated by Brian Baird; produced by Judith Elliott; SHB taking part.

O Rare Amanda! (3 January 1982): an account of the life and work of Amanda McKittrick Ros; written by SHB; produced by Judith Elliott.

John O'Connor (21 February 1982): SHB introduces two stories by the Armagh writer; produced by Paul Muldoon.

The Jew that Shakespeare Drew (16 January 1983): a portrait of the eighteenth-century Irish actor Charles Macklin; written and narrated by SHB; produced by Judith Elliott.

Golden Boat for a Sea God (22 January 1984): account of the finding of and subsequent court case about the Broighter Hoard (1896); written and narrated by SHB; produced by Judith Elliott.

The Most Contrary Region (31 October 1984): sixty years of the BBC in Northern Ireland; written by Rex Cathcart; produced by Paul Muldoon.

Christmas Fare (22 December 1985): produced by Ian Hamilton and James Skelly, with SHB reading excerpts from the New Testament, transposed by him into Ulster idiom.

Television Broadcasting, 1953–1990

SERIES

The Lilt of Music (16 March 1960–17 October 1970).

Make Music (23 October 1963–18 March 1964).

I Remember (1969): produced by G.P. McCrudden and hosted by SHB.
R.H. McCandless (1 April).
John Hewitt (8 April).
Prof. H. Delargy (15 April).
James Mageean (22 April).
Peadar O'Donnell (29 April).
Cahir Healy (13 May).

Profile (1971): produced by G.P. McCrudden and hosted by SHB.
Joseph Tomelty (17 March).

Michael J. Murphy (8 June).

Individual television programmes

Pattern of Ulster (1953): first television programme from N. Ireland; written by SHB.
Rathlin Island (1957): written by SHB.
Shamrock (17 March 1959): with contribution from SHB: 'The Saints Way'.
Countryside (2 December 1959): with contribution from SHB: 'The Boxing-Day Shoot'.
Christmas Eve (24 December 1962): compiled and produced by SHB.
For Heaven's Sake . . . (23 January 1963): compiled and produced by SHB.
Water from the Rock (30 September 1964): written and narrated by SHB.
The Trident Port (25 March 1966): written and narrated by SHB.
William Conor (11 February 1968): written and presented by SHB.

For television programmes involving SHB produced or written after his retirement, see references in text.

INDEX

Abbey Theatre, 88–9, 144–5, 147
Achill Island, 44
Across the Narrow Sea (Bell), 41, 113, 124, 162, 190, 199
  launch, 195, 196
  publication, 183–9
  research for, 183–4, 191
Across the Water (BBC NI), 162
Adair, Tom, 133, 172, 184, 187–8, 190
Agriculture, Ministry of, 15
air raids, 25
Aislinge meic Conglinne, 171
Alexandra College, Dublin, 59
All Saints' Public Elementary school, Belfast, 14
All Souls Night (Tomelty), 145
Allingham, William, 50, 69, 162, 163, 171, 177
Allison, George F., 190
Alpha of the Plough (A. G. Gardiner), 178
'Always Raise Your Hat to a Hearse' (Bell), 33–4, 38
Ancient Order of Hibernians, 108
'. . .and Good Wishes for the New Year' (BBC NI), 90
And the Cock Crew (MacColla), 123–4
Antrim, County, 167
Apollo in Mourne (Williams), 21
Apprentice Boys, 101
Aran Islands, The (Synge), 168
Ariosto, Ludovico, 180
Arlott, John, 190
Armagh, County, 49–50, 104–5
Arnold, A.A.K., 65, 130
Arnold, Phyllis, 197
ARP, 25–6
Arts Ball, 58
Arts Club, Belfast, 137
Arts Council of Northern Ireland, 64, 130, 140, 143, 145–6, 147, 192
Arts in Ulster, The (BBC NI), 88, 120
Arts in Ulster, The (ed. Bell), 64–70
  Bell's introduction, 69–70
Arts Theatre, Belfast, 84, 89, 129, 130, 131, 146
As I Roved Out (BBC NI), 54, 97
Ashleigh House, Belfast, 59
Association of Ulster Drama Festivals, 139
Attlee, Clement, 64
Auden, W.H., 15, 125, 126
Austen, Jane, 122, 179
Autumn Anthology (BBC NI), 90

Awake and Other Poems (Rodgers), 48
Ayr Civic Theatre, 131

Baguley, Michael, 90
Baker, Ruth, 178
'Ballad of William Bloat' (Calvert), 172
Ballybunion, County Kerry, 59
Balzac, Honoré de, 123
Bardwell, Leland, 178
Barkley, Rev. John M., 90
Barnard, Charlotte Alington, 95
Baum, Vicki, 36
Bazaar (RADIO ULSTER), 177
BBC, 10, 15, 30
  Advisory Council, 107
BBC *in Northern Ireland – 1924–1949, The,* 109–10
BBC Northern Ireland, 63, 67, 127, 139, 144
  Bell as Features Producer, 31, 41, 43–56, 102–12, 133–4
    lack of promotion, 88, 192–3
    position in, 133–4
    productions, 102–12
    salary, 47–8
    scripts, 54–5, 83, 89–93
    workload, 95
  Bell post-retirement, 159–68
  Bell writing for, 20–1
  established, 44–6
  pub bombed, 128–9
  recording techniques, 41, 50–1
  Silver Jubilee, 192
  tribute to Bell, 198
  Ulster Tatler competition, 177
Beadle, Gerald, 45
Bebbington, John, 69
Beckett, Mary, 181
Beckett, Samuel, 141
Beef (BBC NI), 131
Begley, Elizabeth, 83
Behan, Brendan, 128
Belfast, 9, 11, 49, 108–9, 164
  bombs, 128–9, 172
  in *The Hollow Ball,* 113–19
  India Street, 13–19
  King's Road house, 60–2
  Second World War, 24–5, 57–8
  sectarianism, 18, 107, 114–16
  United Irishmen, 152–3
  urban folklore, 109–10
Belfast City Hospital, 194–5
Belfast Civil Defence Authority, 25–6
Belfast Corporation, 110
Belfast Drama Circle, 145

'Belfast' (MacNeice), 152
Belfast News-Letter, 29, 88, 91, 128, 137, 139, 171
  reviews, 80, 120
Belfast Public Library, 53
Belfast Reading Society, 21
Belfast Royal Academy, 14
Belfast Society for Promoting Knowledge, 21
Belfast Telegraph, 28, 80, 125, 139, 160, 198
  reviews, 120
Bell, Bobby, 137
Bell, Charles Hunter, 6, 14
Bell, Fergus Hanna, 55, 127, 130–1, 136, 198
  birth, 59–60
  education, 61–2, 63
  father's MBE, 140, 141–2
  marriage, 195, 196
Bell, James Hanna, 4–6, 7
Bell, Jane, 4–7, 9, 13, 17, 24
  death of, 107
Bell, Dr Jonathan, 197
Bell, Mildred, 48, 121, 136, 137, 138–9, 196, 197
  Bell's MBE, 140, 141
  death of, 194–5
  marriage, 58–9
Bell, Robert McIlveen, 6, 14
Bell, Sam Hanna. see also BBC Northern Ireland
  autobiographical note (1980), 24–5, 26–7, 30
  birth, 4
  car accident, 62
  childhood and youth, 6–19
  deafness, 129, 131–2
  death of, 198–9
  diaries, 121–35, 136–7, 139
  drinking, 132–3
  early writing, 20–32
  honorary degree, 109, 136–9, 195
  King's Road house, 60–2
  Lagan, 26–31
  Literary Miscellany, 175–82
  literary tastes, 14, 121–4
  marriage, 58–9
  MBE, 132, 139–42, 195
  physical appearance, 166–7
  plays and features, 83–93
  politics of, 19
  publications
    Across the Narrow Sea, 183–9
    Arts in Ulster, 64–70
    December Bride, 71–82
    Erin's Orange Lily, 94–101
    The Hollow Ball, 62–3, 113–20
    A Man Flourishing, 148–58
    Summer Loanen, 33–42
    Tatler Tales, 172–4
  Within Our Province, 168–72
  retirement, 133, 136–7, 159–68
  'rough notes' (1962), 7–8, 46–9, 51, 102–3, 109, 191–2
  working methods, 183–4, 190–1
Bell, Sam Jnr, 195, 198
Bell, The, 10, 20, 26, 35, 42
  Ulster numbers, 27–8
Bellow, Saul, 123
Bennet, Jill, 140
Bennett, Arnold, 36
Bernhardt, Sarah, 146
Big Drum, The (BBC NI), 97
Big Wind, The (BBC NI), 164
Binchy, Kate, 167
Black, Donald Taylor, 112
Black, Mrs Collinson, 139
Blacker, William, 92
Blackstaff Press, 54, 81, 151, 158, 169–70, 173, 183–4, 196–8
  store bombed, 172
Blair, Doris V., 26
Blakely, Colin, 129
Bleakley, David, 102, 192
Blythe, Ernest, 88
Boehringer, Kathleen, 146
Bolt, David, 148, 149–51
Bonar Law, Andrew, 17
Book at Bedtime, A (BBC), 167
Bossence, Ralph, 171
Boswell, James, 191
Bothy Band, The, 163
Boucher, Billy, 136
'Bound Limp Cloth' (Bell), 16, 35, 36, 40
Bourke, Barbara, 196
Boyce, James, 90, 126, 128, 129
Boyd, John, 14, 21, 22, 57, 63, 110, 130, 138
  Arts in Ulster, 65, 66, 67, 68
  in BBC, 46, 56, 120, 133–4
  Bell interview, 88
  Bell's retirement, 136–7
  on Bell's workload, 95
  Lagan, 26–31
  reminiscences, 23–4, 49, 58–9, 132–3
Boyne, Battle of, 105–7
Braine, John, 122
Brecht, Bertolt, 130
Breslin, Sean, 178, 182
Brief Encounter (Greacen), 22
Broadcasting in a Divided Community (QUB), 51
'Broken Tree, The' (Bell), 15–16, 18, 30, 34, 87
  McLaverty on, 39
  review, 40
Brolly, Francie, 164
Brookeborough, Lord, 128
Brown, Harry T., 163
Brown, Nelson, 66

Bruce, Brenda, 197
Bruce, Edward, 162
Brush in Hand (BBC NI), 103, 111
Buchanan, George, 65
Bullock, Shan F., 70, 171
Bundle and Go (BBC NI), 161
Bunting, Edward, 67, 162
Burke, Barbara, 157–8
Burns, Robert, 10
Byron, Lord, 179

Cabin Hill school, Belfast, 61, 63
Cadbury's, 22
Café Royal, 142
Call My Brother Back (McLaverty), 39
Callaghan, James, 139
Callil, Carmen, 80
Calvert, Raymond, 172
Calvinism, 73
Cameron Commission, 107
Campbell, Arthur, 37
Campbell, George, 22, 37
Campbell, J.J., 14, 171
  Bell's 'rough notes', 15, 102, 109, 138, 144,
    191–2
  broadcasting, 55
  career, 107–9
  Literary Miscellany, 177
Campbell, John Patrick, 170
Campbell, Joseph, 67, 69, 163, 170
Campbell, Mrs Patrick, 146
Campbell's Coffee House, Belfast, 21–2, 26,
  54, 132
Camus, Albert, 131
Canadian Pacific, 15, 21
Canadian Steamship and Railway Company,
  24
Capper, Mrs S.E., 68–9, 130
Capuchin Annual, 108
Carew, Sir George, 189
Carleton, William, 67, 136, 162, 171
Carleton of Tyrone (BBC NI), 102
Carleton Society, 191
Carr, Tom, 58, 128
Carson, Douglas, 46, 103, 105, 121, 159, 160,
  161
  on Bell, 55–6, 166
Carter, Annette, 149
Carty, Ciaran, 197
Cary, Joyce, 122, 177
Casement, Roger, 23
Casey, James J., 21
Cassells, 18, 117, 134, 148, 149, 150
Cathcart, Rex, 44, 45–6, 52, 53, 110
Cavendish, Jonathan, 197
Cemented with Love (Thompson), 112
Central Television, 196–7
Cervantes, Miguel de, 14

Chalet d'Or, Belfast, 112, 192
'Champion of Ulster, The' (BBC NI), 21
Character of Ireland, The, 105–7
Chesney, Alexander, 162
Chieftains, The, 163
Children's Hour, 20–1
Childs, Ted, 196–7
Choice, The (McLaverty), 122
Christian Science Monitor, 141
Christmas Eve (BBC NI), 165
Christmas Garland, A (BBC NI), 90
Chrome Hill Cottage, Lambeg, 60
Church, Richard, 81
Church of Ireland College of Education,
  Rathmines, 179
Cibber, Colley, 129
City Set on a Hill, A (BBC NI), 55, 104–5
Civil Nursing Reserve, 59
Clarke Clinic, Belfast, 63
Clayton and Nelson, 170
Clonard confraternity, Belfast, 109
Club du Livre Français, 81
Clue of the Four Soldiers, The (BBC NI), 90
'Clue of the Four Soldiers, The' (Bell), 173
Clydeside, 6–7, 8
Cnuasacht de Cheoltaí Ulaidh (O'Boyle), 54
College of Technology, Belfast, 15
Collins, 150
Colum Cille, St, 55, 102, 108
Come Day, Go Day (O'Connor), 49, 102–3,
  177
Committee of Ulster Folklife and Traditions,
  192
Communist Party, 19
Conaghan, Rory, 127
Connolly, James, 67
Conor, William, 15, 22, 31, 95–6, 166
Coogan, Beatrice, 158
Coogan, Tim Pat, 158
Corcoran, Norah Meade, 80
Coulter, Phil, 161
Council for the Encouragement of Music and
  the Arts (CEMA), 64, 65, 67, 69, 132, 192
Country Bard (BBC NI), 49, 192
Country Childhood, A (BBC NI), 163, 198
'Country Childhood, A' (Bell), 10–11
Country Magazine (BBC NI), 49
Country Profile (BBC NI), 50
Country Window (BBC NI), 137
Countrywide (BBC NI), 159
County Mixture (BBC NI), 164
Courtenay, Margaret, 140
Cousins, James, 68
Cowan, Barry, 167
Cowie, G.R., 138, 139
Coyle, Kathleen, 177
Craig, Maurice James, 28, 30
Critics, The (BBC NI), 123–4

Crommelin, Samuel Louis, 162
Cronin, John, 178, 181
Crossley-Holland, Kevin, 151, 154, 185
Crozier, Francis, 162
Curry, David, 164
Cusack, Cyril, 105

Dallmeyer, Andrew, 196
D'Alton, Louis, 145
Daly, Padraig J., 176, 178
Danger, Men Working! (Stewart), 62
Dante, Alighieri, 14, 180
D'Arcy, Margaret, 83, 167
'Dark Tenement' (Bell), 35, 37–8, 40
Dark Tower, The (MacNeice), 126
David Higham Associates, 148, 149, 150–1
Davidson, Bob, 22, 23, 24, 58
  Lagan, 26–31
Davidson, Georgie, 23
Davin, Dan, 48
Day, Angélique, 196, 198
Day Lewis, Cecil, 125, 126
de Valera, Eamon, 27, 109
Deane, John F., 176
December Bride (Bell), 29, 31, 36, 38, 68, 94,
    113, 120, 150, 156, 185, 188, 189
  background to, 8, 11, 118–19, 153
  banned, 69
  Bell on, 8, 81–2
  A Book at Bedtime, 167
  dramatised, 128
  film, 196–7, 198–9
  Lallans, 34, 184
  play adaptation, 86–9
  publication of, 41, 71–82
  reviews, 80–1
Delany, Mrs, 170, 171
Delargy, Seamus, 51, 52, 93, 98
depression, economic, 18, 19
Derry, County, 8
Devlin, J.G., 83, 110
Devlin, Joseph, 108–9
Dickens, Charles, 14, 123, 180
Dillon, Gerard, 22
Dobson, Denis, 7, 14, 71, 94, 105–6
'Doctor from Nowhere, The' (Bell), 173
Donegal, County, 8
Donne, John, 123
Dostoevsky, F.M., 14, 121
Dove over the Water (BBC NI), 55, 102, 108
Dowey, Mary, 146
Down, County, 6–12
Downer, Misses, 60
Downer, W.H.N., 65, 68, 69
'Doyle, Lynn' (L.A. Montgomery), 22,
    124–5, 128, 171
Drama Department (BBC), 108
Drawn from Life (Friers), 166–7

Drone, The (Mayne), 125, 143–5
Dublin Corporation, 92
Dublin Film Festival, 199
Dubliners (Joyce), 36
Dufferin, Lord, 171
Duffy, Michael, 136
Duke of Gloucester's Red Cross Fund, 59
Dunbar, Robert A., 179–80
Durham, Colonel, 153
Dutton, E.P., Inc., 71
Dyer, Charles, 131

Eason, Ursula, 20–1, 43–4
East of Eden (Steinbeck), 168
Echo of Voices, An (BBC NI), 164–5, 198
Edgeworth, Maria, 177
Ediphone, 51
Education, Department of, 147
Edwards, Hilton, 112
Elbow Room, Belfast, 111, 128–9, 132–3, 134
Elizabeth, Queen Mother, 141
Elizabeth I, Queen, 189
Elizabeth II, Queen, 100, 139
Ellis, James, 83, 84, 85, 90, 111, 112, 129
Emerson, A.W., 10, 33
Empire Theatre, Belfast, 83, 111, 129, 146,
    147
End House, The (Tomelty), 70
English Folksong Society, 53
Ennis, Seamus, 54, 98–9
Enter Robbie John (BBC NI), 65, 102, 124, 144–5
Enthusiast, The (Purcell), 144
Erin's Orange Lily (Bell), 8–11, 61, 106, 109,
    119, 165, 169
  publication of, 94–101
Ervine, St John, 67, 134–5, 145, 171
Evangelist, The (Thompson), 112
Evans, E. Estyn, 24, 171, 198
Everingham, Bill, 50
Ewalt, Linde, 23
'Eye to Murder, An' (Bell), 173
Eyre and Spottiswood, 150

Faber and Faber, 150
Fairy Faith (BBC), 50, 95, 98
Fallis, Richard, 181
Falls, Cyril, 68
fascism, 19
Father Ralph (O'Donovan), 177
Fay brothers, 27
Feast of Lupercal, The (Moore), 122
Feis in the Glens, The (BBC NI), 97
feiseanna, 98–9
Ferguson, Rev. C.R., 4
Ferguson, Sir Samuel, 67, 69, 177
Festival of Britain, 64
Field, Rachel B., 80–1
Final Harvest (Rowley), 80

Finlay, Jeanne Marie, 184
Finvola, Gem of the Roe (BBC NI), 168
'Fish Without Chips, A' (Bell), 35–6
Fisher and Fisher, 63
Fleming, Tom, 108
'Flower of Sweet Prehen, The' (Bell), 173
Focus, 119
Folk Song Forum (BBC NI), 99
folklore, 12, 163, 192
  collection, 50–3
  Erin's Orange Lily, 94–101
For Heaven's Sake (BBC NI), 165
Fortnight, 146
Foster, A.R., 87
Foster, Nevin, 69
Foster, Vere, 162
Fraser, Lady, 139
French School, Bray, 59
Friel, Brian, 108, 110, 119, 128, 147
Friends and Relations (Ervine), 145
Friers, Rowel, 15, 68, 87, 110, 121, 129, 161
  on Bell, 166–7
Frost, Robert, 179
Fullerton House, Belfast, 61

Gaelic League, 98–9
Galsworthy, John, 125
Gape Row (White), 68, 80
Gardiner, A.G., 178
Gate Theatre, Dublin, 112
Gates, The (Johnston), 167
Gathering of Players, A (Bell), 145
General Foreman, The (BBC NI), 111
General Overseas Service, 89
George V, Silver Jubilee of, 115
'Ghost that Crossed Water, The' (Bell), 173
Gibson, Cathie, 136
Gilbert, Stephen, 67, 68
Gill, Michael, 145, 146
Gill and Macmillan, 143, 145–6, 150, 181
Gillespie, Elgy, 31–2, 41, 176
Gillespie, Leslie, 32
Gilliam, Laurence, 43, 55, 83, 127, 165
Gilnahirk Horticultural Society, 139
Givin, Samuel, 171
Glasgow Herald, 4–5, 7
Glendinning, Robin, 178
Goldblatt, Harold, 83, 84, 111, 129, 136, 138
'Golden Boat of Broighter, The' (Bell), 173
Goldsmith, Oliver, 47, 70, 162
Gollancz, 151, 185
Gollancz, Victor, 19
Gonne, Maud, 27
Good, James Winder, 144
Gorstein, Eva, 23
Government of Ireland Act (1920), 9, 66
Gracey, Diane, 169–70, 173
Gracey, Jim, 151, 169–70, 173

Grand Opera House, Belfast, 61–2, 64, 84, 112, 124, 146, 147
Grand Orange Lodge of Ireland, 91
Graves, Robert, 177
Gray-Stack, Martha, 119
Greacen, Robert, 28, 30, 31, 32, 58, 177
  on Bell, 22
  Bell's death, 197, 198, 199
  Literary Miscellany, 178–9
Greatest Storyteller, The (BBC NI), 136
Green, F.L., 20, 168, 190
'Green Springcart, The' (Bell), 31, 71
Greene, Graham, 122
Gregory, Lady, 27, 122, 146
Gregory, Padraig, 144
Guardian, 198, 199
Guthrie, Tyrone, 44, 64, 65, 68

'Half-hanged MacNaughton' (Bell), 173
Hall, Anna and Samuel, 96
Hammond, David, 110, 160, 161, 164, 165, 167
Hampson, John, 122
Hanna, Denis O'D., 67
Hard Road to Klondike, The (Mac Gabhann), 167–8
Hardy, Thomas, 14, 59, 72, 80–1, 134–5
Harper, Edwin, 150
Harrap, Ian, 65
Harrison, Norman, 102, 138, 178, 192
Hart-Davis, Macgibbon, 151, 156
Hartigan, Anne, 178
Harty, Sir Hamilton, 67
Harvey, Rev. K.D., 94–5
Hawthorne, Denys, 90
He Lies in Armagh Jail (BBC NI), 102
'He Lies in Armagh Jail' (Bell), 173
Healy, Cahir, 52, 93
Heaney, Seamus, 123, 128
Heinemann, 150
Henderson, Doreen, 18
Henry, Sam, 53, 54, 164, 192
Henry Joy McCracken (Loudan), 70
Hewitt, John, 22, 28, 65, 93, 198
  Arts in Ulster, 66, 67, 68, 69
  death of, 196
  on *The Hollow Ball,* 120
  Lagan, 30, 31
  Literary Miscellany, 176
  poems, 171
Hibernia, 81
Higham, David, 150–1, 169–70, 186
Hippodrome, Belfast, 147
Hired and Bound (BBC NI), 97
Hobson, Bulmer, 27, 67, 144, 146
Hobson, Harold, 141
Hogarth Press, 122
Holidays in Britain (BBC NI), 165

Hollow Ball, The (Bell), 29, 62–3, 106, 134, 150, 152, 156, 186
  autobiographical, 16–18
  Belfast in, 11, 36
  publication of, 41, 113–20, 148, 149
  research for, 190–1
  reviews, 119–20
Holly Lodge, County Antrim, 60
Home Rule movement, 17, 75, 109, 145
Home Service, 48, 51, 89, 123–4
Honest Ulsterman, 24–5, 30, 81, 103
Hope, Jemmy, 162
'Hounds of Auld, The' (Bell), 173
Housman, A.E., 121, 191
'How Ilveen Hanna Kept His Promise' (Bell), 20
Howarth, Herbert, 122
Hudson, Jack, 110
Hunter, Barbara, 28
Hunter, Bill, 167
Hunter, Mercy, 15
Huntley, Raymond, 140
Hutchinson, 150
Huxley, Aldous, 132
Hyde, Douglas, 146

I Remember (BBC NI), 49, 52, 92–3, 166
In Praise of Ulster (Bell), 54, 172
Independent Television Authority, 100–1
Inglis, T.P., 7
Institute of Irish Studies, QUB, 24, 51, 196
International Club, 58
Ireland, Denis, 20, 21, 28, 58, 125, 129, 163, 171
Iremonger, Val, 167
Irish, The (BBC NI), 45
Irish Folklore Commission, 51–2
Irish Literary Portraits (Rodgers), 48
Irish Literary Theatre, 27, 146
Irish Press, 41, 81, 158
  New Irish Writing, 176, 182
Irish Republican Army (IRA), 18, 116, 119, 127–8
Irish Review, 55–6, 166
Irish Rhythms (BBC), 164
Irish Sketchbook, The (Thackeray), 96
Irish Song Tradition, The (O'Boyle), 54
Irish Times, 28, 41, 139, 176
  Gillespie interview, 31–2
  MacNeice obituary, 125–6
  reviews, 81, 119, 157–8
Irish Voices (BBC NI), 90
Irvine, Alexander, 177
Island of Love, An (BBC NI), 168
Islandmen, The (BBC NI), 54, 97, 111
'It Takes All Sorts' (Bell), 174

Italy, 198–9
It's a Brave Step (BBC NI), 49, 192

James, Henry, 122
James II, King, 92
Jamieson, Ken, 140
Jenkins, Elizabeth, 81
John O'London's Weekly, 81
'John O'The North' (Harry T. Brown), 163
Johnson, Dr Samuel, 70, 191
Johnston, Denis, 132
Johnston, Jennifer, 167
Johnston, Neil, 198
Johnston, William, 92
Johnston of Ballykilbeg (Bell), 54, 92
Journal of Ulster Folklife, 192
Joyce, James, 122
Judith Hearne (Moore), 25

Kane, Whitford, 144
Kavanagh, Patrick, 69, 177
Keenan, Marie, 103
Kelly, Basil, 110
Kemp, Kenneth, 151
Kennedy, David, 30, 65, 124, 144, 145, 171, 192
  Arts in Ulster, 66, 67, 68, 69
Kennedy, Peter, 53, 54
Kevin, John, 102
Keys, Deborah, 13–14, 21, 29, 183
Kiely, Benedict, 102, 192
Killyglen, County Antrim, 4, 5
Kilt is my Delight, The, 164
Kinahan, Sir Robin, 139
King, Sophia Hillan, 177
King of Green Island, The (BBC NI), 161
Kingdom of Mourne (Bell), 165
Kipling, Rudyard, 177
Kist o'Whistles, A (BBC NI), 54, 78, 90–1
Klaasen, Cor, 143
Knipe, John N., 139–40
Knock Presbyterian Church, Belfast, 198, 199

labour movement, 110, 114
Labour Progress, 19, 24–5, 114
Lady of the Manse, The (BBC NI), 90
Lagan, 26–31, 36, 43, 54, 57, 70, 71, 182
  Summer Loanen review, 40–1
Lagan river, 89
Lake, General, 153
Lallans, 34, 184–5
Lambeg, County Antrim, 60
Latimer, Anne B., 50
Laughlin, P.S., 102
Laurel Cottage, Hillhall, 71
Lavery's pub, Belfast, 132
Law Society, 63
Lawler, Ray, 129

Lawrence, D.H., 123
Le Fanu, Sheridan, 177
Leacock, Stephen, 180
Lee, Laurie, 128
Left Book Club, 19
Leitch, Maurice, 110, 129, 164, 176, 178, 181
Leland, Mary, 158
Lennon, Paddy, 81
Leslie, Sir Shane, 68
Lever, Charles, 177
Liddy, G. Gordon, 181
Lilac Ribbon, The (Doyle), 124
Lilt of Music, The (BBC NI), 165
Linen Hall Library, Belfast, 21, 168, 183, 195, 196
Linen Hall Review, 187
Lissoy, County Westmeath, 47
Listen Here A While To Me (BBC NI), 164
Lit-Phil, 179–80
Little Bird Productions, 197
Little Cowherd of Slaigne, The (Campbell), 144
Littlewood, Joan, 131
Living Stream, The (Longley), 46
Lloyd, Marie, 146
London, Jack, 15
Long Day's Journey into Night (O'Neill), 129
Longland, Sir Jack, 139
Longley, Edna, 46, 176, 178
Longley, Michael, 145–6, 176, 178, 198
Look Stranger: Mountains of Mourne (BBC NI), 165
Lost Fields (McLaverty), 39, 120
Loudan, Jack, 22, 30, 65, 70, 130, 132–3, 171
Loughrey, Pat, 51
Love and Land (Doyle), 124
Lowenthal, Peggy, 23
Lowry, Robert, 81
Lucas, E.V., 178
Lukacs, George, 123
Luke, John, 15
Lynd, Robert, 146, 171, 177, 178
Lyric Players Theatre, Belfast, 86, 88, 130, 146–7

Mac Cathmhaoil, Seaghan, 170
Mac Colla, Fionn, 123–4
Mac Gabhann, Micí, 167–8
McAnally, Ray, 112
McAughtry, Sam, 176, 178
McAuley, Tony, 91, 131, 160, 161, 163–4
McBirney, Martin, 63, 71, 86, 106, 110, 111, 129, 144
  murdered, 127–8
McBirney, Pat, 127
McBride, Jack, 95
McBride, John, 90, 144
McCabe, Eugene, 147
McCandless, R.H., 90, 93, 166

McCann, Bernard, 173
MacCann, George, 15, 105, 129
MacCann, Mercy, 87
McCartney, Aine, 167
McClelland, Aidan, 90, 91
McCollum, Fr. P., 131
McCooeys, The (BBC NI), 102, 144
McCracken, Henry Joy, 152–3, 162
McCracken, Mary Ann, 171
McCrudden, Gerry, 46, 50, 52, 92, 139, 144, 193
  Bell's retirement, 136–7
  I Remember, 166
  Sliddry Dove, 41, 83–6, 129, 144
McEnaney, Frances, 178
McFadden, Roy, 25–6, 28, 30, 31–2, 50, 102, 128, 177
  The Angry Hound, 108
  Literary Miscellany, 178
McGeehan, Terry, 52, 185
MacGill, Patrick, 66–7, 177
McGuckian, Medbh, 178
McGuinness, Frank, 89
McGuire, Waldo, 138
McHenry, Dr Margaret, 143
McIlveen, Jane Ferris McCarey. *see* Bell, Jane
McIlveen, Robert, 7, 9–10
McIlveen family, 72, 192
Mackay, Stewart, 91
McKenna, Virginia, 61
Macklin, Charles, 66, 173
McLaverty, Michael, 26, 28, 30, 31, 120, 122, 196
  Arts in Ulster, 67–8
  on Bell's work, 39–40
  short stories, 40
McLernon, Bob, 130, 136
McMahon, Sean, 133, 177, 178
Macmillan, 151
McMullan, Henry, 55, 144
MacNamara, Brinsley, 145
'Macnamara, Gerard' (Harry Morrow), 144, 145
MacNeice, Hedli, 126
MacNeice, Louis, 47, 59, 67, 69, 111, 112, 127, 128, 142, 168
  in BBC, 43–4, 46, 48, 55, 103, 104, 165
  'Belfast', 152
  Character of Ireland, 105–7
  death of, 125–6
  drinking, 134
McNeill, Fred, 129
MacNeill, Janet, 50
MacNeill, John, 96
McQuoid, Jack, 90, 102, 129, 178, 192
Mageean, James, 93
Maguire, Waldo, 136, 137
Mahon, Bríd, 51–2

Make Music (BBC), 165
Man Flourishing, A (Bell), 11, 113, 159, 185, 186, 188
  dramatisation, 196
  publication of, 41, 148–58
  research for, 191
  reviews, 157–8
Manchester Guardian, 81
Mangan, James Clarence, 180
Marcus, David, 41–2, 158, 176, 182
Marshall, George L., 45–8, 52
Marshall, W.F., 70
Marshall, William, 181
Martyn, Edward, 27
Mason, Ronald, 110, 126, 130, 138
  in BBC, 63, 84, 112, 137, 159
Matcham, Frank, 146
Matthews, Stanley, 190
Maugham, Somerset, 122
Maxwell, Rev. W.H., 96
'Mayne, Rutherford' (Samuel Waddell), 22, 125
  The Drone, 143–5
Mercier Press, 181
Methodist College, Belfast, 61
Middle of My Journey, The (Boyd), 23–4, 27, 46, 95, 132–3
Middleton, Colin, 128
Miles, Bernard, 130
Mill Row (BBC), 102–3
Millar, David, 29, 35, 57–8, 71
Millar, John, 59
Millar, Ruddick, 80
Miller, Arthur, 129
Milligan, Min, 87
Mills, John, 140
Milne, Ewart, 178
Milton, John, 4
Moeran, Edward James, 126
Monteith, Charles, 150
Montgomery, Leslie A. *see* 'Doyle, Lynn'
Moody, T.W., 107
Mooney, Charlie, 26
Mooney's bar, Belfast, 35, 82, 132
Moore, Brian, 25, 122
Moore, George, 122
Moore, Tom, 95
Morgan, Lady, 191
Morrison, Herbert, 64
Morrow, Fred, 144
Morrow, Gerald, 33, 36
Morrow, Harry (Gerard Macnamara'), 144, 145
Morrow, John, 176, 178
Morrow, Larry, 144
Most Contrary Region, The, 110
Mountainy Singer, The (BBC NI), 170
Mourne Press, 21, 24, 26, 40

Mr Doyle of Ballygullion (BBC), 125
Muldoon, Paul, 176, 177, 178
Mullan, William, & Sons, Booksellers, 123
Mullen, Barbara, 110
Müller, H.J., 19
Munro, Henry, 153
Murlough Bay, 23–4, 54, 59
Murphy, Michael J., 136, 163, 171, 196
  broadcasts, 49–50
  folklore collection, 51–2, 96, 97–8
  Literary Miscellany, 177, 178
  TV profile, 166
  music, traditional, 53–4, 98–9, 163–4
Music on the Hearth (BBC NI), 49, 54, 99
My Bundle on My Shoulder (BBC NI), 102
My Lady of the Chimney Corner (Irvine), 177
My Singing Bird (Bell), 163

Nachlat Belfast (BBC NI), 58
Naughton, Bill, 122
Neither Wheel nor Hand (BBC NI), 102
Nelson, Havelock, 108
Neville, John, 61
New Gossoon, The (Shiels), 147
New Theatre, Bangor, 129
New York Times, 81
Newe, G.B., 138
Newry General Hospital, 59
Norman, Barry, 181
Northern Bank, 124
Northern Constitution, 53
Northern Ireland Advisory Council, 52
Northern Ireland Labour Party, 110
Northern Ireland Light Orchestra, 108
Northern Ireland Office (NIO), 140, 142
Northern Ireland Tourist Board, 139
Northern Whig, 80–1
Now in Ulster (Campbell), 37
Nugent, General, 153

Ó Criomhthain, Tomás, 180
Ó Cúisín, Séamus, 68
Oak, Ash and Thorn (BBC), 163
O'Boyle, Sean, 53–4, 97, 98–9, 129
O'Brien Press, 181
O'Callaghan, Maurice, 91
O'Connell, Daniel, 174
O'Connell, James, 181
O'Connor, Emmet, 113
O'Connor, Frank, 128
O'Connor, John, 49, 50, 102–3, 168, 177, 192
O'Donnell, Peadar, 66–7, 93, 177
O'Donovan, Gerald, 177
O'Faoláin, Julia, 177
O'Faoláin, Seán, 10, 20, 27–8, 33, 39, 42, 72, 128
'Old Clay New Earth' (Bell), 38, 40
O'Malley, Mary, 130

One Small Boy (Naughton), 122
O'Neill, Dan, 128
O'Neill, Moira, 176
Orange Lodge of Research, 91
Orange Order, 91, 96, 101, 115, 153
  in *December Bride,* 75–6, 77
  parades, 92
Orangemen, The (BBC NI), 54, 90, 91–2
'Ordeal of Mary Dunbar, The' (Bell), 173
Ordnance Survey Memoirs, 196
Orr, William, 153
Osborne, John, 62
O'Shannon, Cathal, 22, 144
Outdoor Relief riots, 18, 113–14
Over the Bridge (Thompson), 111, 112, 129,
  147

Parker, Dame Dehra, 67, 68
Parker, Hilary, 184
Parker, Kenneth, 148–9
Parkhill, David ('Lewis Purcell'), 27, 144,
  146
Parsons & Parsons, 140, 196
Passing Day, The (Shiels), 62, 63, 147
Pattern of Ulster (BBC NI), 192
Paul Twyning (Shiels), 147
Phil Coulter Orchestra, 161
philately, 179–80
Planted by a River (Marshall), 70
Planxty, 163
'Poisonous Cherry, The' (Bell), 173
Poolbeg Press, 181
Porter, Eric, 61
Porter, Kathryn, 168
Postbag (BBC NI), 161
Praeger, Robert Lloyd, 171, 198
Presbyterian College, Belfast, 90
Presbyterianism, 72–3, 78, 152, 199
Priestley, J.B., 36
'Princess of the Isles, The' (Bell), 20
Prisoner of State (BBC NI), 102
Pritchett, V.S., 142
Professor Tim (Shiels), 147
Protestant National Association, 27
Proud Dunluce (BBC NI), 167
'Purcell, Lewis' (David Parkhill), 27, 144, 146
Putnam, 94

Queen's University Belfast, 24, 51, 107, 109,
  183, 196
  honorary degree, 138–9
Quinn, Archdeacon, 126
Quinn, Hugh, 53, 97
Quote-Unquote (Radio Ulster), 127

Radio Éireann, 48
Radio Four, 165
Radio Times, 50, 86, 104, 191

Radio Ulster, 127, 177
Rafferty, Gerald, 50
Rafferty, Sean, 139
Raffrey, County Down, 4, 6–12
Rainey Endowed School, Magherafelt, 179
Rankin, William, 11
Rann, 28, 31, 182
Rathlin Island, 89
Rathlin Island (BBC NI), 54, 192
Rattigan, Terence, 140
Rea, Stephen, 112
Recordings Library, BBC, 53
Reid, Forrest, 67, 144, 171, 177
Reid, Meta Mayne, 178
Reith, John, 45
Reside, George, 61
Reside, Major Gerald, 138
Reside, May, 61
Reside, Mildred. *see* Bell, Mildred
Return Room, The (BBC NI), 48, 55, 102, 103–4
Return to Northern Ireland (BBC NI), 54–5, 102
Ribbon Round the Coast (BBC NI), 102
Richmond Lodge, Belfast, 138
Rising (1798), 107, 162
  programme planned, 105–7
Riverside Theatre, Coleraine, 89
Robb, Nesca, 65–6, 68, 69–70, 102
Roberts, Graeme, 50
Robinson, Lennox, 128, 145
Rodgers, W.R., 28, 59, 67, 69, 70, 102, 125,
  126, 127, 128, 142, 192
  Arts Council, 130
  broadcasts, 55, 103–7
  career, 48
  death of, 107
  drinking, 134
  Lagan, 30
  Within Our Province, 171
Rogers, Paul, 61–2
Roget's *Thesaurus,* 41
Rolston, Louis, 136
Roof is not Enough, A, 88–9
Ros, Amanda McKittrick, 22, 68, 132, 168
Rosenfield, Judith, 176
Rosenfield, Ray, 58, 176, 178
Rotha Mór an tSaoil (Mac Gabhann), 167–8
Round Britain Quiz, 128, 139
'Rowley, Richard' (R.V. Williams), 21, 26,
  58, 139, 171
  poems, 80
  Summer Loanen, 33–4
Royal Court Theatre, London, 62
Royal Ulster Constabulary (RUC), 114
Royal Victoria Hospital, Belfast, 62, 131
Royle, Trevor, 196
RTÉ, 127, 160
Rugged Path, The (Shiels), 147
Rushlight, The (Campbell), 170

Russell, Bertrand, 122
Russell, George (Æ), 27, 122, 171
'Rutherford, Mayne' (Samuel Waddell), 22, 125
Ruthven, Ann, 178
Ryan, Jim, 138

Sabbath observance, 8–9
St Joseph's College, Belfast, 107
St Malachy's College, Belfast, 107, 122, 144
St Mary's Training College, Belfast, 107, 108
St Patrick's College, Armagh, 53–4
Salinger, J.D., 122
Sam Thompson – Voice of Many Men, 112
Saturday Review of Literature, 81
Savidge, Ken, 164
schools broadcasting, 137, 159, 160–2
Scott, Paul, 148
Scott, Sir Walter, 154, 187
Second World War, 31, 37, 46, 59, 100, 103
  Belfast, 24–5, 57–8
sectarianism, 38, 107, 108, 110
  in The Hollow Ball, 114–16
  Thompson play, 111
Shadwell, Charles, 64–5
Shakespeare, William, 14, 72, 180
Sham Prince, The (Shadwell), 64–5
Share, Bernard, 34
Shaw, Frank, 82
Shaw, George Bernard, 58
Shaw, James, 91
Sherry, Dick, 139, 175, 176, 181
Sherry, Noreen, 175, 176, 181
Shiels, George, 64, 144, 147, 168
Sign, The, 80
Silent Valley reservoir, 89, 165–6
Simmons, E.J., 122
Simnel, Lambert, 162
Simon Community, 198
Sinclair, Peter, 151, 156
Sinclair's, Royal Avenue, 36
Sing North, Sing South (BBC NI), 164
Singing Town, The (BBC NI), 164
Skinner's Alley, Aldermen of, 92
Slanguage (Share), 34
'Slaying of the Black Beast, The' (Bell), 20
Sliddry Dove, The (Bell and McCrudden), 41, 83–6, 129, 144
Sloan, Barry, 130–1
Sloan, James, 92
Smith, Dr Gordon, 131, 132
Socialist Appeal, 25
Songs of the People (BBC NI), 53
Songs of the Street (BBC NI), 97
'Sound Sense' (McFadden), 25–6
Spender, S., 125, 126
Spenser, Edmund, 96–7
Stallworthy, Jon, 47

Stanford, Derek, 177, 178
Starforth, Gail, 130
Steinbeck, John, 168
Stendhal, 122
Stevenson, Patric, 178
Stevenson, Robert Louis, 58, 180
Stewart, Andrew, 52, 53, 104
Stewart, John D., 22, 50, 58, 64, 88, 102, 129
Stowe, Kenneth, 139
Strangford Lough, 197
Strangford Lough (BBC NI), 163
Strangford Lough Remembered (BBC NI), 50
Studholme, Marie, 146
Summer Loanen and Other Stories (Bell), 11, 15–16, 17, 18, 30, 68, 87
  publication of, 21, 26, 33–42
'Summer Loanen' (Bell), 9, 10, 20, 33, 38
Summons, The (Doyle), 124
Sunday Independent, 119
Sunday Press, 52, 185
Sunday Times, 141
Sunday Tribune, 197
Svevo, Italo, 122
'Sweet Dolly Monroe' (Bell), 172, 173
Swift, Jonathan, 91, 146, 162, 170
Synge, J.M., 122, 168

Talking Round the Hearth (BBC NI), 49
Tannahill, Anne, 197, 198, 199
Tatler Tales (Bell), 160, 172–4
television, 100–1, 112, 130, 133–4, 147
  Bell in, 100, 165–7
Tennent, John, 171
Termonfeckin, County Louth, 21
'Terrible Affair at Croft Lodge, The' (Bell), 173
Thackeray, W.M., 96
That Woman at Rathard, 11, 86–8, 89, 128, 144
Thayer, Nancy, 181
theatre, 61–2, 129–31
  Bell's survey of, 143–7
Theatre in Ulster, The (Bell), 27, 125, 143–7, 150, 159
Theatre Royal, Belfast, 146
Theatre Ulster, 89
Their Country's Pride (BBC NI), 49
'Their Country's Pride' (Bell), 47
Third Programme, 48, 51, 52, 124, 145
This is Northern Ireland (BBC), 54, 89, 192
'This We Shall Maintain' (Bell), 10, 33, 35, 38, 39
Thomas, Dylan, 177
Thompson, Beryl, 138
Thompson, George, 140
Thompson, J.M., 123
Thompson, May, 110

Thompson, Sam, 50, 102, 103, 128, 129, 147, 192
  career of, 110–12
  death of, 127
Thompson, Warren, 110
Thompson in Tír na nÓg (McNamara), 144, 145
Thoreau, H.D., 29
Thorez, Maurice, 19
Three-Leafed River, The (BBC NI), 89
Three-O-One (RTÉ), 160
Threshold, 31, 182
'Thursday Nights' (Bell), 35, 36–7, 40
Tilley, Vesta, 146
Times Literary Supplement, 158
Tinker and His Three Wishes, The (BBC NI), 161
Titanic, 6
'To Crack by the Hearth' (Bell), 8–9
Today and Yesterday (BBC NI), 161–3
Tóibin, Colm, 80
Tomelty, Joseph, 21, 25, 28, 31, 58, 63, 87, 128, 196
  Arts in Ulster, 67
  and Bell, 144
  broadcasting, 102, 163
  film career, 65
  Lagan, 30
  Literary Miscellany, 177
  plays, 70, 129, 145
  TV profile, 166
Tomelty, Lena, 87
Tommy Baxter: Shop Steward (BBC NI), 111
Toulson, Shirley, 178
Townshend, Viceroy, 172
Travelling Man, The (BBC NI), 161
'Treacherous Nephew, The' (Bell), 173
Trident Port, The (BBC NI), 89, 166
Trilling, Lionel, 122
Trinity College Dublin (TCD), 59
Tuohy, Denis, 110
Turgenev, Ivan, 121, 130
Turn of the Road, The (Mayne), 125, 144, 145
Turncoats, The (Doyle), 124
Turning Wheels (BBC NI), 162–3
'Two Blades of Grass' (Bell), 35, 37, 39, 40
'Two Gallants' (Joyce), 36

Ulad, 27, 170
Ulster Bank, 139
Ulster dialect, 34, 75, 183, 184–5
Ulster Folk Museum, 90, 140, 159, 166, 168, 170, 197
Ulster Folklife Association, 51
Ulster Folklore Committee, 96
Ulster Group Theatre, 21, 83–4, 86–8, 110–11, 129, 144
  Bell on, 145, 146–7
Ulster Hospital, 194, 195, 198
Ulster Journals, 172

Ulster Literary Theatre, 22, 27, 33, 65, 67, 68, 124, 125, 145
  Bell on, 143, 146–7
Ulster Museum, Belfast, 22, 196
'Ulster Names' (Hewitt), 171
Ulster plantations, 183, 184, 186–9
Ulster Railway, The (BBC NI), 162
Ulster Special Constabulary, 9
Ulster Tatler, 41, 90, 139, 143, 160, 172, 191
  'It Takes All Sorts,' 174, 175
  Literary Miscellany, 41, 172, 175–82
Ulster Television, 139
Ulster Voices, 28
Ulster Volunteer Force (UVF), 9
Unemployment Assistance Board, 21
unionism, 45–6, 55
Unionist Party, 112, 133
United Free Church of Scotland, 4
United Irishmen, 27, 152–3

Vick, F. Arthur, 138, 139
Victoria United Free Church, 6
View of the State of Ireland (Spenser), 96–7

Waddell, Helen, 143
Waddell, Samuel. *see* 'Mayne, Rutherford'
Waiting for Godot (Beckett), 141
Wallace, Martin, 120
Wallace High School, Lisburn, 59
Warm Side of the Stone, The (BBC NI), 90
Wasson, Moore, 130, 167
Water from the Rock (BBC NI), 89, 165–6
Watson, Cowan, 137
Watson, James, 31
Watson, Sheila, 151
'Way to Catch the Morning Dew, The' (Bell), 100
We Build a Ship (BBC NI), 111–12
Wee Joe (BBC NI), 108–9
Wesker, Arnold, 130
Wheatsheaf, Belfast, 134
While Green Grass Grows (Mahon), 51–2
White, Agnes Romilly, 68, 80
White Heather Club, The, 164
White Mare and Other Stories, The (McLaverty), 26, 40
'Who Buried Cock Robin?' (Bell), 21
Wild Sports of the West (Maxwell), 96
Wilkins, Paul, 178
William III, King, 91
Williams, Raymond, 123
Williams, Richard Valentine. *see* 'Rowley, Richard'
Wilmot, Hubert, 84, 146
Wilson, Ian, 177
Windsor Castle pub, Belfast, 128–9
Winter Customs (BBC NI), 163
Witherspoon, Charles, 90

Within Our Province (BBC NI), 28–9, 49, 50
Within Our Province (Bell), 143, 168–72, 173
Wolfe, Ann F., 81
Wolfe Tone, Theobald, 152
Woods, Padraic, 22

Wordsworth, William, 4

Yeats, W.B., 27, 122–3, 146
Young, James, 110–11
Youth Hostel movement, 58